Street Survival Skills

Tips, Tricks and Tactics for Modern Survival

by

Fernando "FerFAL" Aguirre

Illustrated by Fernando Aguirre

First Edition

Published by Fernando Aguirre

ISBN-13: 978-84-09-13417-5

This book is dedicated to my family, my wife and sons who are always there for me and have unconditionally supported me over the years.

For more information visit:

www.themodernsurvivalist.com

And Follow Fernando "FerFAL" Aguirre:

www.youtube.com/user/TheModernSurvivalist

www.instagram.com/ferfal308

www.facebook.com/themodernsurvivalist

WARNING

Please read this full disclaimer as it is of particular importance in a book where such dangerous topics are addressed.

The very nature of the topics covered in this book are extreme and life threatening.

This book is for educational and entertainment purposes only. While the information provided can be very valuable, it does not replace hands-on combat training, qualified medical care or legal advice.

The author and publisher does not in any way condone illegal activities of any kind and disclaim any liability from any injury or financial loss that may result from the use or misuse of the information provided in this book.

The goal of this book is not to cause harm or injury of any kind but to provide information that can be useful during circumstances that are already extreme in nature.

The author and publisher of this book cannot accept any responsibility for the use or misuse of the information provided in this book. It is up to the reader to fully know their local, state, and federal laws and to abide by them.

Index

Introduction

Many years ago I realized how useful it was to keep a small notebook around in which to write down things I needed to remember. Everything from names, phone numbers, to-do lists, it would all go in there. I would also take notes on observations, ideas and random thoughts about survival and preparedness.

Anything I believed was important or potentially useful information I would write it down in a notebook. Sometimes I would include a small drawing or sketch to understand it better later on. As time went by these notebooks would turn out pretty messy but the little pearls of knowledge would still be there, hidden among names, addresses and grocery lists.

That is how I ended up with a number of notebooks packed full of sketches, tips, tricks and techniques on how to get by when life gets tough. Most of it is straightforward practical advice. Some I've picked up from reading books, countless hours researching online, experiencing and figuring out what works and what doesn't. I also took notes during classes and training sessions. Over the years I took several shooting classes, gunsmithing and firearms instructor courses, self-defense courses, with weapons or empty handed. During one of my first defensive shooting classes our instructor encouraged us to take notes so as to not forget what we learned and I applied that to every class I took since then. Sometimes while riding the train, driving to work or after experiencing or observing something as it happened an idea would pop up in my head and I'd quickly write it down.

In a way, this book complements my first book "The Modern Survival Manual: Surviving the Economic Collapse" with many of the skills described there being explained here in greater detail.

All of these skills, tips and observations apply to the philosophy I call modern survivalism. But what is modern survivalism?

Modern survivalism is a lifestyle through which a person makes decisions that significantly increase his chances of success when facing various challenges in life. This may be something as simple as dealing with a car breakdown in the middle of the road, get by during extended power outages during a storm, how to defend yourself on the streets or during a home invasion. Everything from knowing how to stay fit and healthy to knowing what to do if your house is on fire. Some people that identify with all of this refer to themselves as preppers or simply survivalists.

Preppers or doomsday preppers seem to focus mostly on preparing for large scale disruptive events, sometimes overlooking those things that are less dramatic but far more likely to happen. Traditional survivalism has also been linked to the idea of preparing specifically for large scale disasters like nuclear war or end of the world events of that same magnitude. For others it's about focusing on wilderness survival or bushcrafting, surviving and living in the great outdoors.

Rather than focusing on events and circumstances that are very unlikely to happen or downright fantasy, modern survivalism must be above all practical and grounded in reality. The modern survivalist should focus first on what is an unavoidable fact of life (getting old, sick, job loss), what is likely second and that which is very unlikely last. Granted, some of those very unlikely events can have life changing consequences so they may require more attention in a comprehensive preparedness plan.

A word of caution. As you may have noticed already, the world is full of some very strange, sometimes very crazy people and the world of survival and preparedness is no different. Be careful who you end up associating with. There's some amazing people in our community, some of which I greatly admire and consider good friends, but there's also some deeply disturbed individuals out there. Avoid anything that looks fanatic and devoid of logic. The moment you see that everything revolves around one person, take note.

Having lived in Argentina most of my life, crime and violence wasn't that much of an unlikely event. It was more of an unavoidable social reality you had to learn to live with. According to a Di Tella University study[1], violent crime has hit 2 out of 10 homes in Argentina in 2017. That's for 2017 alone. It doesn't take a mathematician to figure out how in such a context having to deal with violent crime eventually is practically unavoidable. Argentina isn't in anyway special when it comes to violent crime. It does happen in other countries, some which have far worse numbers. But in Argentina and Latin America in general crime is indeed a fact of life and people learn to live with it. It is only when you move to a much safer developed country that you grasp the magnitude of it all. In the developed world, middle class houses aren't expected to have fences and burglar bars along with an alarm system and reinforced security doors. In Argentina they are accepted as mandatory for anyone that can afford them. In developed countries it is not common for people to be mugged and carjacked at gunpoint. In Argentina is it downright rare to find an adult that hasn't gone through that at least once.

This is the reason why this book focuses so much on self-defense, security and awareness. My first book was similar in that regard. Some readers were expecting more information regarding the economic aspect. Some would comment "I bought a book about surviving an economic collapse, why am I reading about getting kidnapped?" Because that's what gets you killed when there's an economic collapse.

That's what happens when a country crashes and everything goes to hell. People have two concerns and two concerns only in their minds, all the time: The economy and crime. When the economy crashes you worry every day about making enough money to survive, make it till the end of the month. You worry about not getting fired, not having yet another unexpected bill to deal with. You worry about inflation melting the value of the little money you have in your pocket. You buy stuff today because it will go up in price tomorrow, significantly so. Living like this is terribly stressful. You can't plan anything and it's hard to see any light at the end of the tunnel because there simply is none.

But violent crime, that's in a league of its own. You can eventually find a job, get by with less money, ask friends and family for help and somehow pull through when money is tight. There's nothing you can do once you catch a bullet, or your son is killed or left brain dead in a hospital or when your wife or daughter gets raped while you are hopelessly tied to a chair and tortured for hours. There's no working these out. There's no pulling through. A bullet is final. A wife raped in front of her husband and children is an entire family ruined, damaged for life.

There's plenty of people out there that have lots of good advice on making, saving and investing money. Work hard, get an education, work hard some more. Its valid advice that works anywhere in the world and even during serious economic downturns it's still true. But none of this makes a difference if you fail at being prepared to deal with violence. Protecting yourself and keeping your family safe is what makes it or breaks it during tough times when violence is widespread.

This book also includes plenty of tips about other topics. Some you probably already know. Some are (as far as I know) original ideas of mine based on observations and the life experience of having lived in Argentina, United States, Spain and Northern Ireland.

Some of these are things I've been doing for years, either because I believe it's the smart thing to do or simply because I adapted (like many others did) to a more hostile environment. Most of the tactical shooting information here I learned it in classes from people that know a lot more about shooting than I ever will. You may have been taught the same thing, or something slightly different. In most cases, there's not just one way of doing things. If you've been taught something different and that works for you then that's perfectly fine. I often find myself in that same situation and when presented with a new technique or a different way of doing something I ask myself the following questions: Does it make sense? Is this a logical, sensible approach to address the issue at hand? And finally, does it work? Does it do what it's supposed to do in an effective manner?

Don't be afraid to change if something better or more effective comes along. Don't be afraid to stick to what you know is best either, no matter how much the new cool guy in the block tells you otherwise. There's added value in both gear and techniques that are time-proven.

Dealing with power outages is something I've dealt with most of my life, going back to the times when everyone kept a drawer full of candles for such occasions. Batteries were a luxury and incandescent flashlights burned through them in a matter of minutes.

The younger generations don't know this, and it wasn't *that* long ago, but before the use of LEDs became widespread it was downright expensive to run a flashlight! Keeping food supplies, simple and effective means of cooking it, these are all tips and little tricks that can be put to use when dealing with a number of situations, from minor inconveniences to serious emergencies.

Awareness, detecting potential threats and avoiding them in the first place, these skills should be put to use now and not wait until a disaster happens. Violent crime can happen to anyone, anywhere.

Some places are more dangerous than others, but your number may be up one day and all of a sudden you are dealing with a madman, a terrorist or some other mentally disturbed violent person that only want to kill as many people as possible. Even if it's just a junkie with a cheap knife, you simply never know because that's how life works. What are the chances of having to deal with a life threatening situation? Pretty low if you are lucky enough to live in a good area, but it still happens.

The way I conceive modern survival is more about a way of life than preparing for certain specific disasters. Even if these happen, you won't get a 24hr notification ahead of time. Living in constant red alert isn't realistic but making sure you are aware of what's going on around you and not walk like a zombie with your eyes glued to your cell phone, that's very much doable. Beyond all this, modern survivalism isn't just a lifestyle but a mindset, a way of thinking. To be tough, physically but most of all mentally. To learn to stoically cope with whatever life throws your way, no matter how old or young you are. To stay positive (dear God I can't emphasize this point enough!) when everything seems hopeless, but also when everything is fine yet for whatever reason you can't seem to be able to relax and just enjoy life.

Learn to enjoy the good times.

As for the bad ones, dealing with those is what this book is about.

NOTES:

Chapter 1

Survival Basics

"Be bold and mighty forces will come to your aid."

-Basil King

Survival Rule of Three

Although not always scientifically precise, the Survival Rule of Three does illustrate the main priorities to sustain life:

1) You can't survive 3 minutes without air. Even if taken for granted, air is still essential for survival. Everything from fires and smoke in buildings to volcano eruptions and ash or chemical accidents or attacks, without breathable air you won't be lasting long. It's one of the most overlooked areas in most people's preparedness plans. N99/FFP3 respirators or even full NBC (nuclear, biological, chemical) gas masks can make the difference between being able to breathe (and staying alive) or not.

2) You can't survive 3 hours of exposure to extreme weather conditions. For extreme low temperatures with inadequate clothing the survival time is even lower. Shelter and proper clothing are key elements in survival.

3) You can't survive 3 days without water. Yet another precious resource taken for granted and often overlooked. People feel thirsty in a matter of hours and will become desperate for water within 24hs. Those that wish to be prepared usually understand how important stockpiling food is but not nearly enough stock the minimum amount of water (one gallon per person per day) to make it through a week.

A quality water filter is just as important.

4) You can't survive 3 weeks without food. It can vary greatly but that's about it. Let's just say you won't be around for long without food. Choose shelf-stable food that requires no refrigeration and stores well for long periods of time. Rice, beans, lentils, wheat, dry pasta, canned fruits, vegetables and meats. These are some of the more common staples that have proven themselves over time.

5) You can't survive 3 seconds with a bullet through your brain.

The previous rules are essential for survival but you don't often hear of people freezing or dying of thirst. Suffocation yes, that happens a lot, especially among children during domestic accidents. But of all the rules, the one I know of that kills or otherwise ruins people's lives the most is violent crime. I've seen it happen a lot in Argentina but also in developed countries including the United States. Violent crime does get people killed and it does destroy lives, so prepare accordingly.

Having said this, keep things in context. Cardiovascular diseases and cancer are far more likely to kill you than a bullet.

1.
2.
3.
4.
5.
$

Seven Circles of Preparedness

A good way to understand what your priorities are when it comes to preparedness is organizing them in seven concentric circles.

1) Mindset. The software that runs it all. Without the right mindset nothing else matters. This circle also includes the general attitude you have towards life, the skills and knowledge acquired over the years. The mental resilience you've developed. The spirit always breaks first, not the body. Even with a broken body, he who is truly strong in spirit will always be indomitable.

2) A strong healthy body is your most prized physical tool in this world. Look after it. You need to be healthy, eat well and exercise. It is ironic how many preppers and survivalists ignore the risk of cardiovascular disease, by far the most common cause of premature death.

3) The items you carry with you at all times, your everyday carry (EDC) will be the tools available to you when disaster strikes as it usually does: In the most inconvenient moment. Be honest about what you need but be diligent and consistent as well.

4) When disaster strikes while away from home, your vehicle and the tools in it are all you have to work with. Select them careful. For people working in an office or shop most of the day, this may be the place where they keep additional supplies so as to make it back home during a disaster or emergency.

5) Home, your castle. The place where you are safe and keep most of your supplies. This is where you "shelter in place", the most sensible approach for most emergencies. It may be a house in the city or a homestead in the country with solar, water and food production. Whatever it is make the most of it. Improve its security, make it a hard target and maximize its capabilities and self-reliance as much as you can.

6) The local community. The people you share your town with, do business with and socialize. Stay informed regarding local news and events. Do participate in that school parents social network group. Network and make the time so as to get to know your neighbors.

7) The world around you. Learn to understand what's going on in the world, what the media presents, what their angle is and where their true interests lie. Know what's happening in your country too and know what red flags to look for so as to keep you and your family safe. Know which events are unfolding and know when the time comes to take action.

LOCAL NEWS
WORK PLACE
1
2
3
4
5
6
7
$

Mind and Body

Survival isn't just about managing to stay alive. The point of being alive in the first place is enjoying it, and nothing impacts both your chances of survival and enjoying life like the choices you make every day in regards to your health, both mental and physical.

If we want to expand on the Rule of Three we could say that you won't be enjoying life much by eating poorly for three years. For millions of people, they won't even be *alive* three years from now if they don't make some radical changes to their diet.

Eating healthy, working out but also looking after your mental wellbeing for what it is: A crucial part of your overall health. Avoid worrying about things that are beyond your control but do something about changing for the better the ones you can. Avoid toxic, hateful and negative people. By all means make sure you are not a toxic person yourself. Don't even allow yourself to think that way. Negativity spreads like a disease if you allow it to make itself comfortable in your mind.

Follow a healthy, balanced diet based on non-processed food, the kind that you don't need a degree in chemistry to understand the ingredients list or better yet, has no ingredients list at all because you can tell it's a banana, egg, tomato or piece of beef. Work your way towards healthy eating habits. Learn to cook from scratch and be mindful of the calories consumed/calories spent ratio. Drink plenty of water. Eat fresh fruits and vegetables and a certain amount of quality protein. Some of the most successful, time-proven diets such as the Mediterranean diet revolve around such concepts.

You can't outrun a poor diet, but working out is still important. The World Health Organization[2] (WHO) recommends that adults aged 18–64 should do at least 150 minutes of moderate-intensity aerobic physical activity or at least 75 minutes of vigorous-intensity aerobic physical activity throughout the week.

Given that both time and money are a limited resources, invest them well so as to maximize the benefits. A martial art may be a great way to stay in shape, learn a valuable skill and meet like-minded people. Shooting can be practiced as a sport, become part of a community (develop your networking, mental wellbeing and social skills). It can be combined with hunting and hiking as outdoors activities. Manage your time and don't try to do it all at once but try to incorporate different skills, stay curious and don't allow yourself to stop learning.

MIND & BODY

Bugging Out

Bugging Out has to be, by far, the most misunderstood concept in the world of survival and preparedness. Hollywood carries its fair share of responsibility for this but part of it is also basic human nature.

People understand how food and water would be important in a survival situation. Most folks see the wisdom in knowing how to defend yourself and it doesn't hurt that shooting happens to be a lot of fun. They also quickly understand that a healthy diet along with regular exercise is important and how ridiculous it is to worry much about the end of the world when obesity and cholesterol are effectively killing you right this moment. Most preppers and survivalists love being outdoors and are usually appreciative of their privacy, so a bit of land and growing their own food appeals to them as well.

1) But tell them to prepare to leave everything, all their belongings, and most of them will have an immediate emotional breakdown. In some cases they fire back with a quick "I'm already at my bug out location". Wherever that may be the paradox is that you can never live (as in permanently) in your bug out location given that a bug out location is where you go when your place of residence is no longer viable. A flood, fire, civil unrest, war, whatever causes you to leave the place in which you currently reside, the bug out location is where you plan to go.

2) A bug out location can be a number of places. As long as you can go there when you can no longer stay in your current home, that's a potential bug out location for you, even if it's just a relative's condo.

3) It can also be a holiday home, hunting cabin or dedicated retreat.

4) For some people, they plan on relying on an RV. These are potentially viable bug out locations but they need to be ready to go, along with supplies and an actual plan in regards to where you will be going and where you can park the RV for an extended period of time.

5) Ideally you would have not one but several potential bug out location options. These could be houses of friends and family with whom you have agreed you can count on in times of need. Maybe you have a mutual aid agreement and have not only a place to go but some supplies already in place such as spare clothes, some food, cash and gear.

Whatever it is you have in mind, don't just assume you can count on someone if you ever need them. Actually ask. You may be surprised to learn how wrong you were to assume you could count on someone.

1.
2.
3.
4.
5.

Politics and Media

Awareness also means understanding world events around you, both at a local and global level. At times, understanding how the wheels are turning gives you time to prepare better, make necessary preparations or avoid large scale, life-changing disasters entirely. A neighbouring country about to invade, a president willing to destroy a country's economy long term only to achieve a short term personal victory or simply benefit financially. You must know what's going on. We also happen to live at a time in history when, ironically enough, in spite of having more access to information than ever before we are also more vulnerable than ever before to manipulation.

Technology is a double edged sword. The moment we go online what we see when searching for something is already tainted depending on the search engine we use (I recommend Firefox as a navigator and DuckDuckGo as a search engine). We are bombarded with news that may be entirely fabricated just to influence our opinion. This kind of micro targeting individuals has become so effective, data mining firms know you better than you know yourself. They know what information you want to "consume" and how it will influence your opinion.

Remember: **There are two sides to every story and it is somewhere between those two that you shall find the truth.**

1) Assume everything you read and see online is likely fake. A lot of it is.

2) Look into the sources. Some media outlets are more trustworthy than others but all of them have their own agenda. Who owns the specific company usually says a lot of what news they consider worthy of publishing, its relevance and the angle in which it will be presented.

3) When it comes to politics, apply the same criteria. Where is this person coming from? Who "owns" him? Who are his greatest contributors, what does he owe them and how has he behaved in the past?

4) Politicians come and go so it makes no sense to make big life changes based on someone's temporary job. Having said that, long term trends can affect society and if you see a clear trend in a direction you do not like, consider what action you will take if that trend continues.

5) Left, Right or anything in between, have zero tolerance when it comes to corruption. The only excuse for knowingly supporting and giving power to a corrupt politician who is supposed to represent your best interests is being an utter fool.

FREE $!
VOTE HiM!
VOTE ME!
MSM: VOTE HIM!
100
BUY! 1x$10,000.00

NOTES:

Chapter 2
Awareness

"Be polite, be professional, but have a plan to kill everyone you meet"

- General James "Mad Dog" Mattis

Awareness

Awareness is the ability to recognize people and events developing around you with an emphasis on potential threats. This is without a doubt, one of the most important skills a person can develop.

A heightened level of vigilance can help you avoid dangerous situations entirely. Simply thinking about it, keeping your head up and looking at people around you will significantly increase your awareness level. With practice you will learn to notice suspicious behaviours. Awareness can work at an instinctive level, your "spidey-sense" will let you know something is wrong. This only means that at an unconscious level your brain caught something that is perceived as dangerous.

Colonel Jeff Cooper recognizes four levels of awareness:

1. White. You are completely unaware of your surroundings and unprepared for any kind of attack. You may be using headphones and completely focusing your attention on your cell phone.

   It is not unusual for such people to walk straight into walls, light posts, other people or get hit by cars, let alone get mugged.

2. Yellow. You are moderately aware of what is going on around you. You identify events and people as well as their body language. While being relaxed you are still alert and reasonably prepared for any eventuality.

3. Orange. This is a heightened level of alert. You are not relaxed. You are scanning your surroundings, actively looking for potential threats and planning to take action accordingly. Potential threats have been detected and you already made up your mind about acting if the threat continues or follows through with the action you believe is about to occur.

4. Red. You are in a fight. You are punching, kicking, moving for cover, shooting. You are at your maximum level of awareness, adrenaline pumping.

Ideally you will manage to find a comfortable strong yellow/light orange condition: Aware of your surroundings. Calm but not fully relaxed. Your alarm is set and ready to go on the background while you go about your day.

WHITE
yellow
ORANGE
RED

Controlling Emotions and Body Language

Your mind is your number one most valuable asset, both for survival and life in general. At the end of the day, the purpose of preparedness and survival is to overcome adversity and enjoy fulfilling lives. Being prepared and knowing what to do during disasters and emergencies that would catch the average person completely by surprise not only means you will be more likely to survive them, it means you will also enjoy the peace of mind that comes along with knowing you are capable of dealing with such events.

Key to all of this is our mental stability. A person that crumbles emotionally under pressure struggles through everyday life and just gets crushed by the pressure of greater challenges. During hard times, people need to be tough, both physically and emotionally.

A person that lacks the determination to stay healthy and fit, within a reasonable weight for his size, will often lack the willpower to achieve other things as well. This is why the way a person looks usually say quite a bit about them, including their inner fortitude. Having said this, the mind is truly where it's at. I've known very fit people that when pushed to the limit gave up while less athletic people carried on. Their bodies can go on but the mind just quits and yet for others, even when the body tells them to stop, sheer willpower pushes them forward. There is of course a limit to all of this. Willpower alone won't turn a couch potato into an athlete just because he wills it. This is more about endurance, paint tolerance and pushing yourself to your limits. If those limits are very low though, your mental fortitude won't get you past that.

By controlling your emotions you control you actions and this includes your body language as well. A person that looks physically weak because he lacked the discipline to change that will struggle to go about with an air of confidence and self-assurance he hasn't earned.

Body language is more important than what most people realize. If you look aware and confident then you are far less likely to be considered a soft target by potential attackers. These people are like wild animals. They "smell" weakness, or more like it, unconsciously notice your weakness by your body language and the way you carry yourself.

Being confident, standing tall and speaking with a strong and reassured tone of voice has other advantages beyond self-defense. It also means you are more likely to end up with a better deal when haggling for whatever goods or resources you are likely to need or when negotiating a pay raise with your boss. It simply means you are more likely to get whatever it is you want in life in general.

It's not just about looking the part (physically fit) standing straight with your chin up and looking at people in the eye. It's also about the position of your hands and feet, if you move them nervously while "trying" to look strong and confident when you're really not. It's about how fluid your movements are, how steady your voice tone is and even the minute details of your facial features.

Ideally, you want to be in control, all the time, or at least as much as realistically possible. Work on your "poker" face and don't let emotions betray you. Mentally remind yourself to remain stoic and calm, no matter what you may be struggling with internally.

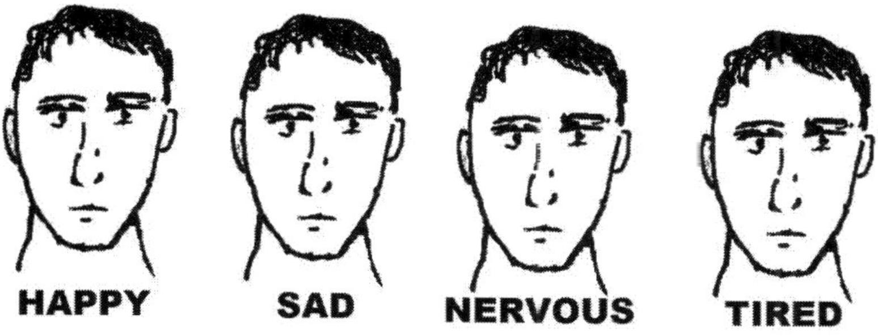

Controlling yourself in this manner not only affects the way others perceive you, it also affects the way you perceive yourself and has very real consequences on your performance. Self-pity because you are in pain when marching for long hours, telling yourself it's okay to quit because you have been injured, these aren't inconsequential feel-good details. These are the difference between winning or losing, living or dying.

These character traits either make you or break you. Like a piece of metal that was thrown into the furnace, beaten time and again and then quenched in cold water (or oil, or your enemy's guts if you believe those stories). It comes down to you making up your mind about what you are made of. If pressure, fire and a cold bath makes you shatter like glass or forges you into strong steel.

Self-pity is never acceptable at any level. Doesn't matter if it's a long whine on how tired you are and how much your feet hurt or if it's a little nervous tsking sound after missing a target. Don't deprecate even for a fraction of a second. Failing means you are training at getting better. Simply do it again. And again. And again until you get it right.

Assessing Surroundings and Resources

Just as you should learn to notice suspicious people around you, learn to keep track of resources available to you in your vicinity.

1) ATMs, police stations, hospitals, pharmacies, pawn stores, gun stores, money exchange shops, make a mental note of them.

As you walk down the street notice which areas provide cover or concealment in a moment's notice. Just a step or two behind a wall or line of trees may keep you safe if you suddenly hear screams or gunfire.

Sewers may overflow during a flood in your area or a manhole may allow you to cover a few blocks underground away from trouble. Pay attention and try to figure out the sewer network. In some areas it may be important to keep track of the community shelters in case of an emergency alert. Know where they are in case you ever need them.

2) The same applies to an office environment or any building you frequent regularly. Notice things such as where the emergency exits and stairs are. Where the fire alarm is, extinguishers, first aid kit. Even where water and food in the form of vending machines may be available. The utility room, supply room or shop may have useful tools and resources during an emergency. The same applies to resources in the form of people. Keep track of what skillsets may come in handy. Someone with medical or emergency response experience, former military, these may be people you can count on during certain events.

3) See, listen, smell and feel the world around you. There may be times in which you hear a loud bang and smell gun power a few moments later. You may hear nothing and just smell it. Don't wear headphones on the street or in public transportation and if you do, only wear one so as to have at least some audio input. Screams, a speeding car, even quick footsteps behind you, these are all things you will notice if you pay attention. This goes for your eyes as well. Keeping your eyes glued to your phone like most people do these days when walking around makes you as vulnerable as a baby. You may as well just wear a blindfold as you walk around.

Learn to notice when things just don't feel right. Pay attention to the people you work with. Notice those that seem off somehow or make extremist political or religious comments. Even when done in a humorous manner there may be something there to be careful about.

24 hr.
PHARMACY
BANK
SAFE ATM
COVER
SUSPICIOUS PERSON
CONCEALMENT
SEWER
STORM SHELTER
1
VENDING MACHINE
FIRST AID
EXIT
WATER
AED
FIRE ALARM
EX MILITARY
UTILITY ROOM
2.
3.

Suspicious Behaviour

You are more likely to notice suspicious people when you know what to look for. Some will be visibly nervous, others may display a dominant body language, feeling bold/empowered because they carry a weapon.

1) People that are up to no good will usually try to conceal their identity. Hoodies, caps or hats may be used. Sometimes sunglasses too.

Loose clothes are better for concealing weapons. Be suspicious of hands kept in pockets and if a weapon is "printing" in the fabric, meaning a visible outline or bulge of a gun beneath the clothes.

Pay attention to nervous people that seem to keep their head on a swivel. They may also pace around, as in struggling to stay put in one spot.

2) Look for guns printing on clothes around the waist area, especially upfront and to the sides (right for most) although some people may carry on the small of their backs too. Also, watch their hands. People that aren't used to carrying concealed will be constantly touching around the area, pulling down their shirt worrying about exposing the weapon.

3) People walk with intent going about their day. Hanging around or just standing in one spot for no apparent reason is suspicious. Most people will have some kind of bag, briefcase or purse. A person that is empty handed with no backpack or bag of any kind is also uncommon.

4) People hanging out in public will usually be engaged in conversation with others or staring at their phones. Someone that is doing neither one and is simply keeping an eye out deserves your attention.

5) Watch the hands. Cops and military are trained to "see the hands". When it comes to a suspicious person, you want to see both hands empty. If not, then there's a reason for concern. Also, a nervous person may have his fists clenched or rapidly open and close his hand. This is a natural instinctive tell for a nervous person about to fight.

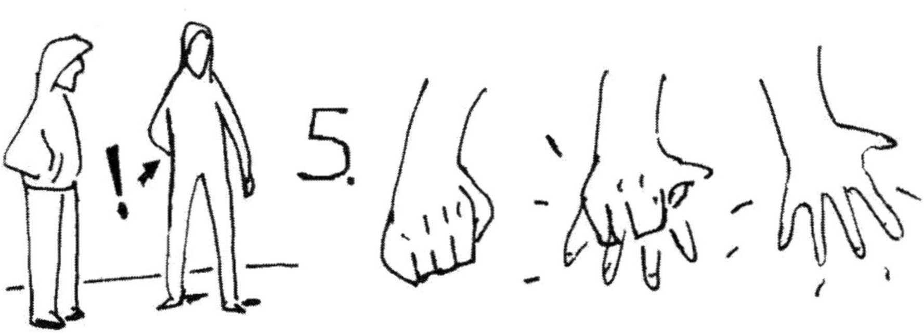

1.
2.
3.
4.

Awareness when Indoors

Every time you enter a building look for the emergency exit. Exits will be clearly signalled in most commercial buildings. Make a mental note of at least two, including the one you just walked through when entering the building. As you move around, keep in mind which exit is closest to you at any given moment.

1) Whenever possible, sit with your back against the wall to cover your six (as in the six o'clock position, 12 o'clock being right in front of you) facing the main entrance. The seat marked "A" would be a good choice. Get used to taking note of who walks in every time the door opens.

"A" is the best place to sit: Sitting against the wall with a clear field of view of both the main entrance and the rest of the people in the establishment. It is also closest to the emergency exit. Should a threat walk in (armed robber, active shooter, etc.) the emergency exit is nearby.

2) When sitting with a companion, do so slightly offset so as to cover each other's back. Among like-minded individuals they may choose to sit organically in this position.

3) In movie theatres, conference rooms or similar settings, the same principle applies: Locate exits and choose a seat that allows for quick exit in case of an emergency. "A" allows the quickest exit while avoiding the more exposed seats in the first two rows. In the case of movie theatres, "B" could be a good choice too so as to quickly reach the main entrance. The back rows are higher and jumping over the wall and falling a small distance may be required. If it's too high you may injure yourself so keep that in mind. In the case of an active shooter (dashed line is the most likely path to be taken by one) it would allow you to escape before the attacker reaches the seats at the back.

4) When sitting at a table, avoid hanging your bag from the chair. It can be easily stolen from there. A bag on top of the table isn't a much better option since it can be snatched by a thief that can take off running, especially when sitting outside or in large food courts.

It is best to keep your bag between your legs, with one of your legs through the strap so that it can't be pushed away from you or accidentally forgotten when leaving.

5) When standing in small stores, it's a good idea to simply wait close to the door in case you need to make a quick exit for whatever reason.

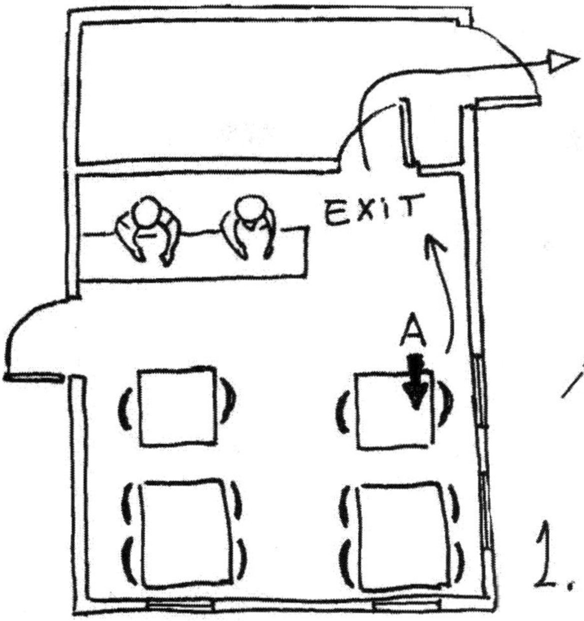

1.

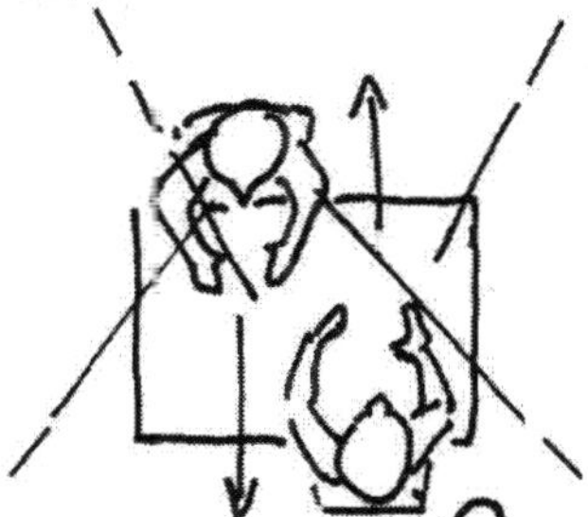

2.

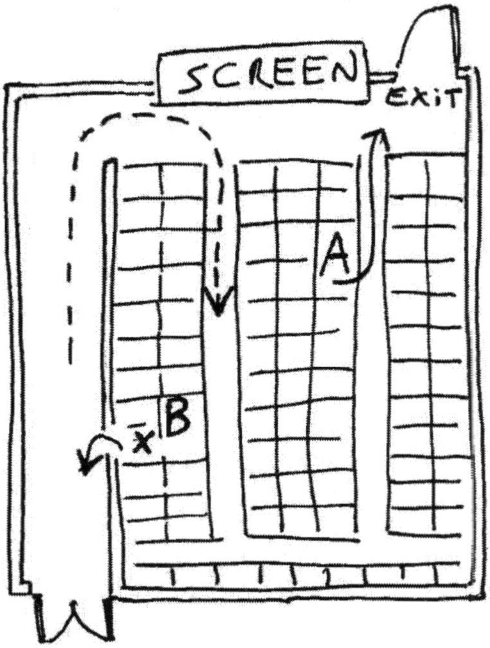

3.

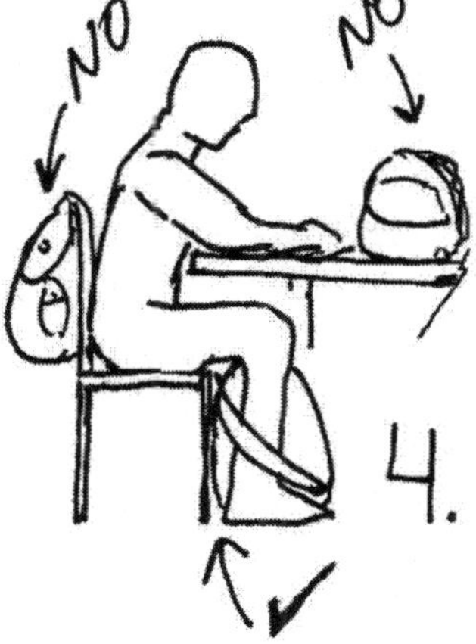

4.

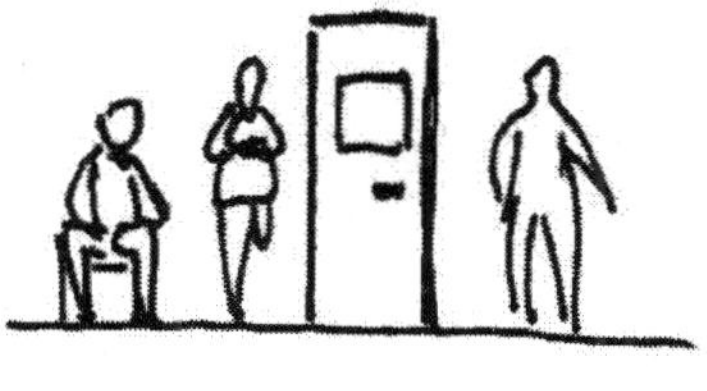

5.

Estimating Distances

In the book "Firing Regulations for Small Arms for the United States Army" by Blunt, Stanhope E. published in 1899, the following advice is provided for estimating distances by sight under ideal conditions:

30 yards- At this distance the white of a person's eye is clearly visible.

80 yards- The two eyes are still distinguishable

100 yards- Facial features can be distinguished and all parts of the body are still seen distinctly. Slight movements are perceivable and minute details of clothes and gear can be distinguished.

150 yards- Some details in clothing and gear can still be distinguished.

200 yards- The outline of the face is confused and the "rows of buttons look like Stripes" (keep in mind the time period of the original text and the uniform worn in 1899)

300 yards- Clothing and gear details are no longer visible.

400 yards- The face is a mere dot, but movement of arms and legs are still distinct.

600 yards- Details are no longer distinguishable, but the files of a squad, if the light is strong, can be counted. The person looks like a short vertical dash or triangle.

800 yards- Men in a squad can't always be counted nor their individual movements distinguished.

1,000 yards- A line of men resembles a "broad belt" the direction of their march can be determined.

1,200 yards- Infantry can be distinguished from cavalry

2,000 yards- A mounted man appears like a mere speck or dot.

Distances can also be estimated using an A65/1 reticle such as the one found on an Eotech holographic sight with a 65 MOA (minute of angle) circle and a 1 MOA dot in the center.

Other sights share similar reticles in which case these estimations also apply to them. It is best to set up a target with the actual height and verify if these estimations are correct for your particular rifle and sight.

Using an M16 rifle or similar AR platform, the front sight post covers the width of a man's chest at approximately 300 meters[3], 2/3 of his width 200 meters away and his entire head at 100 meters. This is a rough estimate and changes with different front sights and barrel lengths.

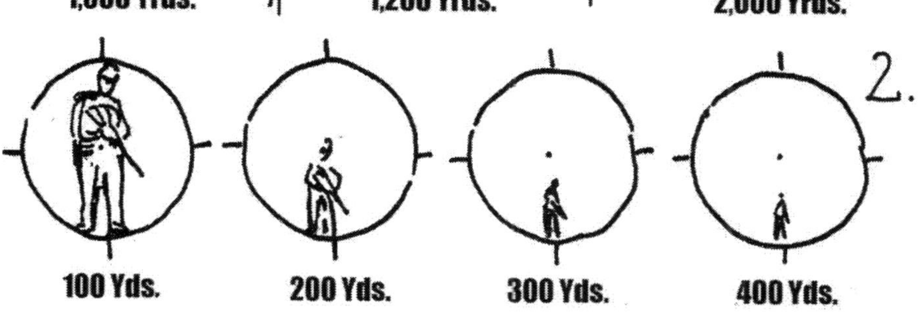

A65/1 reticle pattern with 65 minutes of angle (MOA) ring and 1MOA dot

Crowd Estimation

Crowd estimation allows you to quickly count how many people are in a crowd. The technique isn't very accurate, but an approximated figure is usually good enough for most practical purposes. This technique has many applications, from counting people to stacks or pallets of goods in a warehouse.

Knowing how many people you have in a crowd gives you an idea if the police ratio on the ground would be enough if the protest turns violent.

There's no magic number to know for sure. For a peaceful family event during the day a ratio of 500:1 (1 officer per 500 people) may be enough.[4] For a rock concert, that number may have to go up to 100:1 because such events attract mostly young adult males and there is usually alcohol and drugs involved. During a demonstration or protest that can turn violent, that number can go up to 20:1.

1) Draw imaginary lines in the crowd and divide it by nine.

Count how many people you have in one of the squares and multiply it by ten. Ten is faster to multiply and it conservatively adjusts you margin of error. The edges of a crowd often hold less people as well.

2) For larger crowds, divide by nine and then divide that portion again by nine and count the people in that sector. Now you want to multiply them by 100 to get a rough estimate.

This is just an example. You can of course divide the crowd by whatever number you believe fits the situation best depending on how they happen to be distributed. This method of dividing the crowd in sectors, counting and multiplying is known as the Jacobs's Method.

3) Another effective method of estimating how many people are in a crowd is "Static Crowd Density". This basically means, how tightly people are packed in a specific location.

First, estimate the area. Buildings can be used as a reference with each floor being three meters high. Once you know the area, estimate the crowd's density.

4) If people are standing leaving shoulder's length spaces between them, that's about 2 people per square meter.[5]

5) Shoulder to shoulder one next to the other, that's the upper limit for a standing crowd which is 5 people per square meter.

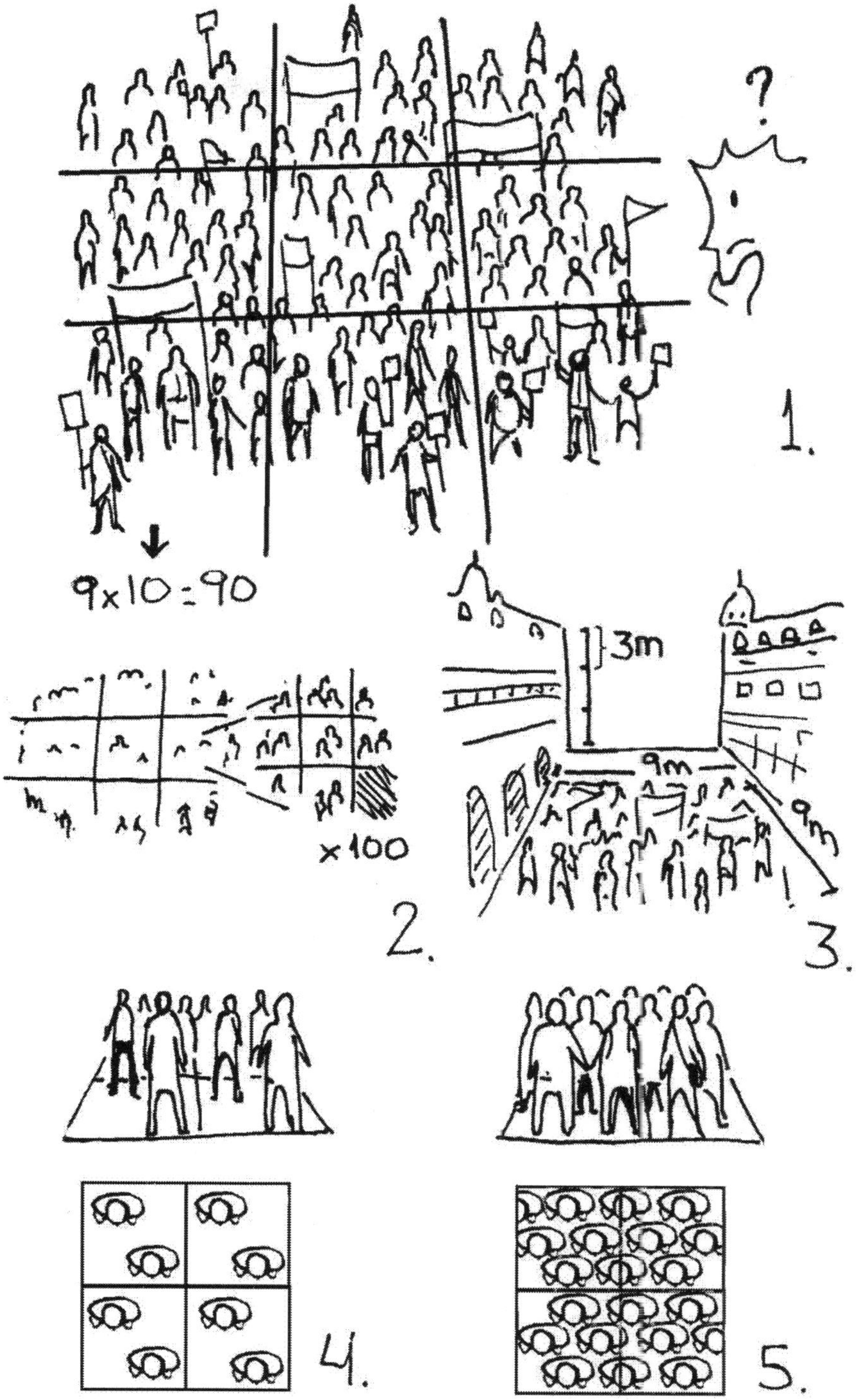
?
1.
9x10=90
x100
2.
3m
9m
9m
3.
4.
5.

NOTES:

Chapter 3:

Gear

"How little you know about the age you live in if you think that honey is sweeter than cash in hand"

-Publius Ovidius Naso, born 20 March 43 BC

Everyday Carry Gear

The gear you carry around with you on daily basis, your EDC (everyday carry), is your first line of defense whenever there's an emergency.

If you get attacked on a parking lot, get hurt in a car crash or get trapped in an elevator or under rubble after an earthquake, what you have with you is all the kit you will be able to rely on to deal with the situation at hand. This is why your everyday carry gear selection is so important.

Ideally, if attacked by an armed criminal in a parking lot (and not being there is not an option) you would have body armor and a Benelli M4 loaded with buckshot. If trapped hanging from a tree for dear life during a flood you'd have a satellite phone and a flare gun. But since all of that is just wishful thinking and not realistic, so as to at least have SOME tools with us we need to go for that word no one likes yet is what life is all about: compromise. The trick to a good EDC setup is finding a combination that covers the basics you don't want to be without yet you can realistically have with you at all times. EDC means every day. What only gets carried sometimes and not always does not count because you will not have it with you when you need it. If you find yourself leaving part of your EDC behind because it's too big or too heavy then maybe revaluate how important it is or maybe go with a smaller/lighter version.

Your EDC should include the following:

1) Wallet. A couple hundred dollars and quarters may be your most useful tool. I know it has saved the day for me several times. Keep one $100 for emergencies hidden in your wallet and some change in $20 or $10 bills. Coins are handy for public phones, parking and vending machines. Choose a wallet that has a pocket for coins.

2) Mobile phone. Choose rugged models or a waterproof model with a protective case and tempered glass screen protector. You don't want your phone to break at the worst possible moment. Choose a phone with a big enough battery. There are still models that have stand-alone FM radio that don't use internet connection. These can be invaluable during disasters when everything else fails. They do use headphones as an antenna so make sure you have a pair in your bag or jacket at all times.

3) Gun. Where and whenever legal to do so, get used to carrying a gun. There's no excuse for not doing so if this is a possibility. Being armed when attacked, either by criminals, kidnappers or mentally unstable people can be the difference between life and death. The life you may be saving may be the one of a loved one rather than your own. A Glock 19 9mm hits the perfect spot of not too big yet not too small. It's a gun you can carry daily yet shoot well during training and competition. A 5-shot snubby 38 revolver in the pocket is far better than nothing but it lacks the capability of a 16 round capacity 9mm. Statistically you are unlikely to need more than 4 or 5 rounds but there's plenty of cases involving multiple attackers and double stack 9mm autos begin shot empty. Choose a gun you feel covers your needs but be honest about it.

4.

5.

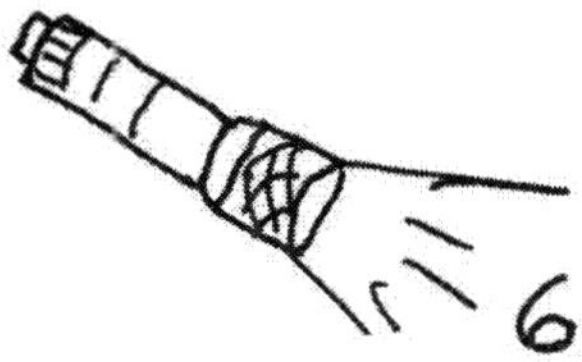
6.

4) Sunglasses. Choose sturdy tactical models that also provide some degree of impact protection. These can be used at the range as well but using them daily means your eyes are well protected not only from UV rays but also dust, debris or any other foreign object. Polarized glasses reduce glare and improve your vision in general. There's also a psychological factor when interacting with people. During arguments and negotiations not showing your eyes while being able to see those of others puts you in a position of power. This may also affect how criminals perceive you when scanning for potential victims.

5) Multi-tool. A quality multi-tool has to be one of the most useful parts of your EDC. After decades of carrying one personally, I don't understand how other people make it through the day without one. In particular the Wave and Charge models by Leatherman, these are very highly recommended, especially with the addition of a pocket clip. The blade is large enough, it can double as a pocket knife for most needs.

6) Flashlight. Without artificial light, it's dark 50% of the time. That doesn't include time spent indoors without light for whatever reason.

After the multi-tool, the flashlight is one of the most valuable tools in your EDC. Pick a model from a reputable manufacturer that uses a single battery. Some models can run both standard AA batteries as well as rechargeable 14500 Lithium Ion batteries. These are similar in power to the CR123A batteries used in tactical lights. The advantage is that you can still run normal AA batteries in them. Some 14500 batteries have an integrated micro-USB port, allowing you to charge the battery directly with a phone charger. This allows for a great deal of flexibility while running a LED flashlight with high lumen output. Flashlights that have low, medium, high and moonlight modes are better because they let you adapt your power consumption during extended blackouts.

7) Folding knife. The knife is the quintessential survival tool. A pocket knife has been part of a gentleman's pocket carry way before the term EDC was coined. The uses for a good pocket knife are countless, but the reality is that a good multi-tool will cover most of your pocket knife needs. Because of this, it makes more sense to go for a sturdy tactical folder, something that can be used for defense and heavy work beyond the uses intended for the blade in your multi-tool. Go with a quality knife. It should include a pocket clip, single handed opening and it should hold an edge well. The locking mechanism should be sturdy and dependable. The blade should be three to four inches long although longer blades can also be carried comfortably throughout the day.

8) Pepper Spray. Pepper Spray should be part of your EDC if carrying a firearm isn't an option. It is compact, light and affordable and when used properly it has a good chance of bringing even the toughest guy to a halt. Even when carrying a gun, pepper spray gives you a non-lethal option to use before escalating to lethal force.

9) Car and house keys. A smart keychain setup allows you to always carry a minimum set of tools at all times. Since you can't drive or get back home without your keys, this forces your to have at least some tools. For people that struggle with the idea of carrying a bunch of EDC gadgets, this is a good way to start. A Leatherman PS4 is one of the best keychain multi-tools available, surprisingly versatile for its size. Victorinox also offers a number of keychain-size models with the Minichamp being the most complete one. Include a small AAA battery LED and run it with a rechargeable AAA battery. These have more power and unlike alkaline primaries, they do not leak. A small peanut lighter or ferrocerium rod will allow you to start fires. This makes for a quite capable keychain setup without being bulky or heavy.

10.

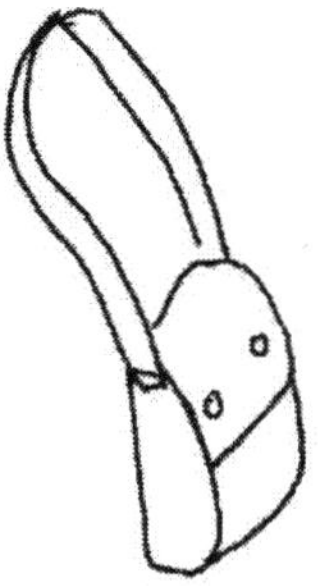

11.

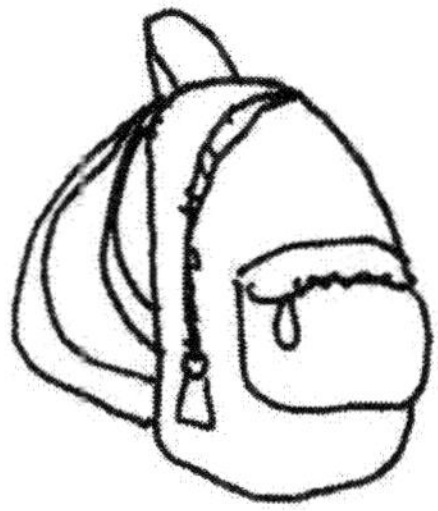

12.

10) Magazine. If you carry a gun, you need to carry at least one spare magazine. In the case of revolvers, you can use speed loaders or speed strips. Ideally your reload would be in a magazine carrier in your belt or in your pocket. If this isn't viable, then it can be kept in your EDC bag.

An EDC bag allows you to carry more gear comfortably. If not fully loaded, the empty space can be practical for whatever you need to carry throughout the day while running errands.

11) The shoulder bag or messenger bag is more practical for opening and accessing the contents often. It is not as big as an actual backpack but it may be enough for your needs.

12) A backpack can carry more gear, comfortably. It is also more convenient for long walks and marches outdoors. In packed urban environments you need to keep an eye on it to make sure no one is opening the backpack and stealing from you. Just hang it from a strap like a messenger bag and keep it in front of you.

An EDC bag lets you carry more gear and a small first aid kit, water bottle, respirator and energy bar are worthy additions. More gear can be added depending on your personal needs but going light and having room for other things you may need to carry has its advantages as well.

Try blending in and avoid bright colors, logos or military looking gear unless these are common in your area. Plain black or dark green are good choices that usually don't warrant much attention.

1) Tilting your head forward bringing your chin down is a natural instinctive reaction in the presence of danger. It covers your neck better, gives you a more solid structure if punched in the head and it improves your peripheral vision.

This can be quickly verified by standing straight, looking forward with your arms stretched and thumbs up. While keeping your eyes focused on an object in front of you, move your hands to the sides until your thumbs are out of your field of view. Tilt your head and you'll see your thumbs clearly again within your peripheral vision

2) The lines in a plaid shirt allows you to break the printing of a gun much better. The exact same gun "print" was drawn on both cases. The one on the right with the chequered pattern hides it much better. When keeping a weapon concealed is a high priority, details like these make a big difference. You can adapt the kind of plaid you go for depending on the environment you are trying to fit it. A red and blue plaid shirt would go well in most rural areas. A blue, green and white shirt would be perfectly at home in an office environment along with khaki pants.

3) Knife pocket clips, usually black, are very visible against khaki, sand and other clear color fabrics. This may attract unwanted attention. Police officers and security personal are often trained to look for these. Darker color pants and deep carry clips reduce the chance of detection and the hassle of explaining what you are carrying and why.

Having said this, there may be times when you are better off keeping the folding knife entirely in your pocket and not risk it being noticed.

4) Keep a cuff key and scalpel blade hidden in your belt. These can go under a strip of duct tape on the inside of your belt. Right side of your waist for right handed people, left side for lefties. This will make it easier to access if you are cuffed in front or behind your back. The cuff key will help you escape if captured by kidnapers or other criminals. The blade can be used for cutting ropes and cord if tied and also as a thumb knife as a last resort defensive tool.

Tip: A neat thumb knife can be made using a piece of a hacksaw. Put an edge on it with a grinder and you have a nice little thumb knife. The piece of saw can also be used, with enough patience, to cut through chains or even bars.

5) Get used to keeping your strong arm, the hand with which you shoot, unoccupied as you go about your day carrying packs, bags or even when holding hands with a girlfriend, wife or your children.

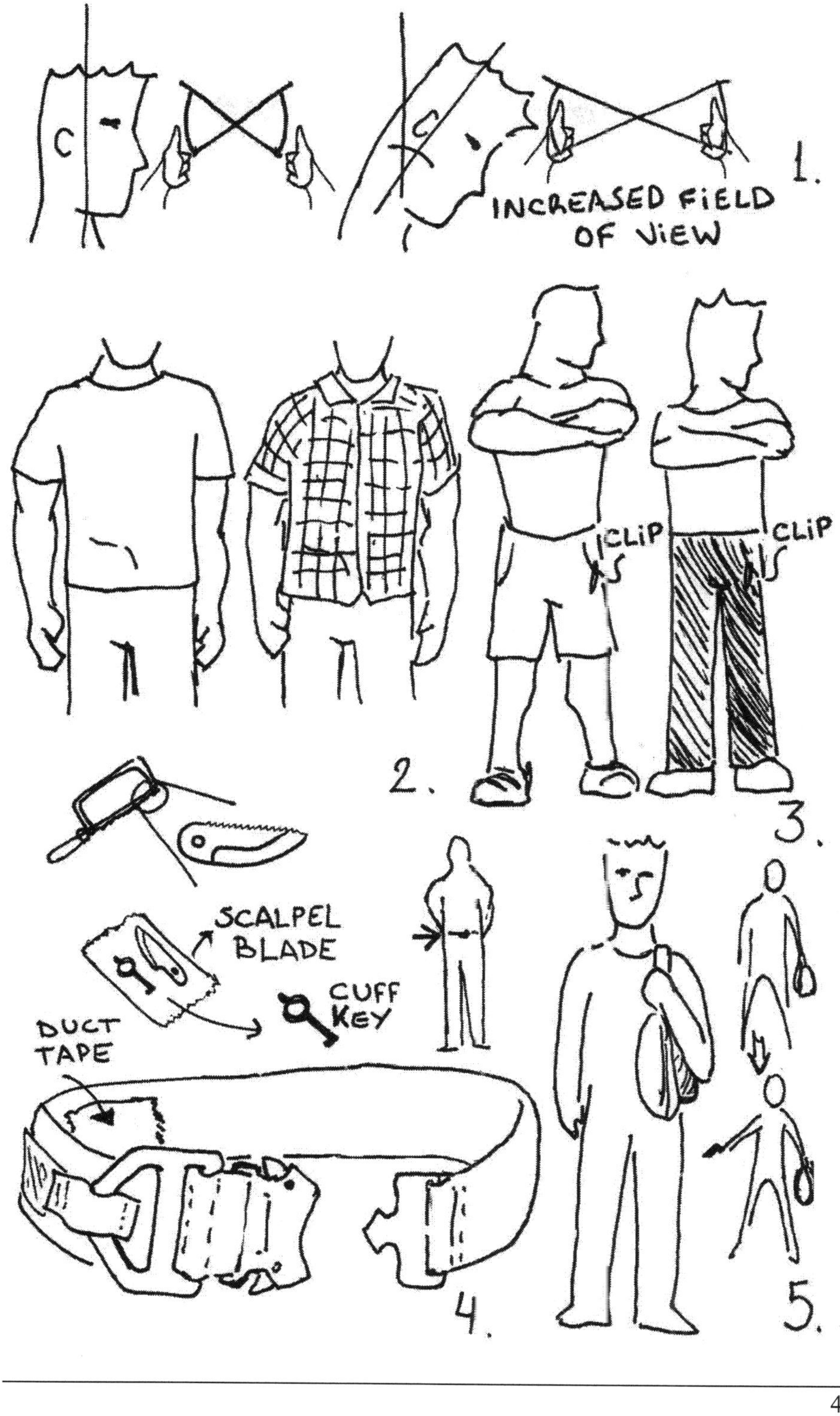
1.
INCREASED FIELD OF VIEW
CLIP
CLIP
2.
3.
SCALPEL BLADE
CUFF KEY
DUCT TAPE
4.
5.

Clothing

The clothes you wear play a far more important role than most people realize. They strongly influence that first impression people get of you. This can work in your favor or against you. For an executive, a fancy suit projects an image of success. That same suit may catch a criminal's attention who probably assumes the person wearing it also has a fat wallet and carries an expensive phone or watch. Criminals are always looking for gold and other types of expensive jewellery as well.

What you wear may also say too much about you. Sometimes literally so. While expressing yourself and having strong political views is fine, maybe having it written all over you isn't the smartest thing to do. At times, it just may not work in your best interest. Police also pay attention to these kind of things.

A t-shirt that says "I don't call 911" catches people's attention. Extremist political slogans also raise a red flag. In 2019, a man wearing a "Smash the patriarchy" shirt was gunned down by police after confronting the officers with a firearm in an Oregon middle school.

In today's overconnected world, a simple image can haunt you for the rest of your life. Once a picture or video goes online, it's there forever.

Your clothes are also your first line of defense when it comes to shelter. Those clothes you happen to be wearing that day may be all you have to work with during an emergency. They may end up being used for walking back home unexpectedly in the middle of winter or walking for miles to reach safety under the scorching summer sun. Maybe you will have to run so as to literally save your life or move around during a fight and your footwear may end up making all the difference.

It is important to find the right balance between what you may be required to wear given your lifestyle and line of work and the technical capabilities of those clothes. If you have to wear a suit in the office all day, plan accordingly. Leave a bag there with some supplies, including a set of clothes and well-worn hiking shoes to change into.

If a less formal attire is an option for daily wear, there are many options to choose from. Outdoors or tactical clothing can be combined with more casual clothing in a way that it doesn't stick out in the crowd. We want quality clothing that is versatile yet nondescript so as to not attract attention to ourselves. Bright colors and large graphic designs and logos are to be avoided. The objective is to be tactical but not look tactical. Tactical in terms of capability, not in appearance.

Learn what type of clothing material fits your needs best.

Cotton: The most commonly used fabric. Cheap, comfortable, cotton is not a bad choice for the average Joe going about his day. But as the saying goes, "cotton kills". This means that cotton retains humidity which in low temperature conditions can indeed be fatal. Wet socks and wet underwear aren't fun in hot weather either, causing chaffing and blisters. This is why athletes will mostly stay away from cotton and chose synthetic underwear instead. Cotton is also harder to dry after washing.

Wool: Wool has several advantages over cotton. Wool wicks moisture away from your body. Even when humid, wool helps you retain body heat. Wool has natural antibacterial properties and is ideal for staying warm. Merino wool is softer and less itchy than traditional wool.

Synthetic fibers: Synthetic fabrics are tougher than natural ones. They dry faster and wick humidity away from your body. They do a good enough job at keeping you warm although it's not as good as wool. When it comes to filling in winter jackets, it is not as good as down feather. While "cotton kills", synthetic fabrics have a saying of their own: Synthetic stinks. Synthetic fabrics are known to be a bit smelly even after washing but there are some that have antibacterial treatments, which in theory should help reduce the smell.

Down: Down is the fine, fluffy feathers found under the tougher exterior feathers in birds. While rain and wind is kept away by the tougher exterior feathers, down works as a bird's natural insulation layer. Down is very warm, packable and light. It's found in high-end jackets and sleeping bags. On the other hand, down forms clumps when wet and loses all its properties. Cheaper synthetic insulation, while heavier and not as good when it comes to insulation, does resists humidity far better.

Blends: Blends of cotton, wool and synthetic fibers are fairly popular. The US military uses 50/50 nylon and cotton Battle Dress Uniforms (BDU). It is more comfortable than 100% synthetic, yet it is more durable and dries faster than 100% cotton.

1) The base layer is the foundation upon which everything else goes. A wet cotton t-shirt defeats the advantages you could get from the best jacket. A poor fitting tube sock from the discount store will leave your feet full of blisters even when wearing the best shoes money can buy. Synthetic socks and underwear are the smart choice so as to stay dry. Merino wool is an excellent choice for colder climates. Buy athletic socks that are intended for your foot size and shape. These are made to fit your right and left foot like gloves for a perfect fit.

2) Polar fleece or wool mid layers are good choices. Fleece won't be as warm, but it is more durable, easier to clean and dries much faster than wool. For an exterior layer, either a windbreaker or jacket are good choices. Soft shells are a good all-purpose option. It keeps wind and rain away relatively well. It's a breathable layer yet provides some insulation.

3) For hats, go with baseball caps or wool caps for cold climates.

4) Jeans are comfortable but since they are cotton, they can be a nightmare when wet. Jeans made of synthetic fabrics or blends are available. Cotton jeans with water repellent and stain-resistant treatments are available in the market, but the repellent properties are lost after a few washes. 5.11 tactical pants and shorts are a great alternative, durable with large pockets. They are well made and offer the same arrangement of pockets, keeping everything the same as you go from pants to shorts.

5) For general use, light or intermediate hiking boots are a reasonable alternative. They tend to look better than sports sneakers. The right color of hiking boots doesn't look all that bad with jeans or khaki pants. Salomon makes the Quest 4D boots which are some of the best boots in the market. Well-made working boots are a viable option. The nicer models are durable, offer a good bit of foot protection and can be comfortable for standing or walking all day.

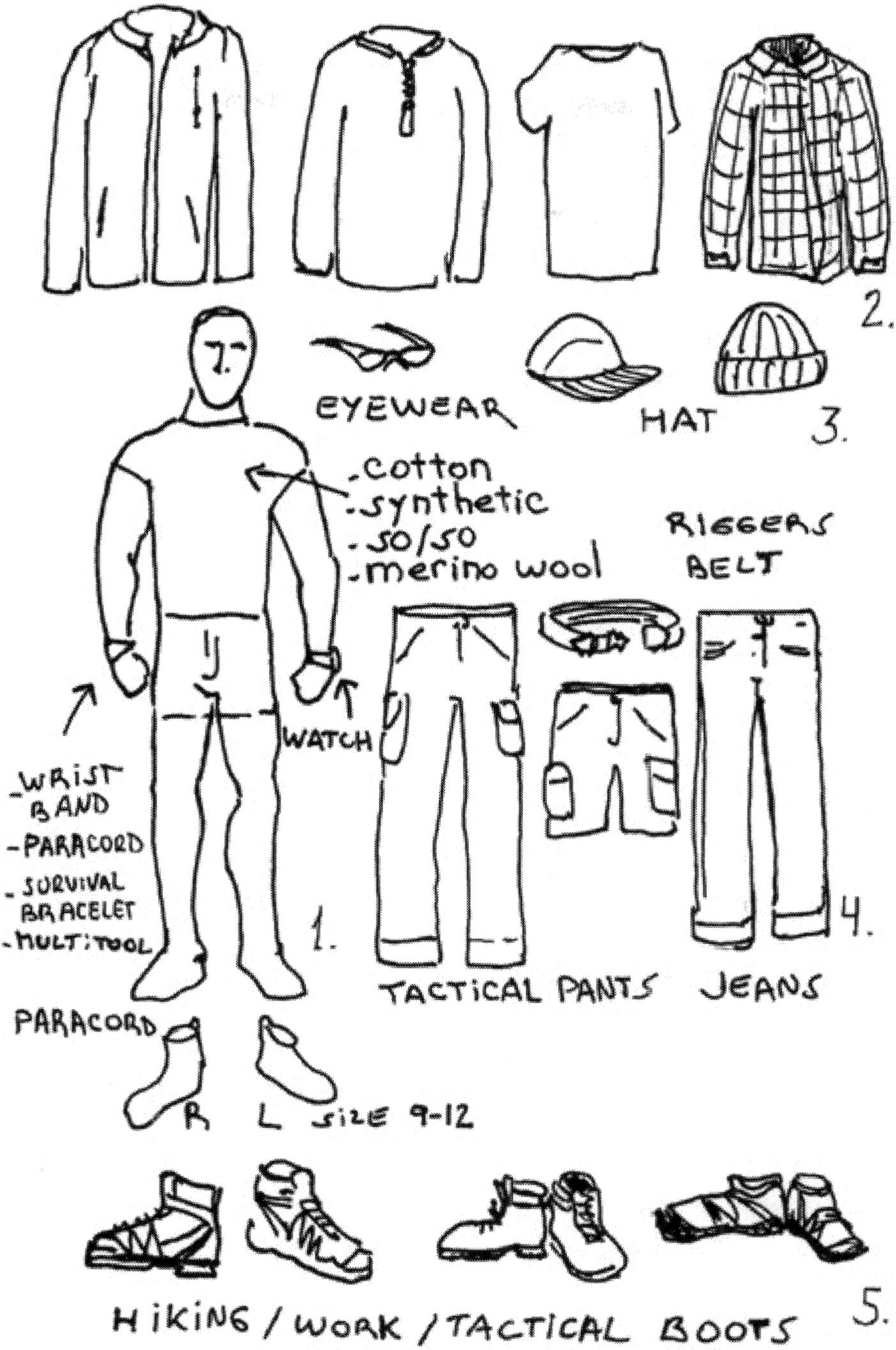
2.
EYEWEAR
HAT
3.
-cotton
-synthetic
-50/50
-merino wool
RIGGERS BELT
WATCH
-WRIST BAND
-PARACORD
-SURVIVAL BRACELET
-MULTITOOL
1.
TACTICAL PANTS
JEANS
4.
PARACORD
R L SIZE 9-12
HIKING / WORK / TACTICAL BOOTS
5.

Shemagh, Scarf and Tie

Shemaghs may seem like a "tacticool" fad but they are pretty useful pieces of kit. Keep in mind that cowboys were rarely without a bandana or "wild rag" of some kind, made of cotton or silk. It wasn't for covering their faces when robbing banks. Beyond the countless uses, from picking hot pots from the camp fire to making a tourniquet or used as a towel, a shemagh or traditional square scarf is also versatile when worn on the head. It can protect from the sun and wind, protect the face from dust and snow, or keep the head or neck warm during winter.

1) Start by folding the square cloth in half to make a triangle and place it over your head, the tip of the triangle pointing back.

2) Make sure one end of the triangle is shorter than the other.

3) Wrap the short end first bringing it under your chin. Then, bring the long end across your face, covering your nose.

4) Wrap both ends around your head and tie them together.

5) Adjust so that you are comfortable and have good visibility. Pull a bit on the top end of the scarf so that it protects your eyes from the sun like a baseball cap.

6) You can now adjust the scarf anyway you want. Covering the head only and pulling down the part that covers your face, bring both of them down and up as needed throughout the day. Eventually it may loosen up and require to be wrapped again.

7) Traditional scarves have their place as well but these can be used against you in a fight. The last thing you want in a fight is a leash around your neck for an attacker to use against you. Don't tie it or wrap it around your neck. Just fold it and tuck the folded end inside.

8) Arrange the scarf so that it stays in place and keeps you warm but would easily come off if someone pulls from it.

9) The same applies to ties. While you may need to wear a tie depending on the kind of job you have, you can still be smart about it. Cut your tie so that the narrow end is shorter and ends up just a couple inches past the knot.

10) A tie gives an attacker something to hold or even choke you with.

Tip: It's not just about fighting. Ties are banned in certain workplaces where they may get caught in heavy machinery. With a shortened narrow end, if an attacker (or machine) pulls your tie it will just come off.

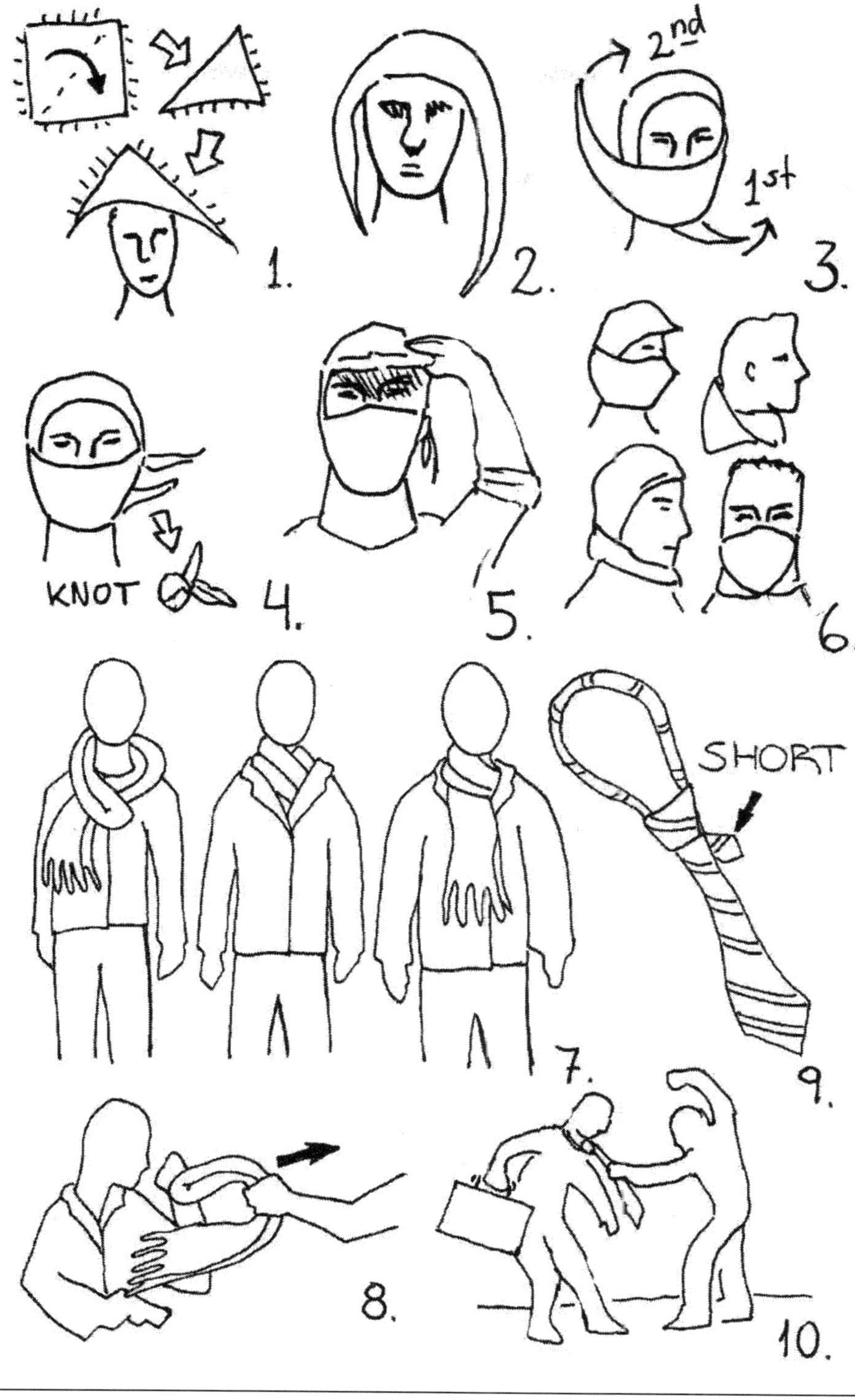
1.
2.
2nd
1st
3.
KNOT
4.
5.
6.
7.
SHORT
9.
8.
10.

Home Survival Kit

You need a number of supplies to be prepared for most disasters and emergencies. The American Red Cross[6] has a list of supplies which would be a good place to start. Some supplies are useful in numerous emergency situations while others are more specific.

The American Red Cross recommends a 2-week supply of food. That's better than what most people have and it is a good place to start, but 4 weeks or ideally six months gives you far more peace of mind when dealing with an extended crisis. Rather than buying survival rations (which are fine for 24-48hs) the rest should be food your family is already used to cooking with and consuming. This also makes it easier to rotate, keeping your supply well within its expiration date.

Your supplies should be well organized. A good solution is keeping them in clear plastic containers with lids so as to see what's inside. Keeping them in the garage would make it easier if you need to load up your vehicle during an evacuation. These can be kept next to camping supplies such as tent, cookware, and camping gas stove. You'll need a way to cook food if there's no power. If a camping stove is what you plan to use, make sure you have enough fuel for at least two weeks. Food needs to be organized in a food rotation system such as first-in first-out (FIFO). Expiration dates in medical supplies and batteries need to be checked and water needs to be rotated at least once a year.

Tip: Because of its simplicity and efficiency, a quality **kerosene heater** and enough fuel to get you by for a week or two is essential in cold climate regions. Some models can also be used for cooking and lighting.

Besides these basic supplies, there are other kits you need to organize.

Bug Out Bag: A Bug Out Bag (BOB) is intended to get you safely from point A to point B. This means having an actual plan on where to go and how to get there. A typical BOB may include spare clothes, food, water, a weapon for self-defense, map and GPS among other supplies.

VIP Bag: The Very Important Papers bag is where you keep your documents, passports, birth certificates and a USB flash drive with important information and family photos. Include your emergency cash, precious metals and spare keys for the house and car.

This bag should be small. A waterproof satchel would be ideal.

The VIP Bag is to be kept locked, preferably in a safe and it is the one thing you take if you must leave in a hurry unable to carry anything else.

- Water[1]
- A quality Water Filter
- Food[2]
- Flashlight
- NOAA Weather Radio
- Extra batteries
- Family first aid kit
- Medications
- Multi-purpose tool
- Sanitation Supplies
- Personal hygiene items
- Copies of personal documents
- Cell phone with charger
- Emergency contact information
- Extra cash (small denomination bills)
- Emergency blanket
- Map(s) of the area and compass
- Whistle
- N95 or surgical masks
- Matches
- Portable stove
- Fuel[3]
- Rain gear
- Towels
- Work gloves
- Tools/supplies for securing your home
- Extra clothing, hat and sturdy shoes
- Plastic sheeting
- Extra set of car keys and house keys
- Manual can opener
- Duct tape
- Two-way radios
- Scissors
- Household liquid bleach
- Children Games and Entertainment items
- Blankets or sleeping bags
- Baby supplies[5]
- Medical supplies[4]
- Pet supplies[6]

1) A Gallon per person per day, at least two weeks.

2) Non-perishable, easy to prepare with minimum use of fuel and water.

3) Enough gasoline in metal Jerry cans to reach your bug out location, treated with fuel stabilizer and rotated accordingly.

4) Prescription medications, hearing aids, glasses or contact lenses.

5) Bottle, formula, shelf-stable baby food, diapers, wipes, fever medicine.

6) Spare collar and leash, ID, food, bowl and pet medication.

Car Survival Kit

Your car becomes your "home away from home" when you are out an about. The gear you keep in it may come in handy when involved in an accident, when stranded on the road or when you have to make it back home on foot.

Get Home Bag: The Get Home Bag (GHB) is the kit you use when the car breaks down, the roads are blocked or for whatever other reason you need to walk back home. The GHB is different for each person. You need to look at your routine, how far your home is from your work place or other locations you frequent and how you would get back home if stranded there. You need to look at how fast you walk, the distance you will need to cover and the route you are planning on taking. For people that work near from home, the best approach isn't to plan on stopping for the night every 5 miles but travel light and fast. If you are walking back home then the situation is likely to be complicated and dangerous. Moving fast and getting home as fast as possible is your main priority, even if you have to walk all day or night.

Depending on your location, this may involve winter hiking or doing so under extremely hot summer conditions. Plan accordingly so as to be dressed properly for such events. Extra warm clothes, hats and gloves for winter. For hot climates you want a hat, extra water and sunscreen.

For walking twenty or thirty miles, food isn't nearly as much of a priority as water. A couple energy bars will be more than enough food for short distances. It is not a good idea to waste time cooking if you can avoid it.

A firearm may be added for self-defense. Depending on your area, defense against four legged predators may be important too. Just keep in mind that anything left in the car has to stay there all the time and there's a chance it may get stolen one day.

Vehicle Emergency Kit: This is the kit you keep in the vehicle for car accidents and various roadside emergencies. This is very likely to be used one day given that accidents on the road are fairly common.

The car itself should be considered part of this system. Pick a model known for its reliability. Four wheel drive and at least some off road capability is highly desirable. Pay attention when you have your car serviced and know how to do at least basic maintenance, change light bulbs, filters, etc. Know how to get your vehicle unstuck from snow, mud or sand. Keep an E-tool in the car or a dedicated shovel if you find yourself off-road often for whatever reasons. Some of the items you should include are the following:

- First Aid Kit
- Food[1]
- Clothes and footwear[2]
- Water
- Flashlight and spare batteries
- AM/FM radio
- Tool Kit
- Jump Starter and Air Compressor[3]
- Fire extinguisher[4]
- Duct Tape
- Spare Tire, Lug Wrench and Jack
- Jumper Cables
- 50 Feet of 550 Paracord
- Tow Strap
- Lighter
- Work Gloves
- Map
- Compass
- Hand Sanitizer
- Wet Wipes
- Sunblock
- Bug Repellent
- Toilet Paper
- Cellphone with charger
- E-tool/Shovel
- Ice Scrapper
- Emergency Flat Tire Repair
- Blankets or sleeping bags
- Reflective vest[5]
- Reflective triangle or road flares

1) You don't want anything that requires cooking. 48hs worth of emergency rations, MREs (meals ready-to-eat) or energy bars will do. Keep in mind that temperatures can get pretty hot or cold so check the food often and rotate as needed.

2) A spare set of ordinary clothes and underwear kept in a sealed bag is one of the most useful items and is likely to be used if soaked wet or if your clothes are torn or bloody after an accident.

3) This can be invaluable, allowing you to jump-start your car without the assistance of another vehicle. Some models have a compressor for the tires and USB ports for charging cell phones. Get a complete, quality made model from a reputable manufacturer.

4) Check often to verify the pressure and service or replace as needed.

5) Keep them in the glove compartment along with a flashlight so as to put it on before exiting the vehicle when on the road.

Firearms

Shooting is an enjoyable sport. For some of us, firearms are a way of life, essential to freedom, but self-defense doesn't require a massive arsenal.

1) Most people looking to arm themselves for self-defense just want something simple, reliable and effective that is within their budget.

A good 357 Magnum revolver made by Smith & Wesson or Ruger with a 3", 4" or 6" barrel is ideal for that role. A 6" barrel is longer and heavier, but the long barrel also means it is easier to shoot accurately thanks to the longer sight radius and the extra weight upfront allows the shooter to control recoil better. A 2" or 3" barrel is more compact and often the choice for those that conceal carry revolvers, but the shorter barrel makes it harder to shoot accurately (shorter sight radius). It's harder to control the recoil and muzzle flash is also more noticeable. A 4" barrel is often considered the best compromise. Having said that, a 5" or 6" barrel is about ideal for home defense for a new shooter that won't be investing much in firearms training beyond a basic safety course. Longer barrels also give an attacker more real estate to hold on to in a fight and for small apartments and condos where distances are minimal a shorter barrel can be more desirable. Still, the idea that criminals always go around grabbing guns successfully is somewhat exaggerated and when it does happen, pulling the trigger tends to fix that problem. 357 magnum revolvers typically have a 6-shot capacity, hence the name "six shooters", but some models have 7 or 8 round capacity. They also tend to be larger and heavier guns. Of the most commonly available models, for home defense I recommend the Smith and Wesson 686, 586, Ruger GP100 and Security Six. More compact frame revolvers are better suited if the intention is to conceal carry the gun as well.

357 magnum revolvers have the advantage of shooting both 357 magnum which is a powerful round ideal for self-defense and 38 special.

38 special is slightly shorter than 357. It is also less powerful and has less felt recoil, making it a good alternative for beginners.

2) There's a reason why every military and police department around the world issues automatic pistols. Auto pistols are simply better fighting guns. They are more rugged compared to the intricate revolver mechanism, have greater firepower and do that while being lighter and easier to carry. A revolver dropped in the mud in the field will likely experience a malfunction if mud gets between the cylinder and frame. Most modern pistols will run just fine in those same conditions.

The disadvantage with automatic pistols is that they require more training so as to be used proficiently during stressful self-defense situations. Any person can learn how to operate a pistol in a matter of minutes and shoot it accurately at a paper target. But learning how to instinctively clear malfunctions so that the hands do it without thinking in the heat of the moment, avoid limp wristing the gun, become confident in the use of the gun so that it is always carried with a round in the chamber and always remember to disengage the safety if the pistol happens to have one, that takes considerably more training than your basic safety course. These problems simply don't come up with revolvers. There's no safety or empty chamber to mess up and ammunition related problems are solved by pulling the trigger. This is why revolvers are better for most beginners.

But if a person will take professional training and practice at least once a month or even better, every week, if he commits to taking one or two self-defense courses every year, then a pistol is the way to go. People with such dedication will often get involved in practical pistol shooting such as IPSC or IDPA. The gun I recommend is the Glock 17 or the slightly more compact Glock 19, both in 9mm. These are the ones I've seen most firearms experts carry themselves, in USA and around the world. With a 15+1 round capacity, compact enough for concealed carry yet handles like a bigger gun, you just can't go wrong with a Glock 19.

3) Although you will eventually want a 22LR handgun, 22LR Conversion kits are available for Glocks. By simply changing the slide and using the provided magazine, 22LR can be fired. 22LR is ideal for beginners, plinking, cheap practice, even pest control and small game hunting if the shooter is good enough. Glock pistols in 40 S&W and 357 SIG can shoot either caliber by simply swapping barrels. They can also shoot 9mm with an aftermarket barrel. One of these guns with a couple spare barrels and a 22LR Conversion Kit can be a very flexible platform to have.

You want to stock at least 200 rounds per gun. 500 would be even better.

4) A handgun is often enough for most people's self-defense needs but a semi-automatic carbine offers significantly more firepower. In the country or more isolated residences it is not a bad idea to have a home defense carbine along with your handgun. The AR15 platform is by far the most popular choice in America and most countries around the world. The platform is not perfect but it is accurate, lightweight and popular for practical shooting sports. If possible, an AR with short-stroke gas piston system is desirable. It takes advantage of the AR platform but having a piston means it's easier to keep clean and more likely to be reliable during periods of less than ideal maintenance.

5) The AK47 and AK platform in general is well suited for the needs of preppers and survivalists. Tough, reliable, it's a gun that requires less maintenance, has larger and stronger parts and is easier to keep running during hard times. The 7.62x39mm round the AK typically fires also has more stopping power than the 5.56mm NATO round the AR platform is usually chambered in.

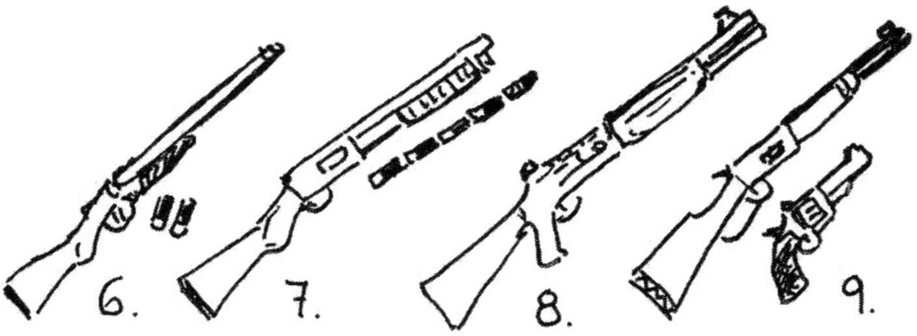

6) Even in countries with awful gun laws, in most cases a double barrel shotgun is still legal to own. It's not ideal, but it is better than nothing.

7) Still in the shotgun category, pump action shotguns are also fairly popular even in restrictive countries. Loaded with buckshot or slugs, a pump shotgun is a formidable home defense weapon. It does require frequent training so as to stay proficient in its use.

8) An even better alternative is the semiautomatic shotgun. This closes the gap with auto rifles with its semiautomatic capability and whenever possible, the auto shotgun is the way to go. Auto shotguns are sensitive to ammunition given the wide range of shells available. They tend to prefer powerful, heavier shells. Learn what your shotgun runs reliably and stock up on that ammunition.

9) Pistol-caliber lever action carbines are another good choice, especially if you need longer range accuracy than the one you can expect from handguns. For defense, a 357 magnum revolver combined with a 357 magnum lever gun allows you to use the same round in both guns. Some auto carbines also fire 9mm and even share magazines with Glocks pistols. These 9mm combos are a good alternative to simplify logistics or if semiautomatic rifles aren't legal in your location.

10.

10) Rounding up the gun battery, a 22LR carbine such as the Ruger 10/22 is a handy gun everyone should own for hunting, plinking, pest control and cheap trigger time. A 22LR semi-automatic carbine is one of the most practical guns a person can own. For hunting, a bolt action rifle in a powerful caliber is preferred. A 308W bolt gun with a sound suppressor and a good scope on top can be used for hunting but also for "reaching out and touching" someone if there's ever the need. A battle rifle such as the FAL Para in 308W with a folding stock is a bit heavier than your intermediate caliber carbine but it can be used for hunting, defense and long range shooting with a good scope.

Try stocking no less than 500-1000 rounds per long arm.

NOTES:

Chapter 4
Security

Be kind, passionate and generous of heart. But when the time comes, dispense violence with that same passion and generosity.

Home Security

Any house can be broken into with enough time and dedication, but a few simple measures can greatly increase you home security level.

Your goal is to make your home as hard a target as possible. The harder it is to break into, criminals are more likely to go looking for an easier place to burglarize. Criminals are dissuaded by different defensive measures depending on their modus operandi. The more defensive and dissuasive measures you apply, the safer your house becomes.

1) Doors are the most common point of entry for home invaders. The fact that most doors are cheap, fragile barriers doesn't help much either. A quick and easy way to improve the security level of a house is to replace the existing hinge and strike plate screws with longer ones, three or four inches long. These will go through the weaker frame and into the structure of most houses. Replace the standard cheap front door lock with a better one, hardened with bump proof and pick proof features.

Ideally, your would have a metal door frame with poured concrete and a dedicated reinforced safety door made of steel plate with a lock that has bolts on all four sides of the door.

2) Every safety feature adds up. An alarm system and a medium to large dog are two of the things criminals take into consideration the most. Security cameras, flood lights, these help as well. Some large estates may require motion detectors and exterior cameras along the property's perimeter. Tools can be stolen and used to break in so keep sheds locked.

For better security, some areas demand bars on windows. Spanish-style wrought iron bars can integrate well into some architectural styles. It is hard to have much security without a proper perimeter, secured with a wall or fence. This keeps anyone that comes to the house at a safe distance until you buzz them in. A video intercom allows you to interact with strangers from a safe distance without opening your door.

3) Be mindful of the conversations you have in public, either with friends or neighbors on the sidewalk or even on your cell phone when walking. You never know who may be listening. Overhearing even a few seconds of a typical conversation can mean a goldmine of information for someone looking to make some money. For example, going out for dinner means your house is left unattended for a couple hours. It is common people, sometimes with regular jobs, the ones that pass along the information to others or maybe organize a break-in themselves.

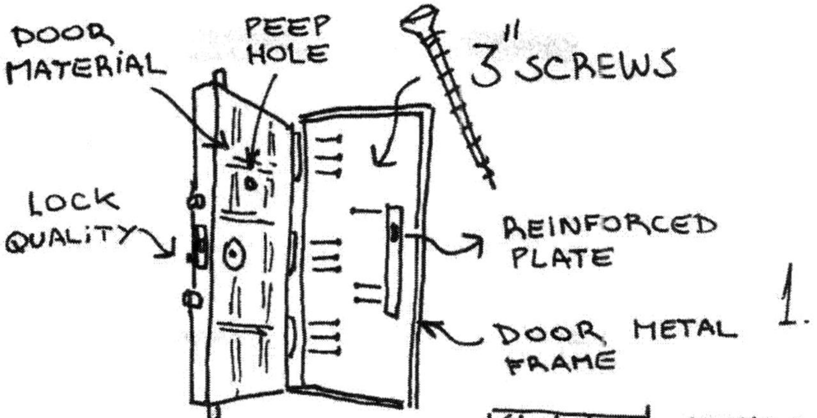
DOOR MATERIAL
PEEP HOLE
3" SCREWS
LOCK QUALITY
REINFORCED PLATE
DOOR METAL FRAME
1.

MOTION SENSOR LIGHT
SHED\ TOOLS
ALARM
CAMERAS
DOG
INTERCOM
2.

8PM TONIGHT MY PLACE?
PIZZA GUY
3.

4) Indoor cameras are affordable and they are a great investment for home security. They let you know if someone breaks in while you're away, takes a picture or video clip and notifies you to your cell phone. You can immediately call the police when this happens. Police can use these images to catch the criminals and recover any stolen belongings.

5) The video intercom is another high value addition, but it needs to be used right to work. Don't just let people in because they claim to be the police or wear a uniform. Don't let anyone in until you are 100% certain of who you are dealing with. Ask for ID. Look at the name and take the time to call the company they claim to work for, calling a number you find yourself online. Criminals will try to hustle and hurry you into making bad decisions. Don't let anyone boss you around.

6) Tools left around the yard can be used to gain access to your home. Ladders are often left outside and these can easily be used to climb to an open window in an upper floor. Sometimes, it's even poorly trimmed trees and bushes that not only provide concealment for criminals, but they can also use them to climb up a roof. Large branches too close to the house may also be a hazard during storms, causing thousands worth of damages at the worst possible moment.

7) Having bars on your windows is ideal but they can be an eyesore in some cases, too expensive or not allowed by your HOA. A possible solution to harden your windows is to install safety and security window films such as the ones sold by 3M™ and other manufacturers. These aren't as good as bars when it comes to stopping criminals but it has proven to be a reasonable compromise and it will keep a criminal from just throwing a rock through your window and walking inside.

8) An old yet time-proven trick is having a couple timers set so that they turn lights on when you're not home. Even better, get a radio or TV turned on as well. Criminals do pay attention to such signs and if they have any doubt that someone is inside, those looking to avoid confrontations will not risk it and go looking for a home where all the signs point towards it being unoccupied at the moment. This may even dissuade some criminals that are willing to go inside with people home, but are looking to do so when the occupants are asleep.

It is also true that a number of criminals will not care either way and just kick the door down and catch everyone by surprise. Not the most commonly used tactic but it does occur, which makes a strong case for planning your home security strategy so as to always have weapons within reach or keep your concealed carry weapon on you even at home.

4.
5.
6.
7.
TIMER
?!!
8.

Avoiding Scams and Frauds

All the home security measures and all the awareness in the world won't do you any good if you don't learn to avoid scams, frauds and other tricks used by criminals.

1) We already talked about never opening the door unless you are 100% sure of who you are dealing with. Even when keeping the door closed, you have to be cautious. Criminals may drop by and engage in conversation, trying to gain information about your daily routine, where you work, what school your children go to, names of family members and their whereabouts so as to use that information later. Some criminals have even befriended their victims, meeting them on several occasions over long periods of time before finally making their move.

2) Get used to saying no to strangers on the phone as well. If they don't know who you are then why are they calling you? Don't reveal any personal information such as your full name, date of birth, or names of companies you deal with such as your bank or internet provider.

3) These days most scams reach people through the internet. Emails and social network scams have gone a long way since the times of the Nigerian prince emails. Today people send emails pretending to be large, well-known companies. Usually you can find small discrepancies in their email address. When in doubt, contact the company yourself to verify. Never send money orders or personal transfers. Never believe anyone you meet online, especially when asking for money. Assume that whatever sad story they share is entirely fabricated to attract donations.

4) Don't post sensitive personal information on social networks. Leaving on holidays or because of work and posting about it lets everyone know your house is unoccupied. Posting about a new job, new car or house sale lets everyone know what kind of money you may have at your disposal.

5) Be careful about signing or agreeing to contracts, loans or other obligations before having them checked by a trusted professional. Some of the worst "scams" people get sucked into are perfectly legal once your signature is on that paper.

6) Be careful of clicking and accepting prizes or unknowingly giving consent on your computer or phone. You may be installing a Trojan and allowing access to your personal computer and your bank accounts.

7) Distrust strangers "helping" you on the street. Especially anyone trying to get you out of your car. Simply ignore them and drive away.

ID
1.
NO
2.
Dear Mr.
3.
4.
5.
YOU WON!
CLAIM PRIZE
6.
!
?
7.

Formation when Walking

Some dispositions are safer than others when walking along the streets.

In more urban settings, especially in larger cities, attacks are likely to come from vehicles moving along the street. This can be anything from muggings, kidnap attempts or purse snatchers. Any vehicle slowing down should be considered suspicious. A motorcycle with two people is by far the most common choice among criminals: It easy for one of them to get off, snatch a purse, bag or mug you at gunpoint and then get on and take off in seconds. The motorcycle is also more agile than cars and this allows them to quickly get lost in the traffic and avoid capture.

1) Because of this reason, the hardest target (adult, male) should be on the side of the road when walking. If there's children or any other more vulnerable person, it's best to put yourself between them and the threat.

2) In this case the husband is on the side of the street, the child is in the middle and the wife is on the side closest to buildings. Depending on the setting, threats can come from this side as well. For example, a reckless driver leaving his driveway without watching his rare-view mirror, an unleashed dog in a house attacking pedestrians that are walking by or someone waiting to ambush you. These incidents are very common. In some locations, such incidents may be more likely than getting attacked by criminals. If that's the case then the disposition should change accordingly.

If you have a guard dog, put him between you and the threat. A guard dog is good insurance, especially as we grow older.

3) Criminals will often target females for a number of reasons: In general, they are physically weaker than men and less prone to fight back. They carry more valuables, more expensive phones, purses and jewellery. The typical recommendation is to carry the bag strap across the chest. This makes it harder for a criminal to snatch it. Having said this, women have been beaten, dragged and injured after criminals take off in their motorcycles with the victim still caught by the strap. Also, if mugged, the side in which the bag is may force you to let go of the hand of a child you may have with you. Instinct kicking in, women have resisted letting go and criminals have pushed away children to get to the bag.

The best choice is to hold the bag close to you but not in a way that you may be injured if forced to surrender the bag or if someone takes off with it in spite of your attempts to retain it.

1.

2.

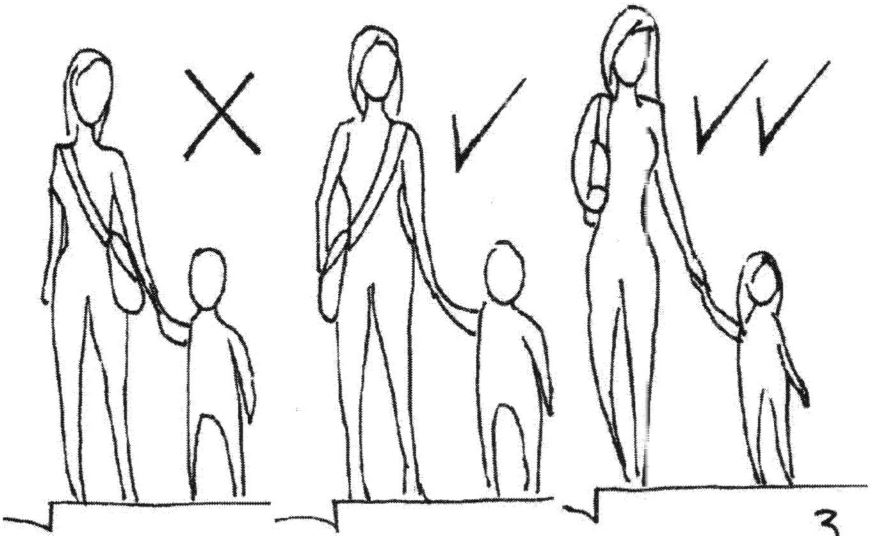

3.

Safety when Traveling on Foot

When going from point "A" to point "B", safety should be taken into account. There are a number of considerations such as general level of crime in the area, time of the day, illumination and the number of pedestrians on the street. None of these mean much by themselves but together they give us an idea of what precautions we should take.

1) The drawing depicts a typical situation: When going from "A" to "B", should you cut across the park, where there's less people, more shade, trees to hide among and risk being ambushed and mugged, or take the longer route along the sidewalk where there's more people, streetlights and a mugger would be more exposed? The second route, the one along the sidewalk, is obviously safer. Having said that, there are times in which that's precisely where criminals do attack when they no longer fear getting caught. There's parts of the world where people frequently get mugged in broad daylight with people all around them.

Having said this, there are times in which you may want to take the route across the park. Being in a heightened state of awareness, visibly fit, maybe even armed, you may choose to move in the dark for your own reasons. If you *are* the thing that goes bump in the night yourself there's a good chance social predators will perceive just that. If that's the case, you are likely to be left alone.

2) When walking in the city, especially when using public transportation such as subways, trains and buses but also at airports in some cases, make sure to keep your backpack in front of you. It is easy to open or even cut your bag and remove any valuables inside while you are distracted.

I have seen this happen to people standing in a crowded bus, but also to people as they walked at a steady pace running errands.

3) In a similar manner, it is not a good idea to keep wallets or cell phones in your back pocket. An experienced pick pocket can slip it out without you noticing, even if you believe to be well aware of your surroundings.

In some cases, an accomplice may pretend to bump into you, confuse you with some other person or distract you in any other way while the thief behind you takes advantage of the confusion created. Some even bump into you with a drink or food, the liquid or food stain suddenly becoming the focus of your attention.

Tip: In dangerous areas, you may want to keep a "throwaway" wallet. This is a wallet with contents you don't care for so as to hand over if mugged. A broken or old cell phone may work in a similar manner.

1.

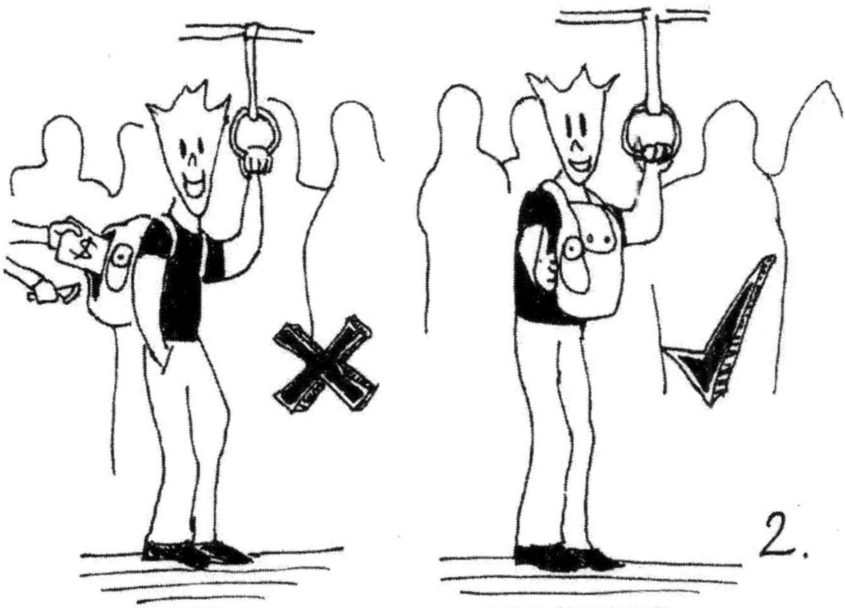

2.

3.

Stalkers and Creeps

If there is a stalker or some creep following you, you need to take action.

Both women and men can be followed by either a stalker, mugger or someone looking to attack them in some other way, but the reality is that according to the National Violence Against Women Survey (NVAW), four out of five stalking victims are women.

Try to remember a couple basic tips on what to do if you happen to find yourself being followed:

1) Unless you are a spy that is actively trying to sell sensitive information to a Chinese agent, there's no reason why you should pretend not to notice that a person is following you. Turn around and look at him. Let him know you know what he's doing.

Pretending that you don't notice when someone is following you is some of the worst, most dangerous advice I've ever come across.

If you are not a secret agent, there's no reason why you should act like one. It doesn't benefit you in any way. It simply makes your stalker believe he continues to hold the upper hand, encouraging him to continue doing it.

The first thing you should do when you know you are being followed is to look for a store or public space with people. Get inside, alert the people in the store and call the police.

2) If there are no stores or buildings you can enter, then hurry towards more populated areas. Run if you have to. Call 911 and prepare any weapons you may have available so as to defend yourself.

3) If you believe someone is following you, cross to the other side of the road and start walking in the opposite direction. If the person you believe is following you changes direction as well then you can be pretty certain you are indeed being followed. Crossing the street also puts some much needed distance between you and your stalker.

If there's heavy traffic, you can time your crossing so as to cross right before vehicles cut you off, blocking the path for anyone chasing you.

4) If you know you are being followed, don't be afraid to ask for help.

Just look for any other person and start a conversation with them. Ask them for directions or simply tell them what's going on, ask them if you can walk with them because there's a strange man following you.

COFFEE
STAR
SUCK
COFFEE
1.
911
2.
YOU
CREEP
3.
4.

Safety at the ATM

Extra precautions should be taken when using ATMs. The risk of getting mugged is higher, but there are also traps and tricks used to steal people's money or their credit card information.

1) Use ATMs only at banks, preferably branches of a bank you have an account on. While this seems inconvenient (and it often is) this is particularly important when extracting large amounts of cash. If there's ever a problem such as the ATM failing to give you the money for whatever reason but the funds do leave your account, any discrepancy is far more likely to be sorted out if you can actually walk into the bank in charge of the ATM and do so as a client. The same goes for any other problem you may have such as the machine failing to return your card. ATMs that aren't in banks are also more likely to be tampered with.

2) Criminals use different tricks to steal money from you at ATMs. A "Fish hook" is simply a device that can be inserted into some ATMs, either directly into the cash dispenser slot (folded piece of metal) or after modifying the front of the machine more extensively. A fake panel can be placed right on top with a fake slot. The ATM fails to give you the money and the criminal comes and takes it after you leave. Cameras can be hidden to steal personal information, including your PIN number. These small cameras can be concealed about the ATM or somewhere else nearby. Given how small and powerful spy cameras can be, it is almost impossible to detect some of them. Assume you are being filmed. Deposit slots can be modified to steal your deposit. The front of the ATM can be modified and your deposit falls into a fake compartment.

3) A card reader can be attached to the machine right on top of the card slot. It looks like an original part of the ATM, it allows you to insert and extract your card with no issues, but while doing so it also scans and copies your card. After a few hours the machine is retrieved with information to clone several cards.

4) Your card can be cloned when paying at restaurants or other establishments. Never lose sight of your card when paying. Always make sure your card is only used on a real payment terminal and not swiped or approached to any other devices.

5) Always cover the pad with your hand when entering your PIN.

6) Be smart about using ATMs. Use ATMs during office hours when the bank is open and has security. Don't use them if you notice suspicious people in the vicinity.

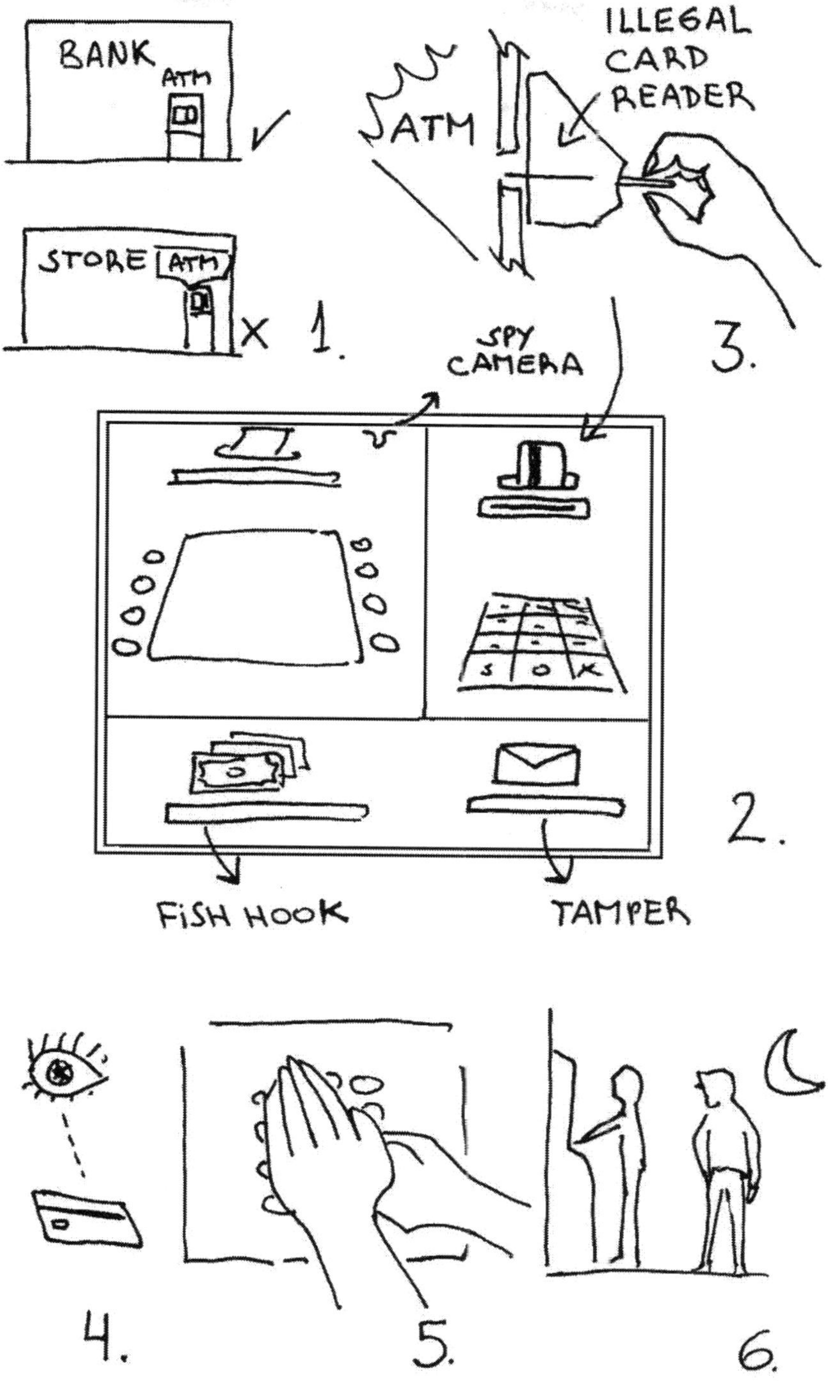
BANK
ATM
STORE
ATM
1.
ATM
ILLEGAL
CARD
READER
3.
SPY
CAMERA
2.
FISH HOOK
TAMPER
4.
5.
6.

NOTES:

Chapter 5

Firearms and Self-Defense

"Si vis pacem, para bellum"
("If you want peace, prepare for war!")- Latin adage

Firearms Safety

Statistics regarding firearms safety are often tainted by the political agenda of the group financing said research. Still, it is safe to say that swimming pools, cars and fast food kill more people in a day than guns in the hands of law abiding citizens kill in a decade.

It is also true that if everyone took to heart a few simple gun safety rules the number of gun related accidents would be practically zero.

1) All guns are always loaded and should be treated as such. It seems that when there's a tragedy, nine times out of ten it involves one of these fabled "unloaded" guns that still manage to fire. If you need to pull the trigger to disassemble, test or dry fire practice, still do so in a safe direction (bookshelf, dresser) as if expecting it to fire.

Even after unloading the gun for storage or transportation, remember to still treat the gun as if loaded. Always verify an "unloaded" gun yourself.

2) Keep your finger off the trigger guard until ready to fire. This needs to be practiced during training until it becomes second nature. Getting into the habit of resting your trigger finger on the trigger can have fatal consequences, especially when adrenalin is flowing, fine motor skills are compromised and more pressure than intended can be easily applied discharging the firearm.

3) Keep the gun pointed in a safe direction at all times. Never cover yourself or others with the muzzle of your gun. Imagine there's a laser coming out of the barrel that cuts through everything it touches. Be sure of your backstop and what's behind your target. The power, penetration and range of a cartridge is often underestimated.

4) Never shoot without positive identification. Especially in your own home and your own community, that person you failed to clearly identify may be a family member, friend or neighbor. Failing to ID a target before pulling the trigger is a tragic mistake that happens way too often.

Use some common sense. Everyone needs a gun safe and that is where you should keep unsupervised guns in households frequently visited by people outside the family circle. Secure unattended firearms, especially with small children in the house.

Children are incredibly resourceful and unsupervised guns are one of the leading causes of gun related accidents around the world. Teach them to never touch a gun without your supervision, to leave it alone and alert you if they ever find one.

1) ALL GUNS ARE ALWAYS LOADED

2) KEEP YOUR FINGER OFF THE TRIGGER

3) KEEP THE GUN POINTED IN A SAFE DIRECTION

4) ALWAYS ID YOUR TARGET BEFORE SHOOTING

Handgun Grip

A correct grip is essential for accuracy, speed and recoil control and even for the correct functioning of the handgun. A poor grip on a semiautomatic pistol can cause "limp wristing", meaning the gun lacks the support for the slide to cycle properly causing a malfunction.

1) Grab the gun like you would when giving a firm handshake, the backstrap deep in the "v" of your hand between your thumb and index finger. Check the gun slide and forearm. From a top view, the muzzle of the gun and your forearm should be aligned.

2) When shooting single handed in a typical target shooting stance, this axis line would continue along the arm and end in your spine. On a two hand grip, this support structure is now composed of two arms. These are the two lines through which the recoil travels to your shoulders. A two handed grip is of course preferable whenever possible but the truth is that a great number of gunfights involve one-handed shooting for numerous reasons such as speed, injury or because one hand is needed to fight the attacker or keeping his own gun away from you.

3) On a two hand grip, the palm of the support hand (also known as weak, off hand or non-dominant hand) goes on the other side of the grip, the fingers closing on top of the ones of the strong hand, surrounding the grip on all four sides. The support hand should be pulling back while the strong hand firmly grips the gun and pushes forward. This counter pressure helps control recoil as the gun tries to flip up as you fire.

4) The thumbs go on the side of the frame, pointing forwards. Depending on the gun, you can apply some downward pressure on the frame with the thumb of your support hand. Thumbs are strong and this can help control recoil.

5) Grip your gun as high as possible. Every millimeter counts.

The backwards force when firing a gun takes place along the bore axis of the barrel where the round is discharged. This means that the closer your wrist is to that bore axis, the less muzzle flip you will experience. The recoil will still be there but it is distance "d" the one that makes the muzzle of the gun go up and your sights to go off target.

The smaller you manage "d" to be, the less moment of force (torque) you will have. A very firm grip helps reduce recoil considerably. Make sure to apply force with your support hand. The little and ring finger in your support hand, even these play an important role in reducing muzzle flip

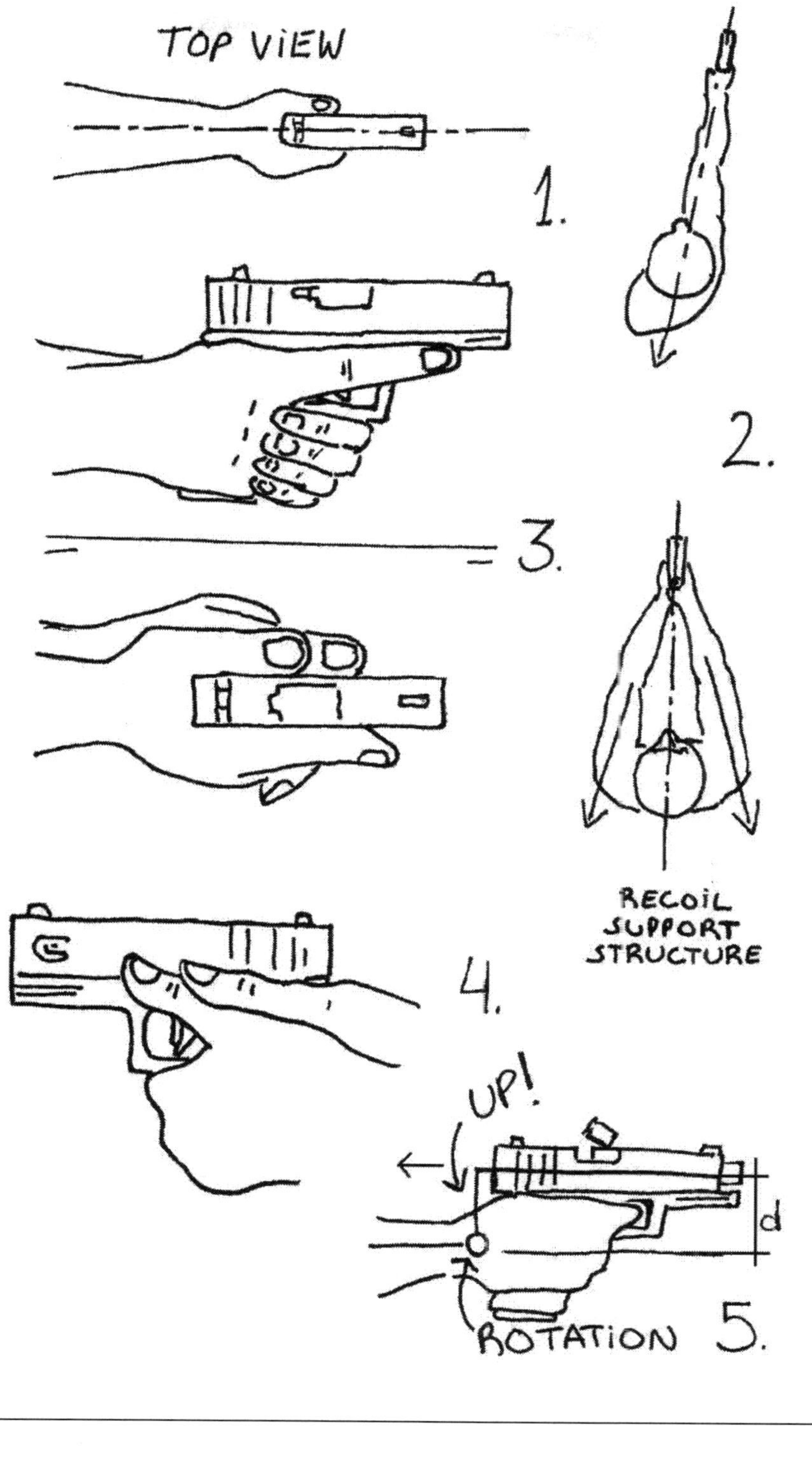
TOP VIEW
1.
2.
3.
RECOIL
SUPPORT
STRUCTURE
4.
UP!
d
ROTATION
5.

How to Hold a Gun

When holding a gun, it is important to handle it in a safe manner so as to avoid accidents. Keeping in mind the gun safety rules learned earlier, keep the gun pointed in a safe direction and never point it at anything you don't intend to destroy. When at the shooting range, simply keep the gun pointed downrange at all times. But on the street or during more advanced training involving other people, the correct stance is needed.

Position Sul (South for Portuguese) keeps the gun pointed down. For most situations (not all, it depends on the specific scenario), position Sul is the better choice. It also feels more natural and comfortable. Because of the shorter muzzle, keeping a handgun pointed up (Temple Index or High Ready position) means the hand must be held high as well so as to avoid accidentally sweeping people with the muzzle of your gun.

1) For Sul, the gun is held with your dominant hand, resting over the other hand with arms flexed at about 90 degrees. You want the gun kept in a central position that is comfortable yet ready to be used if needed.

2) As the slide rests on top of the knuckles, the gun is pointing at a slight angle away from the body.

3) Position Sul allows for the gun to be pointed in a safe direction yet quickly be brought into action by bringing the hands together into a two-hand grip. Already from this position the gun can be fired if necessary at a target at very close range.

4) The non-dominant hand can be used for defense, striking, grabbing people, opening doors and turning on lights. The gun stays in the same position.

5) At times you may want to keep the gun ready yet somewhat better concealed. While gripping the gun, pointing down, the slide can be hidden behind the leg. At a distance, this creates the illusion of both hands being visible and empty. The hand simply looks balled into a fist. This works even better with a black or mate finish gun and dark pants or blue jeans. Distance and poor lighting helps too.

6) In Position Sul, the slide of the gun rests on top of the knuckles of your non-dominant hand. While gripping the gun, both thumbs go together and the middle finger of your dominant hand rests on the index finger joint of your non-dominant hand. This becomes the rotation point for when the gun is brought up and the two hands come together forming a proper two-hand grip. The trigger finger stays on the side of the frame the entire time until ready to fire.

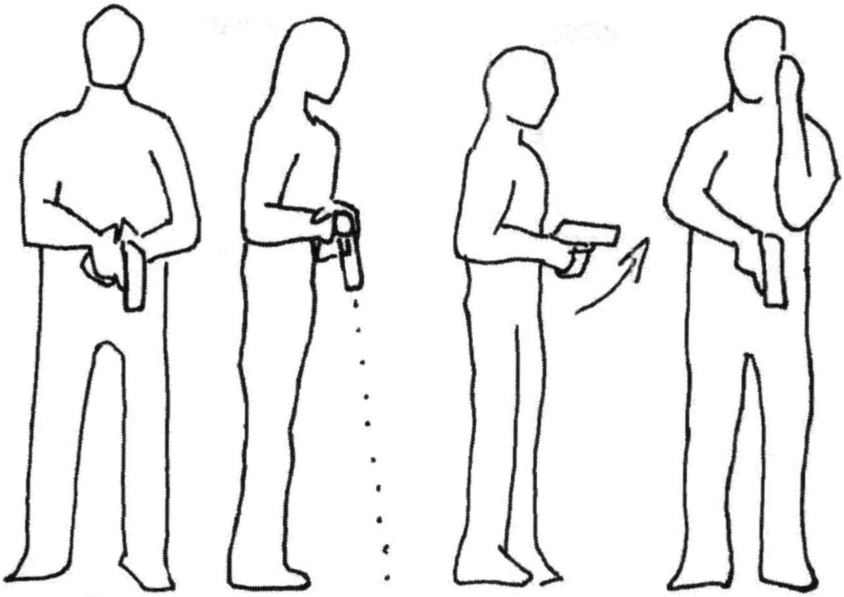

1. 2. 3. 4.

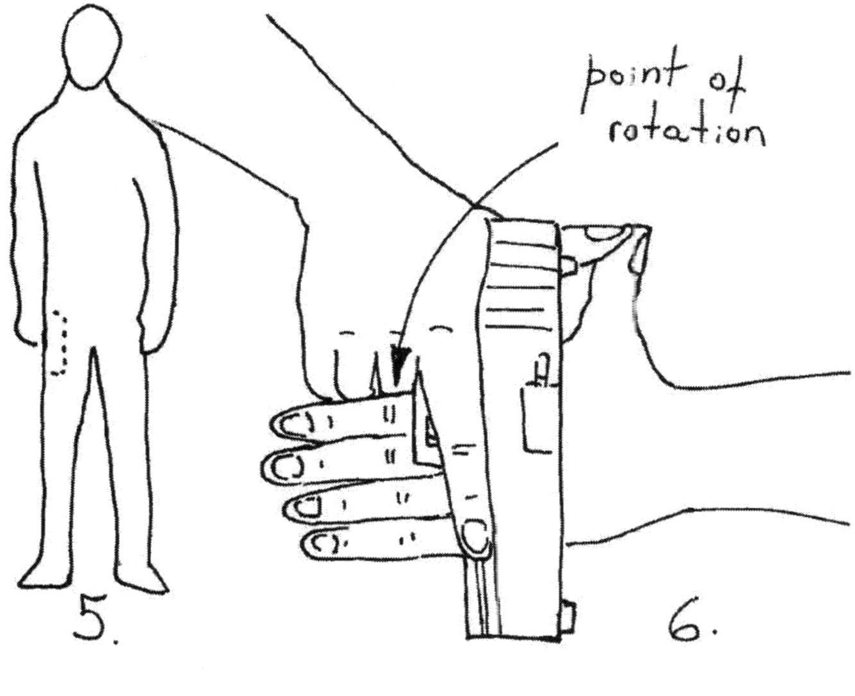

5. 6.

Point Shooting

Point shooting can be surprisingly accurate when done properly. Most veteran cops will have one or two stories about how an escaping suspect would be running away, suddenly turn and take a shot without aiming. They would just point the gun at them and pull the trigger with bad enough luck that a cop gets hit. There's more to these stories than "bad luck" and that's why they happen surprisingly often. A person spends his entire life pointing at things. The mechanics that go into pointing are not all that different from those used when reaching for a cup of coffee or pushing a button on the elevator. How often have you missed when doing either one? That's because our biomechanical accuracy is spot on. When pointing at any random object, if a laser came out of the tip of your finger it will likely be on target, especially at close range. People that try point shooting at the range often fail to hit their target not because there's something wrong with their hand but because they are thinking too much about it. More likely than not they are a) jerking the trigger anticipating the recoil (which is the main cause of lack of accuracy in general, poor trigger control) or b) trying to point with the gun instead of the finger. When a criminal runs from the police with adrenaline pumping and takes a shot he doesn't think about any of this.

1) Point at any object with your index finger and check the position of your hand.

2) That hand position while pointing at something with your index finger, that's the right angle and position for you and your bone structure. Simply hold the gun while keeping everything else the same. Your index finger still being off the trigger guard as it always should (until ready to shoot) even while holding the gun your index finger should still be on target as it rests on the side of the frame of the gun.

Point shooting is simply a matter of that finger going to the trigger and pulling it while everything else stays in the same place without moving. Some people are naturally better than others at point shooting, but done right everyone is capable of surprisingly good accuracy with it, especially at close range.

3) For most people, the natural hand position while pointing at an object and for point shooting will be with the palm of the hand canted inwards. A gross exaggeration of this hand position is the gangster stance with the palm of the hand parallel to the floor. Some people can still shoot accurately with a "gangster stance" but an angle closer to 45° feels a lot more natural.

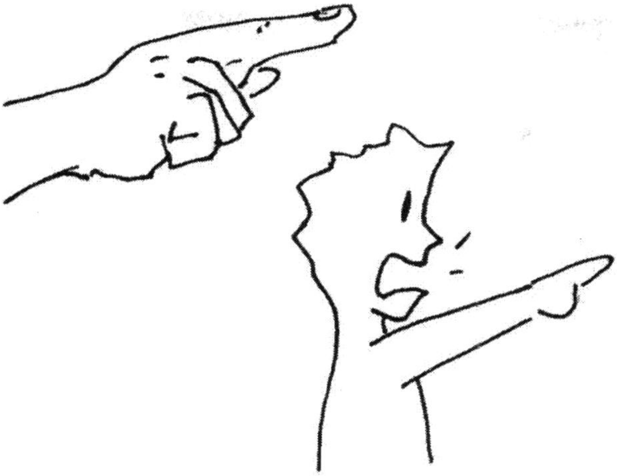

1.

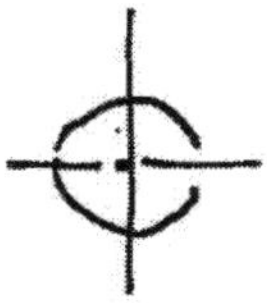

2.

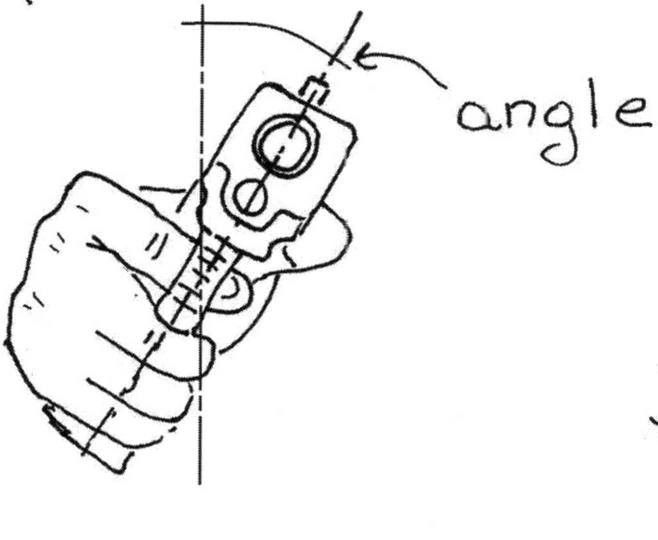

3.

How to Draw a Handgun

Proper technique when drawing a handgun is one of the most important skills to master when using a gun for self-defense.

It is also at this moment when most accidental discharges occur, people shooting themselves in the foot or worse. Proper technique means you will be both fast an accurate for that all-important first shot.

1) Eyes towards the threat, weak hand balled into a fist. The weak hand is placed against your chest, your fist covering you heart. Knowing where the weak hand is supposed to go reduces the chances of accidentally shooting it and since it is not in use at that moment it might as well be used to cover a vital organ (your heart). When shooting one handed, this is where the weak hand stays. Some shooters prefer to keep the support hand open against the chest or stomach, that's fine too.

With the strong hand, the handgun is firmly gripped while keeping the finger off the trigger guard. This is important so as to avoid accidents: Finger off the trigger guard until ready to shoot, no exceptions. The gun is firmly pulled out vertically until the muzzle clears the holster.

2) Once the muzzle of the gun clears the holster, it is immediately rotated towards the threat. At this point you can fire if needed. Accuracy will be poor but point shooting is accurate enough at very short range.

3) While pointing towards the threat, the gun comes up to eye level. When the gun is closest to the weak hand (usually around the center of the chest), the weak hand then moves and completes the two hand grip.

4) With the two hands on the gun, the movement continues and stops at eye level with the sights aligned with the eye and target. Having a correct technique and stopping the movement at precisely that point means you have a correct presentation. Notice how the arms are extended but the elbow isn't locked but slightly bent for better recoil management.

With a perfected presentation the shooter can pull the trigger as soon as he sees the front sight reach that point. If the stance practiced is correct this means elevation should be on target with enough accuracy for a quick center of mass shot.

5) Isosceles stance top view. The barrel of the gun is aligned with the axis of symmetry of the body, slightly bent arms forming the triangle. With the chest and arms forming the triangle and the gun at its tip all aligned.

With the right stance, windage (horizontal deviation) should be on target.

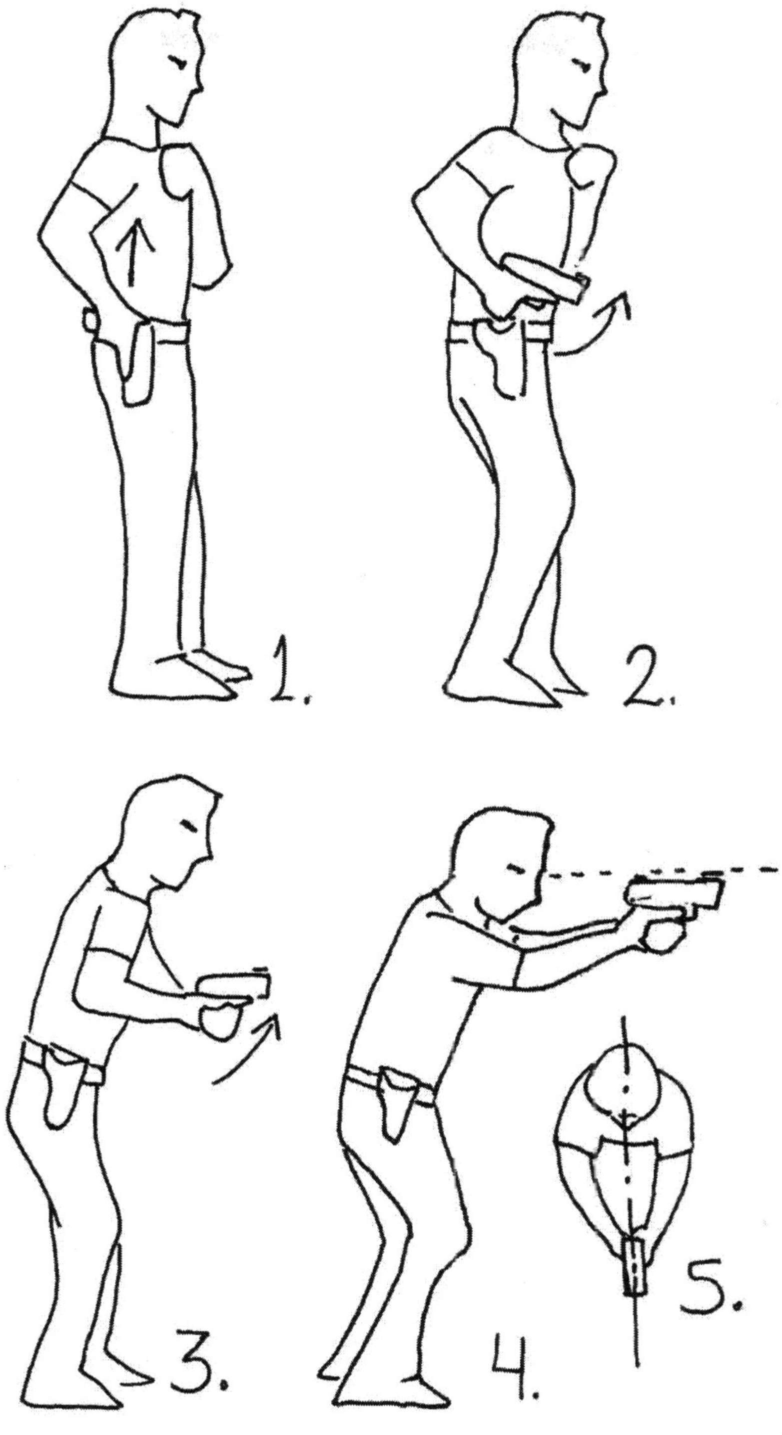
1.
2.
3.
4.
5.

Drawing from Concealment

Carrying concealed every day not only involves a certain level of training, it also requires an important amount of commitment. Concealed carry requires a solid gun belt, a good holster, but also dressing appropriately for it. Pants will need to be a bit larger, shirt longer and not very tight fitting. Even certain fabrics, colors and patterns reflect light in a different way which makes printing more noticeable.

1) Reaching for a firearm in an Inside-the-waistband holster means you will have to reach for the grip of the gun that is being concealed under a garment. Reach and lift your top garment. Hook your thumb under the bunched up fabric. Now you can slide your hand towards your firearm. This works for guns carried appendix (front of your torso), three, four or five o'clock position (clockwise, with your belt buckle being 12 o'clock).

Three or Four O'clock is a good balance between comfort standing and sitting, a position similar to the one used in practical shooting sports and concealability. Once you reach and grip your gun, you finish the draw like you normally would depending on the situation you are involved in. If using a jacket or vest, sometimes having keys or coins adds a bit of weight making it easier to swipe away to reach your gun.

2) Another option is grabbing the garment directly where the gun is, pulling up to clear the gun and then pressing the rolled up garment against your side with the heel of your hand and sliding down to grab the gun. One of the advantages of carrying past three o'clock compared to appendix carry is that after drawing the gun, the muzzle can still be somewhat concealed behind your hip or leg. This is far less visible and obvious for someone in front of you.

3) The weak hand pulls the garment up and out of the way, clearing the gun to be drawn. You then draw with your strong hand. This is the most positive and secure way of drawing from concealment but it can be slower, more noticeable and requires the use of both hands, which may not be available at that moment.

4) If your strong arm is injured, bend forward, your chest pointing towards the ground in as much of a 90 degree angle as you can manage. The weak hand then reaches around your back, moves the shirt away and draws the gun. The gun must be pointed down as it comes around your back, careful not to cover yourself with the muzzle.

Tip: The more you bend forward the easier it is to reach for the gun. This technique should be practiced frequently.

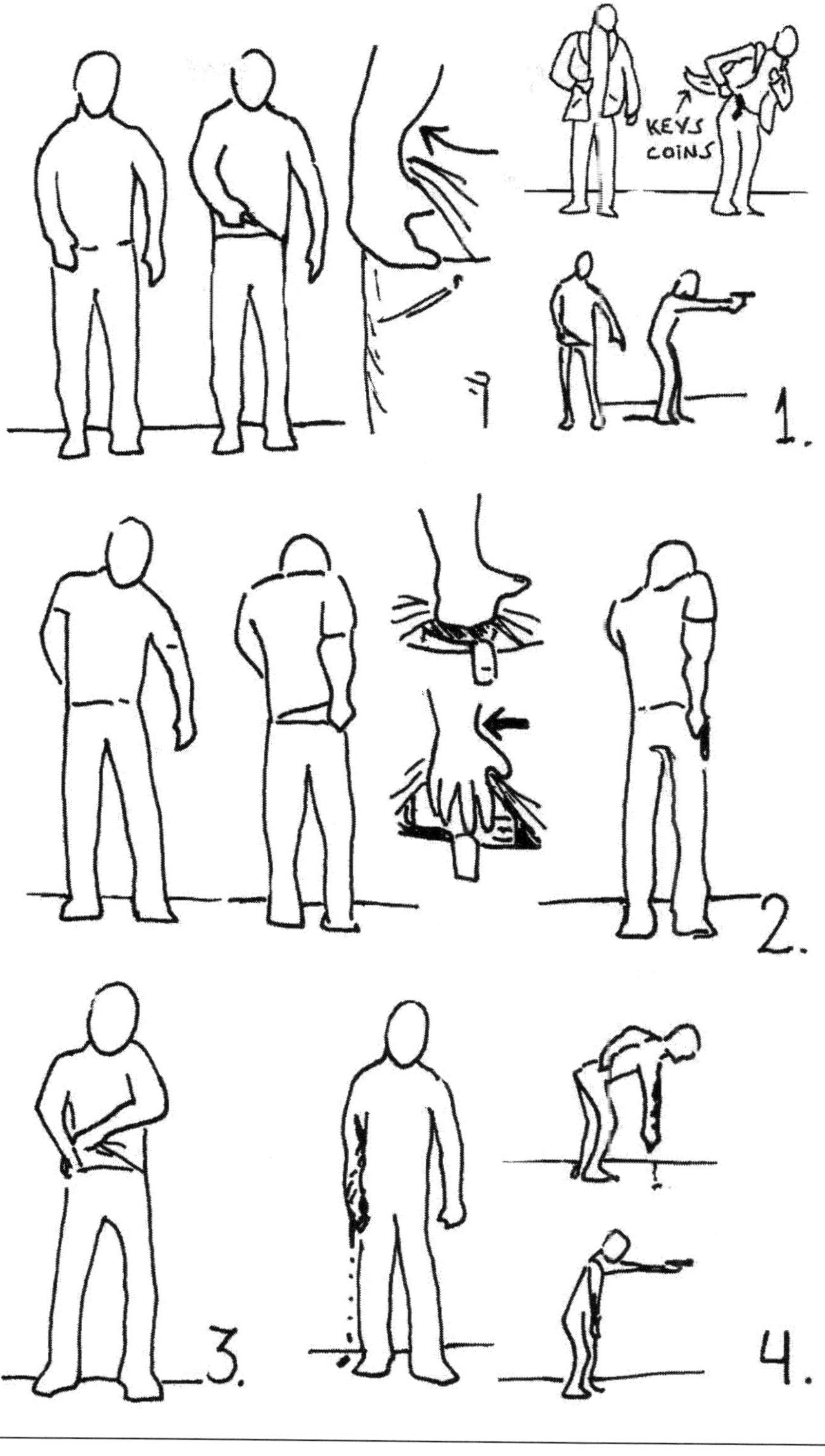
KEYS
COINS
1.
2.
3.
4.

5) Ankle holsters, belly bands and pocket carry are all viable options with advantages and disadvantages to each.

With the right ankle holster and a light and compact gun, it is easy to carry and you will eventually forget the gun is even there. The gun is not on your waist so there's no concerns of your clothes rolling up with movement and exposing the gun. This makes it ideal for certain clothes that are tighter around the torso. You do need to go with a smaller lighter gun, it won't be nearly as fast as more traditional waist carry and the holster needs to be of good quality so as to not drop the gun.

The belly band is a good option because it conceals the gun well, yet if correctly positioned it can be drawn fast. It can get hot and uncomfortable and it is far more complicated to reholster.

Pocket carry is one of the most practical ways to carry simply by slipping the gun into your pocket. You do need a proper pocket holster, a light and compact gun (J-frame revolvers and subcompact autos are a good choice) and to frequently practice drawing.

6) Carrying in a purse or messenger bag is not ideal since you want to have the gun on you at all times. If the purse or bag itself is being snatched, then you probably can't draw your weapon. There are bags, fanny packs and purses designed with interior holsters which can be used effectively. The person carrying this way also needs to practice often.

For women consistently carrying a gun in such a manner, they should start thinking of their purse as a shoulder holster or turn of the century sling holster rather than an actual purse.

Many of these carry options have the disadvantage of not integrating well to most shooting classes and training or the muscle memory you are likely to develop in practical shooting sports.

7) Inside the waistband appendix carry allows for fast and convenient drawing. Unlike "Mexican" carry, appendix carry is done with a proper holster, usually hard polymer ones made specifically for appendix carry. The disadvantage of appendix is the barrel may end up pointing at your groin or upper thigh where your femoral artery is when sitting down.

If clothes get caught when drawing the gun, if your belly pushes down on an improperly holstered weapon with something putting pressure on the trigger or if there's an accidental or negligent discharge of any kind, there's a greater chance of suffering a more serious injury than with more traditional three or four o'clock inside the waistband carry.

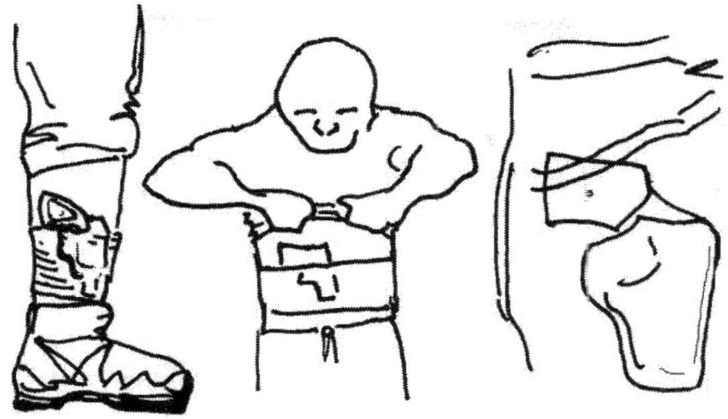

5.

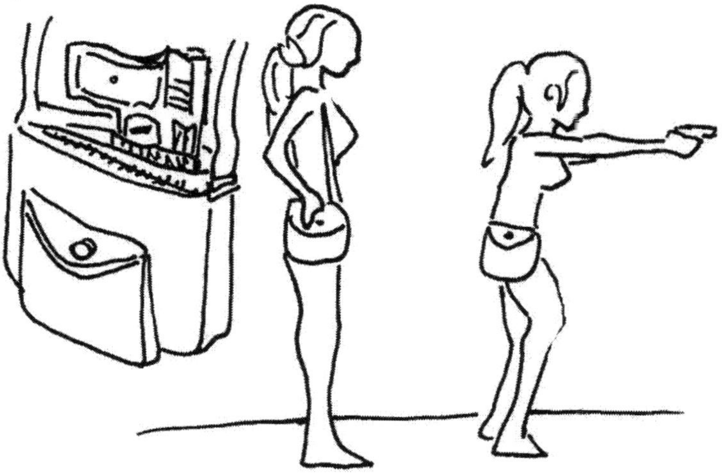

6.

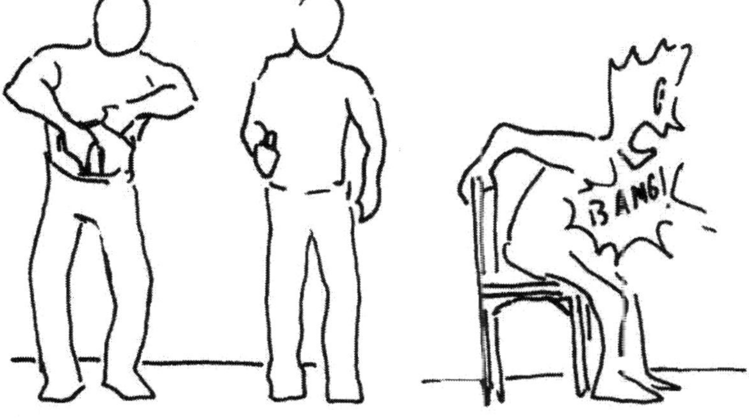

7.

Extreme Close Quarters Shooting

Close quarters combat (CQC) shooting requires the use of different stances and techniques so as to adapt to each situation. Moving around narrow corridors, bumping against walls, furniture or even people, there's no 'One Size Fits All' solution. Extreme Close quarters involves situations where the attacker is at contact distance or right on top of you.

1) Positon "Sul" allows you to move comfortably and safely in close quarters while still being able to instantly ready your weapon to fire.

2) From "Sul", the gun is brought up to the Isosceles stance, sights at eye level, arms extended, elbows slightly bent. This feels more natural and manages recoil better. Some small-frame shooters prefer to fully extend the arms and lock the elbows which presents a more stable structure, reducing muzzle flip and transmitting the recoil to the back. Professional shooters, including most practical pistol competition shooters who have well developed muscles, prefer to keep elbows slightly bent for better shock absorption during recoil.

Either way, eye, sights and target must all be in the same line. The gun can be brought back along the line of sight, reducing the distance for moving indoors or for better retention. This is not a stance for pinpoint accuracy but for engaging close range threats or allowing better movement in tight quarters.

3) The low ready position provides a better field of view while keeping the gun ready pointing downrange. Move the gun back along the axis into a compressed position to shorten the distance when needed.

4) In doing so, the elbows naturally shift positions. The support hand elbow going down, the strong hand elbow going up and to the side and the gun itself at an angle like when point shooting single handed.

5) From a compressed position, the support hand can come forward to push people out of the way, strike an attacker or grab his weapon.

6) At extreme close or contact range the gun is brought further back to the Retention Position, hand pressed against the side of your ribs. The gun is firmly held against the body but with the hand making contact, not the gun. This could impair the movement of the slide, jamming the gun.

7) The gun will be at an angle given the "V" shape of your chest and the position of the arms. In the Retention Position the support hand goes up, protecting the face and head. The elbow can be used to strike or create distance.

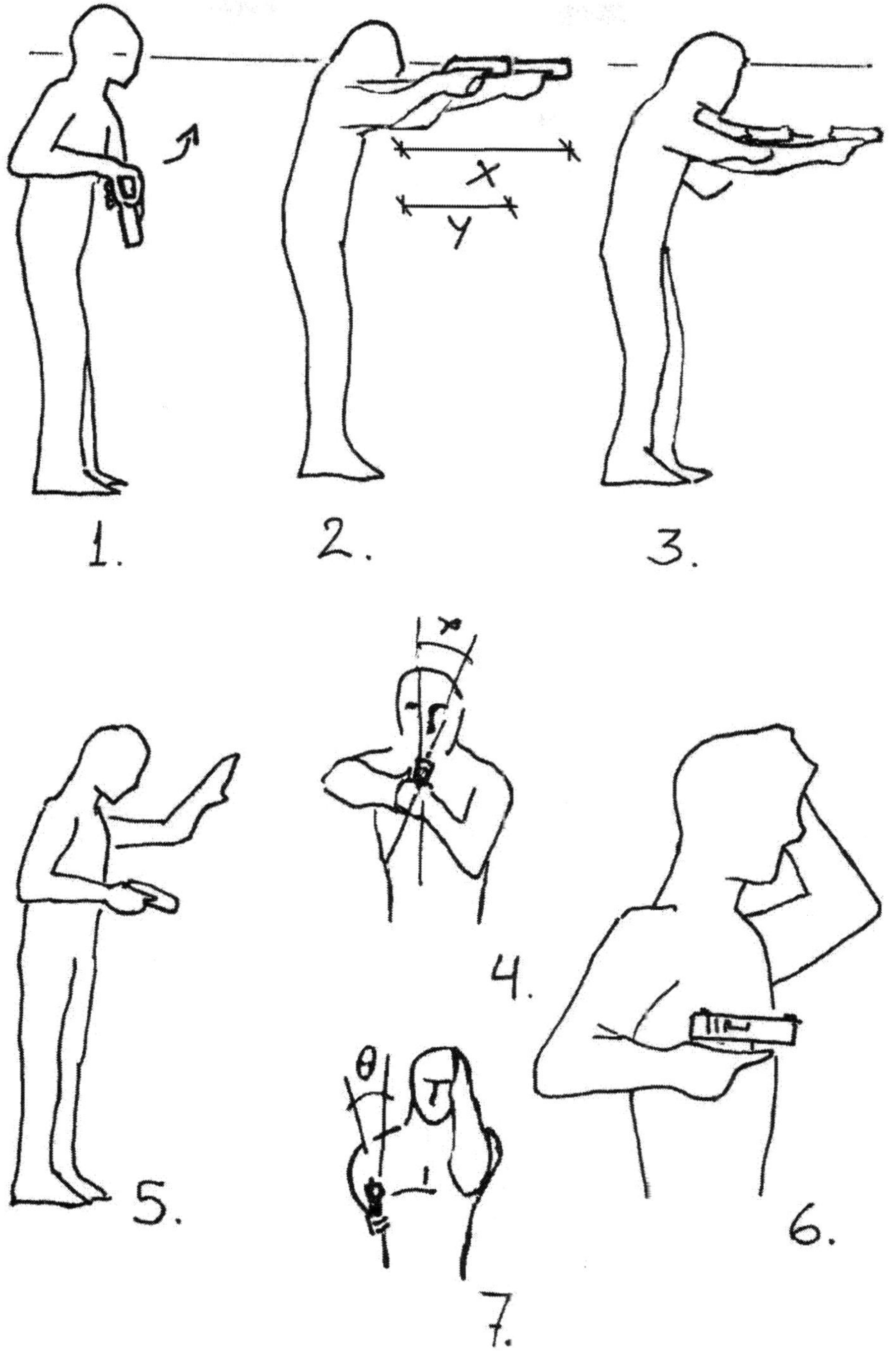
1.
2.
3.
X
Y
4.
5.
6.
7.
θ

Room Clearing

Room clearing is one of the most dangerous operations a person can be involved in. When tactical units perform them, they are carried out by professionals that specifically train for that, training every week, sometimes every day. For full-time SWAT officers in large cities in America, executing search warrants, kicking down doors and clearing rooms is just part of their day job.

Having said that, there may be times when you are on your own and knowing how to move around with a gun when something goes bump in the night can save your life and the lives of your loved ones.

Clearing a room can be done either slowly and deliberately or as more often seen in movies, rapidly and aggressively. This type of Dynamic Entry is intended to overwhelm the enemy, breach the door and flow into a room to take control. This type of tactic requires not only specific training and equipment (a ballistic shield would be a nice tool to have), but also a number of people.

1) When alone, a slow and deliberate approach is best. Move carefully and pay attention to doors and openings where you may be exposed to attackers. Approach the corner carefully "cutting the pie", one slice at a time, and be ready to either fire or pull back depending on the situation you encounter.

2) Move in a way that exposes you as little as possible. If necessary, change the hand you are holding your gun with to achieve this.

This is yet another reason why it is important to practice shooting with both hands.

3) Careful not to expose your lower body. Make sure your feet are behind cover as you peep around the corner.

4) Adjust your stance moving the gun back and compressing as needed so as to not bump into walls or expose your gun so that it may be grabbed by attackers. Simply flex your elbows brining the gun back while keeping the sights aligned with your eye.

5) As you move cutting the pie, maintain as much radius distance "R" as you can, given the room you have to work with. In most cases, the more distance you have the safer it is. Range tends to benefit the best shooter in a gunfight. Train so as to make sure you are the best shooter in the fight that fateful day.

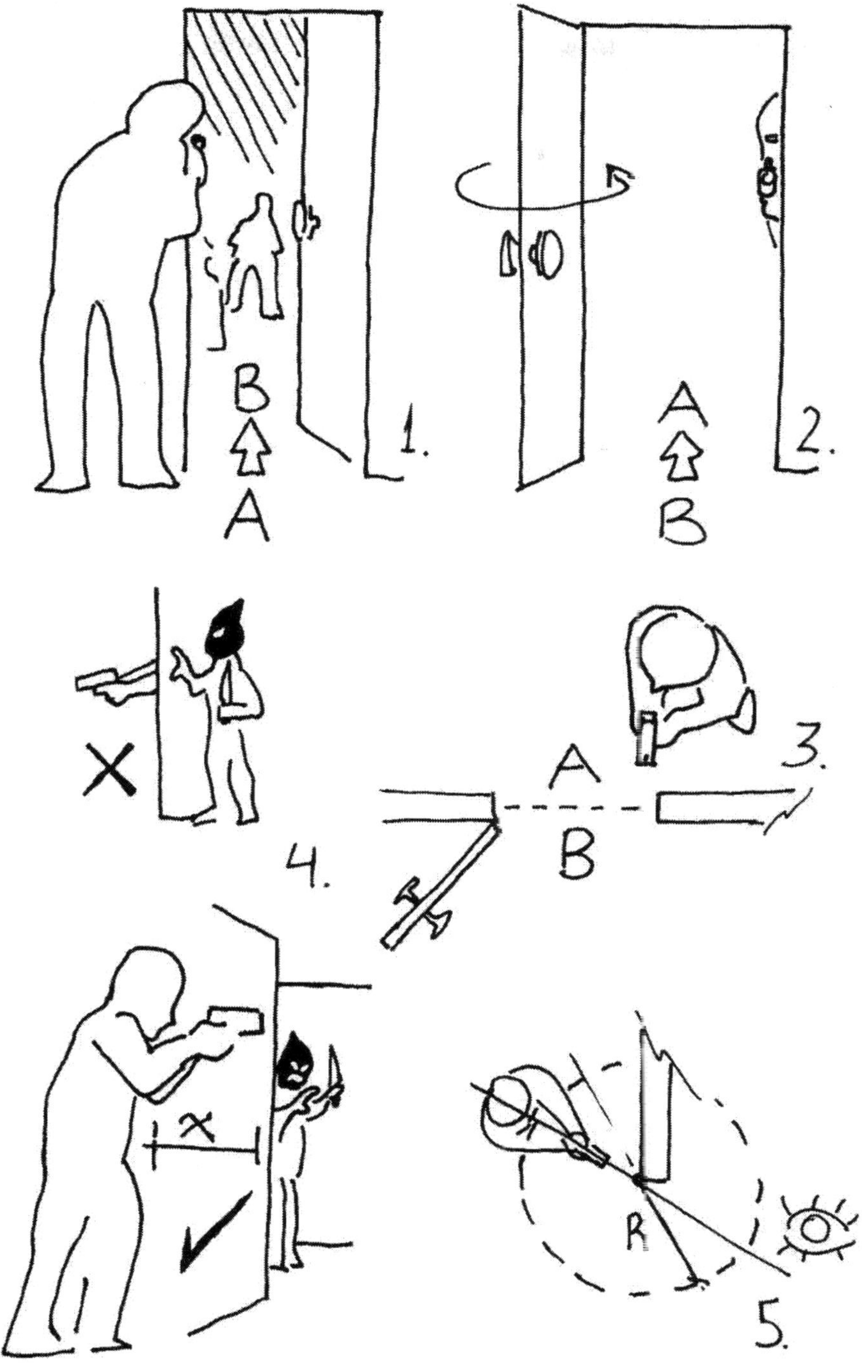
B
A
1.
A
B
2.
A
B
3.
4.
x
R
5.

Moving and Shooting

Most of the shooting done in beginners courses is likely to be stationary, shooting from a fixed position. More advanced classes will incorporate movement, shooting and moving as well as shooting while you move.

In reality a gunfight is a very dynamic situation and for the most part standing still is ill-advised. Standing still makes you an easier target. Hitting a moving target is far more difficult. Moving away from your attacker, creating distance or moving towards cover, moving in and closing the distance, these will all depend on the situation you are involved in but rarely is standing still the best course of action.

1) Shooting (accurately) is already hard enough. Moving adds yet another level of difficulty. Ideally you want to move creating as little disruption as possible. Walking normally makes your gun go up and down as you try to take aim (center line). Taking shorter steps and reducing how much you lift your foot with each step reduces this vertical movement significantly and you are able to stay on target better (top line). You want quick, short steps, knees slightly flexed and a rolling motion that looks more like sliding on a skateboard rather than walking.

2) Sometimes you need to move fast, you need to run and maybe do so on uneven terrain. This makes accurate shooting even more difficult.

When running in such conditions there's no point in fighting the vertical movement. Your sights will bob up and down no matter what you do. One thing you can do is time your shots so as to get a sight picture and shoot when your foot comes down and hits the ground with each step. At this point, for a fraction of a second, your aim is steady.

A holographic sight or red dot sight would help greatly in such instances where you need to take quick shots. If using iron sights, one useful tip would be to use the "poor man's holosight" technique. (page 120)

3) Tip up or tip down with handgun or rifle, what works best depends on the given situation. For handguns, tip down (Sul) makes the most sense in most situations. For rifles muzzle down is better in close quarters and when moving in and out of vehicles. Muzzle up is better for running.

4) Muzzle up makes it easier to hit the floor, the gun already aiming downrange, then get back up supporting the weight of the rifle rather than dragging it.

1.

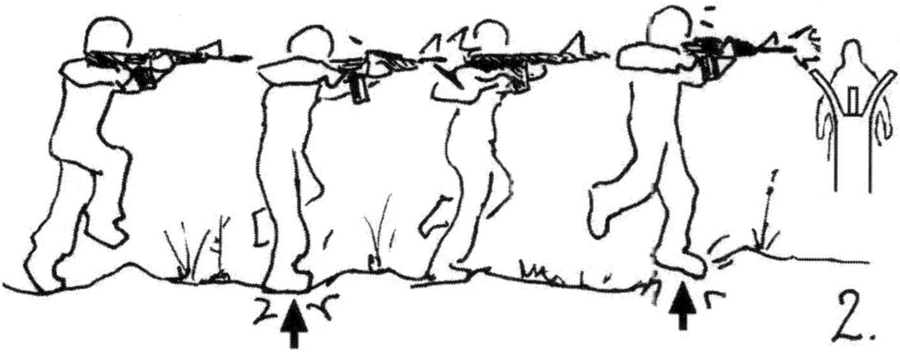

2.

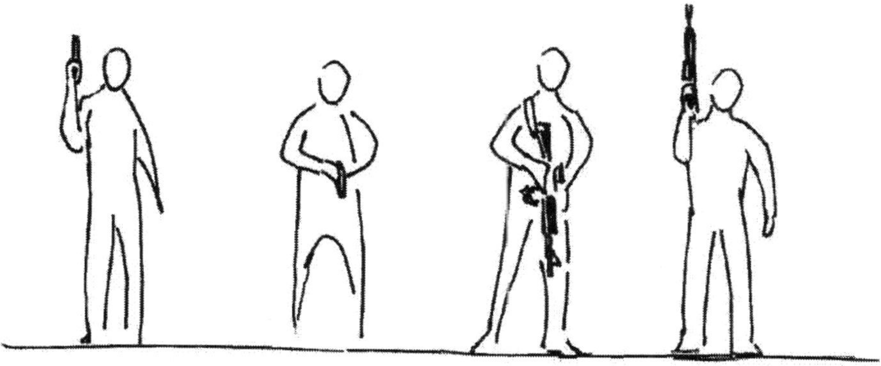

3.

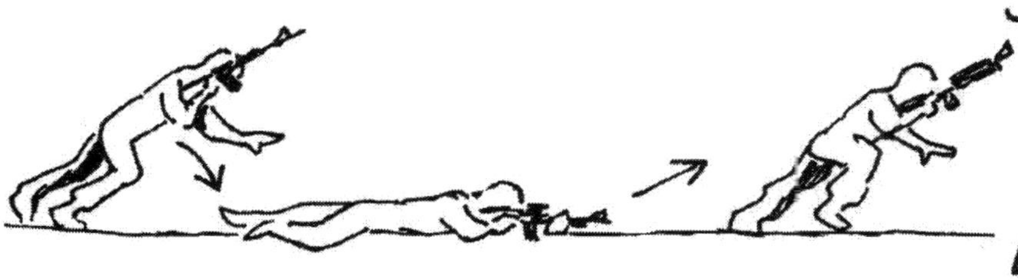

4.

Using Cover

Know how to take cover and move around corners correctly.

1) Distance is your friend. When shooting through windows, back away from it as much as possible. Light is less likely to reflect on you and reveal your position to others. You are a smaller target and less likely to be hit.

2) You don't want to bring your gun and arms through the window.

It may create a large shadow with any exterior light, revealing your position and you may be hit by rounds that impact on walls nearby and ricochet or spall.

3) When working around corners, expose as little of your body as possible. Ideally, only your eye, part of your head and your hand with the gun is exposed. If peeping around corners, don't pop out on the same spot twice. Lowering your body and shifting the position a few inches can make the difference between catching a bullet to the head or not.

4) When looking around corners, bring your knees together and move them in the opposite direction. This changes your balance and makes it easier to peep with minimal exposure.

In some cases you may want to take a second or third look to gain more information, but each time you do so you risk being detected and you risk getting shot. Bring your head around the corner in different places. Look for a new lookout position whenever possible.

If someone is taking aim and expecting you to pop up in one spot, taking a knee will lower your body enough so that your head is not in the same place as before. Even small sight adjustments work in your favor.

One of the best places to peep from is the angle where the wall meets the floor. At a distance it is far harder to notice the disruption, compared to half a head protruding from the perfectly straight line of a wall's outline.

5) Most people carry around a cell phone and the camera can be used as a tool to peep around corners without exposing yourself at all.

Turn on the camera and use it to see around corners, exposing only the camera portion. Make sure the flash is off and the phone is muted.

You can use the zoom function to take a closer look, record video and take photographs, safely gathering valuable information.

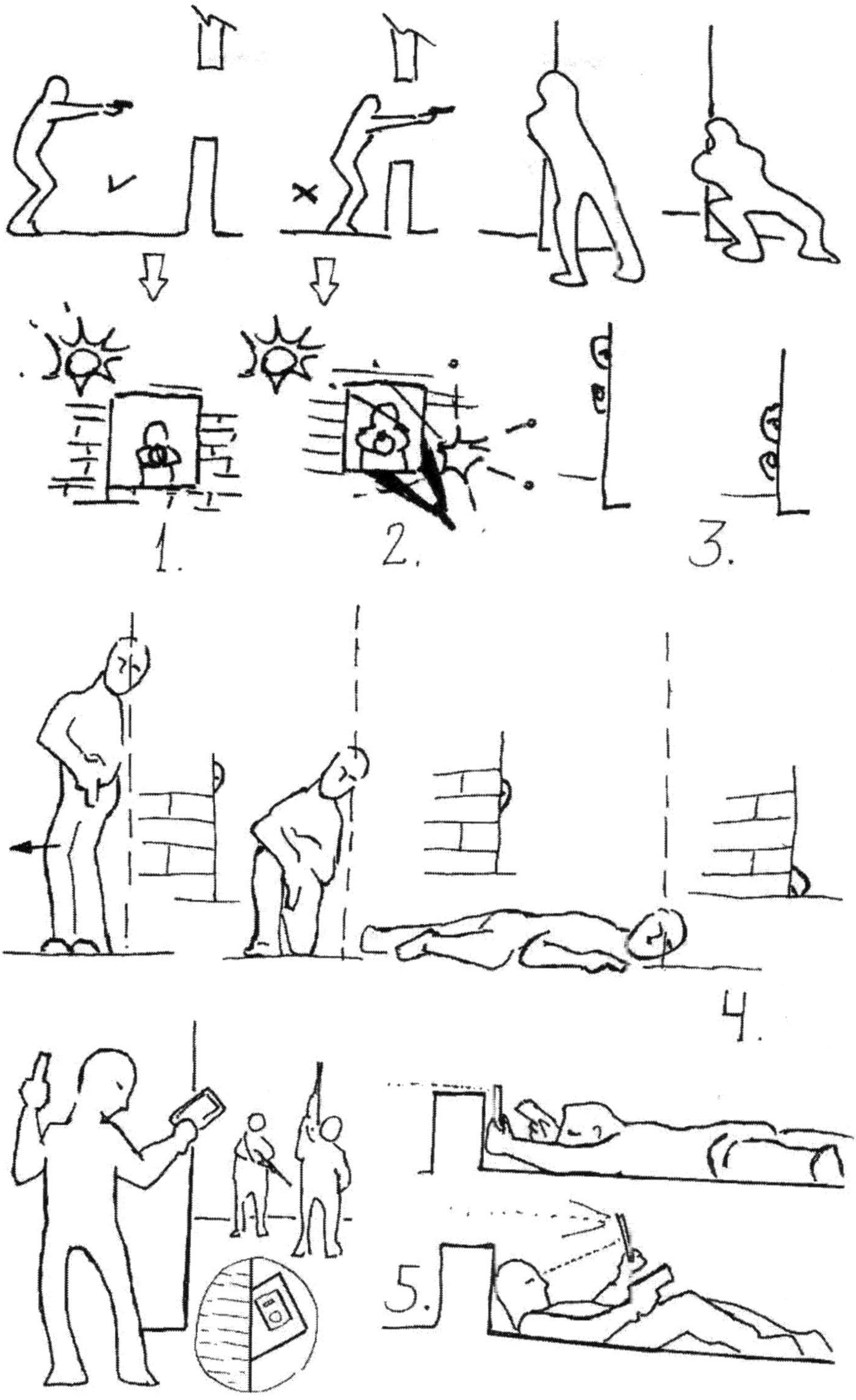
1.
2.
3.
4.
5.

Gunfight Dynamics

Gunfights are violent and chaotic fast-paced events. In spite of the chaos, when all hell breaks loose having a plan gives you a huge advantage.

1) When the fight starts, move. Get off the point X where you stand. Lack of mobility significantly increases your chances of getting shot so program yourself to start moving as soon as you hear gunshots.

2) When you move away from an attacker, move diagonally. Moving backwards is not just slower and you are more likely to fall, you are also staying in the same line of sight. From the perspective of the person shooting at you, you're not moving at all, you're just becoming a smaller target and a center of mass shot is just as likely to hit you. Moving diagonally on the other hand means that the shooter needs to adjust his aim horizontally which is more difficult and more likely to miss.

3) At extreme closer range, you want to move your attacker's gun away from you, close distance and stay on top of him. Shoot from the retention position, gun close to your body and away from your attacker.

When facing multiple attackers, engage the closest one and manoeuvre so that he's between you and the other attackers. This will make them less likely to shoot at you and even if they do, you have a human shield. Against multiple attackers, everyone gets "served" once before repeating.

4) A "double tap" (two shots) is typically fired when engaging an attacker. This doubles your chances of incapacitation and with practice it takes a fraction of a second to perform. A "controlled pair" would be similar but while a double tap is considered an "aim once, shoot twice" affair, a controlled pair involves a fast but deliberate aimed follow up shot. At close range the difference is academic but you want to practice putting two shots on target as a standard procedure. Get used to shooting twice and you will do it when shooting instinctively in a gunfight. Two shots per target is also standard for most practical shooting sports so the muscle memory you are reinforcing is the same.

Having said this, it will all depend on the situation at hand. Against a single armed attacker a quick string of five or six shots may be best. Shoot fast and keep shooting until the attacker is incapacitated.

Another drill worth practicing is the 2+1 or Mozambique drill. After two shots to the center of mass, a third shot goes to the head. This drill makes sense when: a) the attacker is wearing body armor (it's getting more common among criminals) b) when the shots to the torso fail to stop the attacker, due to being under the influence of drugs or alcohol.

1.
y
y
x
NOT MOVING, ONLY GETTING SMALLER
MOVING TARGET
2.
3.
DOUBLE TAP
2+1
4.

5) Closing the distance and using an attacker as a shield by keeping him between you and his accomplices can sometimes be combined with other structures and elements around you. A wall, a narrow corridor used as a choke point, these should be taken advantage of whenever possible. Cars can also be used in such a manner. Attacks often take place in parking lots and garages where such opportunities may present themselves. During home invasions, an attacker may rush in as you park your car. Use your surroundings to your advantage.

6) Understand the nervous system and circulatory system. In popular "gun culture" it is believed that only a round to the central nervous system (CNS), the brain and spinal cord, guarantees to stop an attacker. This theory is not backed by practice though, where we see that the human body is far more complex than that and a number of factors may influence what stops a person or not.

7) It is still safe to say that the center of mass of a person and the line going up to the brain is a prime target area. We not only have the spinal cord, but also the heart and main blood vessels along this line. The closer rounds land along this area, the more likely it is to effectively stop an attacker. Shooting at very close range, shooting upwards along this line, "zipping up", is likely to be highly effective.

8) Target practice is fun and helps increase accuracy. Practical shooting is also a great way to develop valuable skills. Shooting fast and accurately is always good. Practicing draws, reloads and solving malfunctions on the go, these are all very important.

9) But don't lose focus of what you are trying to do. Practical shooting sports are a great way of practicing valuable skills and being part of a social group that is likely to be composed of like-minded people but it does not replace defensive shooting and tactical training.

It is easy to let yourself get lost in the "sport" side of practical shooting sports and forget about situational awareness.

Just like a boxer needs to role-play in his head when shadow boxing, a shooter needs to put himself in a situation where those targets are shooting back. That while shooting around a corner needlessly exposing your torso may save a second or two, in the streets it is reckless to do so. It makes the difference between getting shot or not.

More than two rounds are likely to be needed to effectively neutralize a threat. Naturally moving away after two rounds fired without assessing can be a bad habit to incorporate.

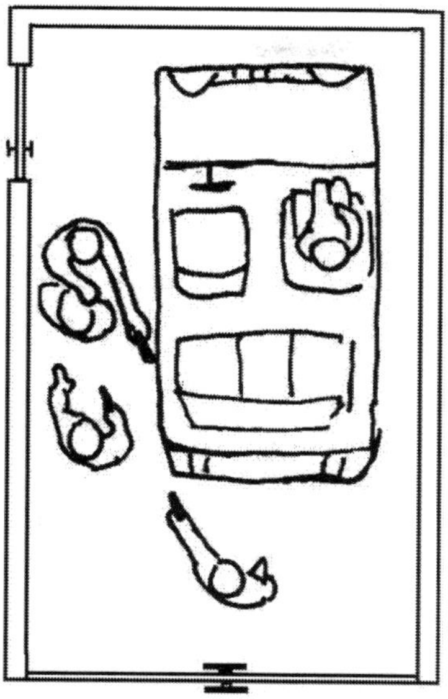

5.

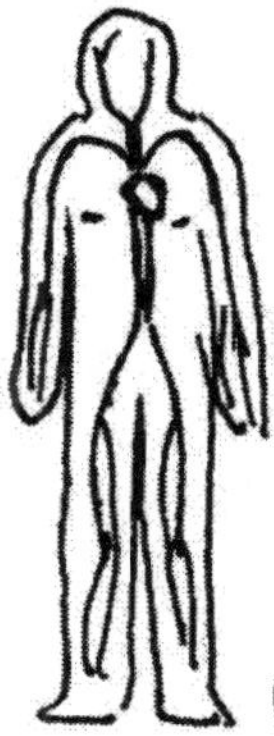

6.

7.

8.

9.

What to do after a Shooting

So you armed yourself, followed the advice presented here and one day you get into a gunfight and make it out alive. That's just half the battle. Now you get to deal with the part Hollywood rarely shows in cool action movies which is defending yourself in court. Here's where bad advice from "experts" can land you in jail for the rest of your natural life.

1) Burning corpses in steel barrels or sinking them in a river is fantastic advice… if you want to end up in prison! Tampering with evidence alone can get you 20 years and turn a clear self-defense case into a homicide.

2) The first thing you should do is take a deep breath, calm yourself and call 911. Let them know you've been attacked, a person has been shot, give them your name and address. Answer the questions but keep replies short. Right after calling 911, call your lawyer. You should have one you trust on your contacts list. Don't touch the body, don't try to help the person you shot. Unless you are a doctor, you can only make things worse and get yourself a lawsuit. Holster or secure your firearm. Keep your hands up when the police arrive and follow their instructions. Be polite. Resist the urge to "explain" things but be reasonable. Tell the police if an accomplice wearing a red shirt took off or where a weapon has fallen during the fight. Other than that, say you've been attacked, you defended yourself and that you will fully cooperate once you get the chance to talk to your lawyer. Since you are likely under a lot of stress, nothing else you say can help you but it could be used against you.

3) If the shooting took place on the street after a disaster and the police aren't responding, take pictures of the scene, record any witness's name and contact information. Take plenty of pictures so as to explain what happened and assist any investigation once order is restored.

4) Use common sense. If during a large scale disaster you shoot someone in self-defense and no one is responding for days or weeks, you can't leave a rotting corpse in your living room. Before touching anything, take pictures of the body and the general setting. Insist on calling the police regularly and keep track of when those calls were made and the officer you spoke with. If no one is responding and you need to move the body, don't burn it or sink it in a river. Move it away from home so as to avoid sanitary hazards (at least 60 meters), burry the body and mark the location. Using a clean bag, pick the weapon the attacker used against you without touching it, grabbing it by the muzzle with minimal contact. Secure it as evidence which you will present to the authorities once order is restored and they can respond to your call.

1.
911
LAW
YER
2.
3.
RIP
200 feet
60 meters
4.

Ballistics

The actual power of most small arms cartridges is greatly exaggerated in popular culture, (no, none will send a person flying across a room) yet at the same time even the smallest round commonly available (.22 Long Rifle) is capable of killing and will easily penetrate most of the materials used as effective cover in movies.

1) Typical terminal ballistics for 9mm FMJ (Full Metal Jacket) on a block of ballistic gelatin which somewhat resembles the behaviour of flesh. 9mm, the most common handgun round for military, law enforcement and for civilian self-defense use, will penetrate 18" to 22". Of course, men aren't made of gelatin and rounds may fragment or deform when they hit bone, slowing down, penetrating less. 9mm FMJ is used by most military forces. Its tendency to overpenetrate is a disadvantage for law enforcement and self defense but for military applications better penetration is desirable. The lines in the block show the permanent cavity (continuous line) and the temporary cavity (dotted line). The permanent cavity is the actual empty space left. How much tissue was destroyed and how profuse the bleeding will be. The temporary cavity shows the elastic deformation, how far the tissue was stretched before returning to its place. While often considered less effective than the permanent wound channel, not all tissue is capable of equal elastic behaviour without damage and a larger temporary cavity means greater disruption to organs, blood vessels and nerves, increasing the chance of incapacitation. The larger the projectile and the more velocity it has, the larger the wound it creates tends to be. This is why high powered rifle rounds, often thanks to higher velocity alone, are much more effective than handguns.

2) 9mm Jacket Hollow Point (JHP) creates a larger permanent and temporary cavity but penetrates less. This makes it statistically more effective when it comes to incapacitating an attacker.

3) Wooden doors, garbage cans, interior hollow walls, plastic or thin metal signs, none is likely to effectively stop 9mm or other big-bore rounds. These can provide concealment, meaning you can hide behind them and that can be better than nothing, but expect a round going through it to be lethal.

4) A tree large enough to hide behind, bricks walls, flower pots, a foot of dirt or sandbags as the ones used by the military, these provide cover, meaning most small arm rounds will be stopped. Keep in mind that some powerful rifle rounds can penetrate materials handguns cannot. Rifle rounds can also destroy cover quicker.

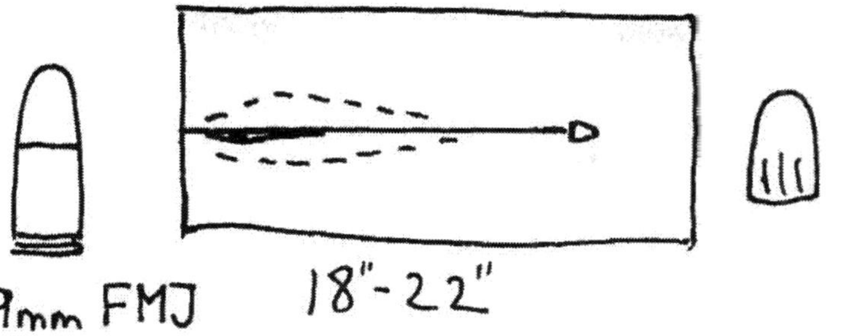

1.

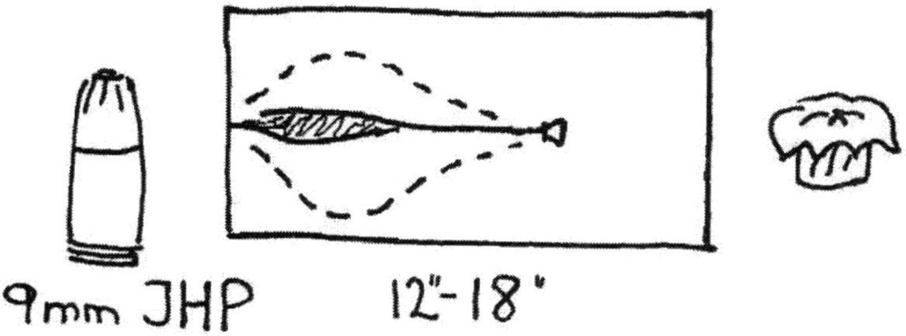

2.

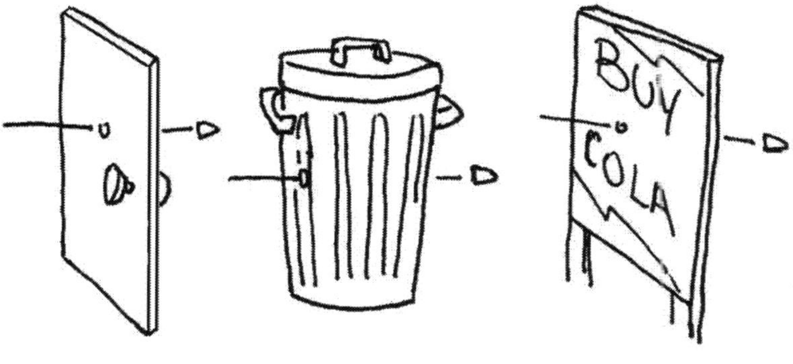

3.

4.

Force Multipliers

Force multipliers increase the capabilities of the shooter or of the tools he uses.

1) Body armor isn't just likely to save your life in a gunfight, it also means you are harder to bring down. Given its relatively low cost when compared to firearms, it is curious to observe that the same people that believe having body armor at hand is going overboard or trying to be "Rambo" don't think twice about owning half a dozen guns for "home defense". Ideally, you should have a IIIA concealable vest for when greater discretion is required and a rifle plate carrier set with magazine pouches to use with your rifle for more serious social occasions.

2) An accurized battle rifle, a .30 caliber rifle properly set up with a scope allows you to engage targets at greater distances and to deliver a more powerful round downrange. It is a common military approach to have a good shooter in the team equipped with a more powerful scoped rifle. Sometimes refers to as "Designated Marksman" this is the person in the team that actually gets hits at a higher rate. While in a civilian role long range self defense shots are almost unheard of, in certain settings (homesteads, farms, isolated residences) the ability to do so can be a great asset. A more powerful round will have greater stopping power and can turn cover into concealment, effectively penetrating barriers smaller caliber rounds will not.

3) Night vision is one of the greatest force multipliers an individual can use. This is particularly true in military operations where they are used during night time or in blacked out buildings. They can be valuable for civilians as well, especially during long term civil unrest, blackouts or out in the country. Suppressors also have many advantages including hunting or shooting firearms in urban settings more discretely. A person using night vision, a suppressor, and infrared laser will be literally picking people like fish in a barrel when going against adversaries without such technology and training.

4) Full-automatic fire has somewhat of a bad reputation among some shooters. They believe it means one must always "spray and pray". The price of full auto firearms doesn't help either, putting it beyond the budget of many. Properly used, full auto does have its applications. Use it in short three or four round bursts sweeping in tight angles. Use it against attackers packed in tight quarters such as narrow corridors and hallways, flights of stairs or people inside vehicles.

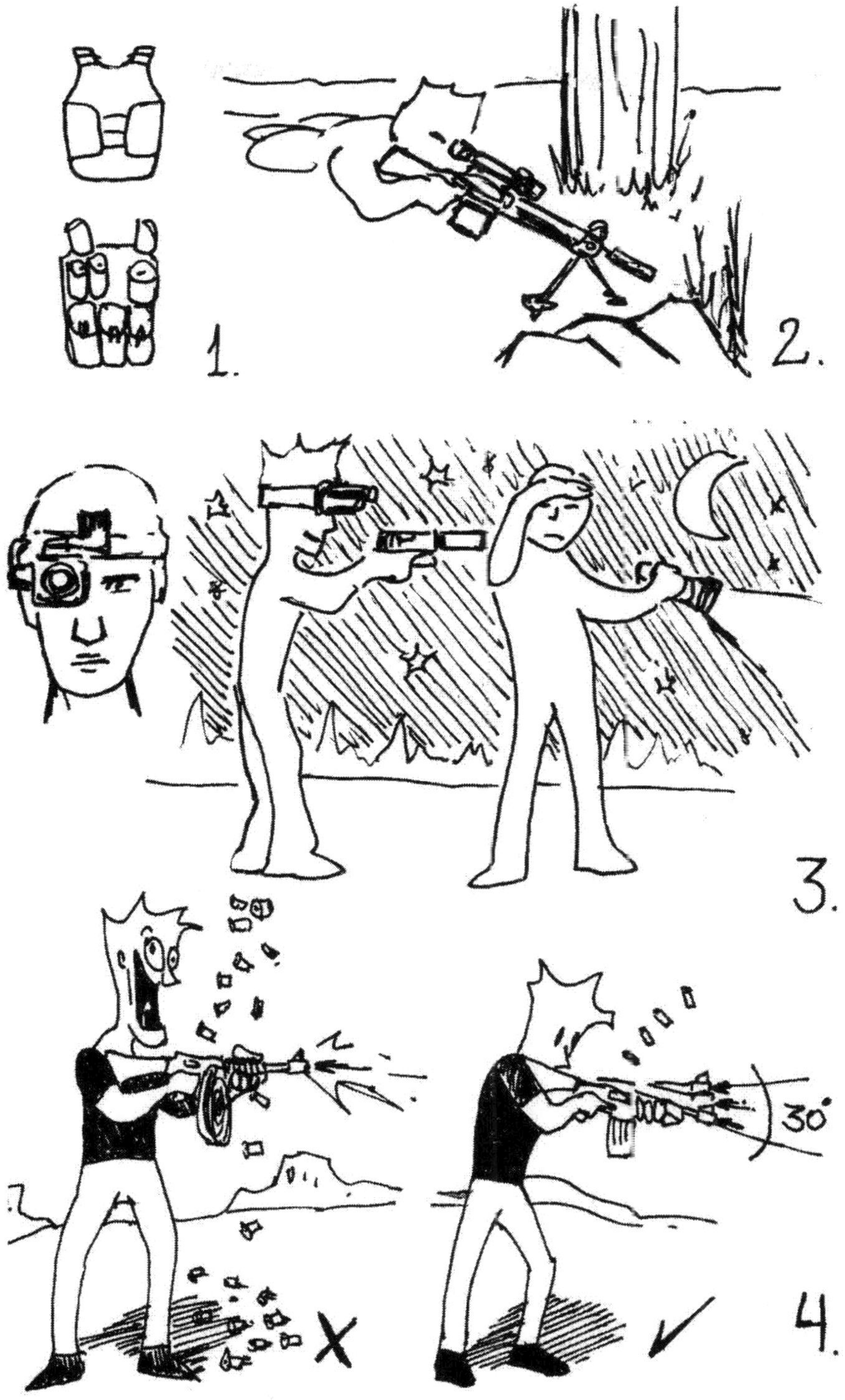
1.
2.
3.
30°
4.

Punches and Gunshots: Reality vs Fiction

Understanding what truly happens during violent encounters will prepare you better to deal with them in real life. It is often the case that Hollywood presents an unrealistic view of what it's like when people get beaten or shot.

1) The face of a person (A) is a rather delicate structure with small bones and blood vessels. When a person gets fictionally beaten on TV (B), they will often put some makeup, a few drops of blood and they are done. In reality, (C) a person that is severely beaten will not only profusely bleed, but as bones get broken, tissue and blood vessels damaged, the face of the person gets swollen, eyes swollen shut, bumps appear on the head and face and in some cases the face can be so severely disfigured that even close relatives may not recognise the person in front of them. It will take days or even weeks to go back to normal and for the purple and black skin discoloration to go away.

2) Handguns are not death rays. According to the Annals of Emergency Medicine publication[7], mortality rate for gunshot wounds is roughly 33% (7.7% for stab wounds) with handguns being less powerful and less lethal than long arms. People shot with handguns don't fly through the air. If they do drop when shot, and they don't always do, it will seem to be more of a collapse, knees buckling. The shooter rarely sees the hits, and if there is any arterial bleeding, it is unlikely to be immediately noticeable. Blood isn't likely to squirt by the buckets, flying in every direction like in the movies. Spraying will be minimal.

3) Service rifles fire high velocity cartridges. These are more powerful than handgun ammunition (low velocity). A person that has been shot is more likely to drop (as if tripped or punched) but again, no one flies through the air. Depending on where they are hit, blood spray can be visible. The damage is more visible, creating larger wounds. Bleeding is likely to start faster and more profusely than with handguns.

4) All shotgun shells pack a good amount of power and the person shot with them will feel the punch, probably fall to the ground. With shotguns it depends on the kind of ammunition used. Birdshot (A) at close range will produce shallow, gruesome wounds even if lacking penetration. Birdshot will fail to do much damage past 25 yards. Buckshot (B) produces wounds similar to handguns, but with 9 pellets or more hitting at the same time its stopping power is multiplied as well. Slugs (C) are a single large lead projectile. These are low speed but heavy (typically 1oz) projectiles which penetrate a great deal with devastating results.

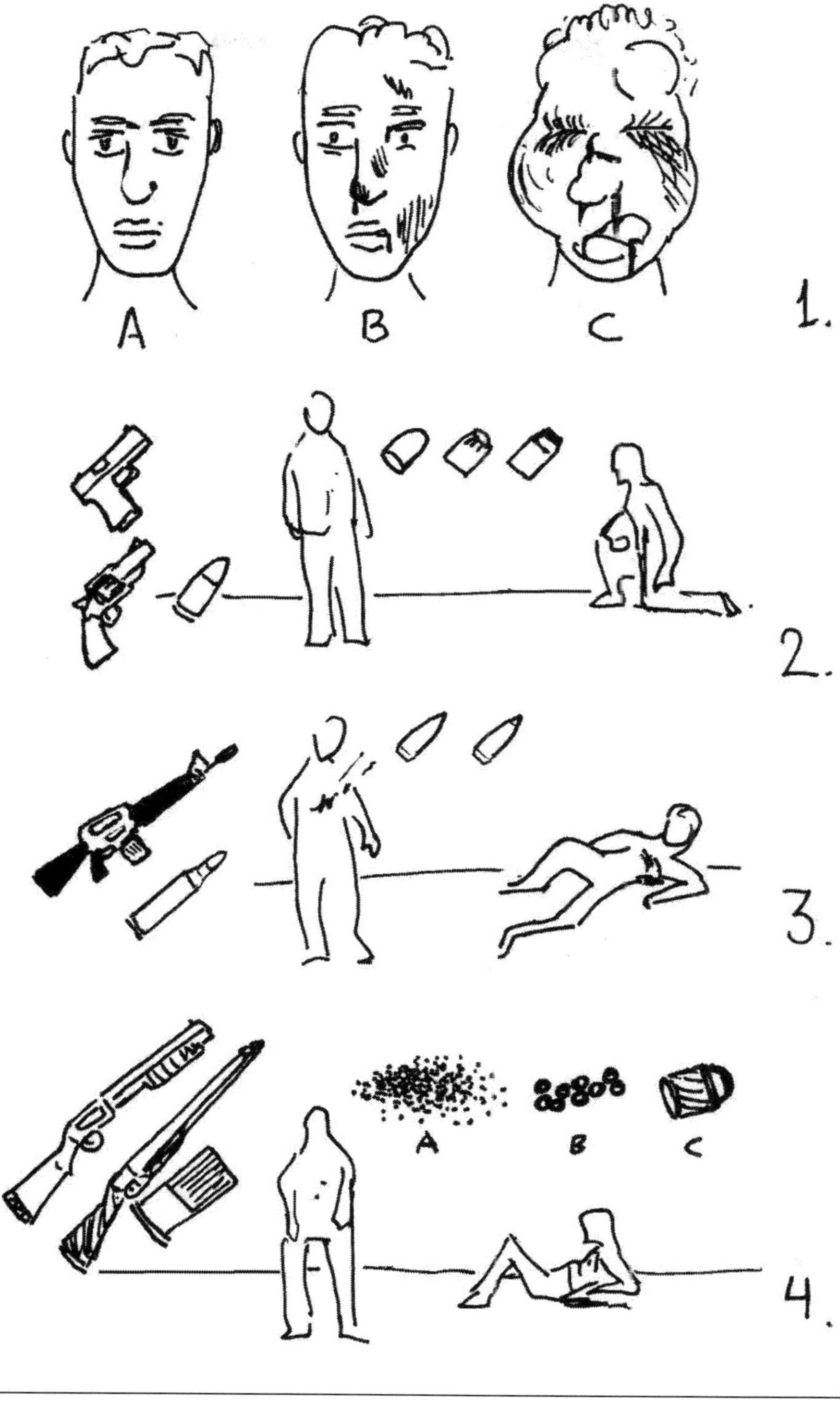
A
B
C
1.
2.
3.
A
B
C
4.

Using a Handgun as an Impact Weapon

Guns can jam, run out of ammo or malfunction in a number of ways. In a worst case scenario there may not be time to do much about it other than keep on fighting. If that's the case, you still have a tool you can use to strike with. All-metal guns aren't as common as they once were but even with extensive use of polymer the metal slide can cause plenty of damage when used correctly.

1) The easiest and most instinctive way to strike with a handgun is simply punching with it in the same way you would throw a jab in boxing.

With a firm grip, muzzle pointed forward, the objective is to strike the face of your opponent with the tip of the muzzle. If the gun is empty with the slide locked back the barrel will still be protruding so as to strike with it. Aim for the face. The metal slide will easily break teeth, nose and cheekbones or damage the eyes.

2) Striking sideways using the slide. The motion is similar to a hook in boxing. In this case, aim for the jaw, cheekbone, temple and head in general. Enough force can be delivered to crack a person's skull with a heavy enough gun. Striking this way, if there's a metal front sight with sharp edges it can cause lacerations to the face.

Don't expect your opponent to stand still while you strike. You may need to keep your attacker at bay with your other hand. Try creating openings with it so as to strike with your gun.

3) Another common way of using a gun as a striking tool is just bringing it down over your attacker's head like a hammer. This will be more effective with an all-metal firearm. Guns that have a lanyard ring in the bottom like certain 1911 pistols can be very effective when used in such a manner. Polymer-framed guns with polymer magazines won't be as effective but can be used in a pinch.

Compact guns will be problematic as well when used to strike this way. Some of them have little in the way of grip and the small finger hangs under the magazine. The smaller and lighter the gun, the less of an effective blunt weapon it becomes.

Magazine plates with glass breakers are available for some of the most popular handguns in the market. These would turn them into more effective striking tools.

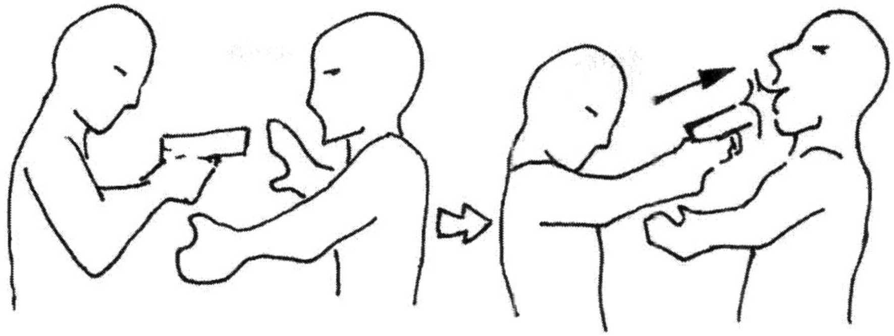

A B 1.

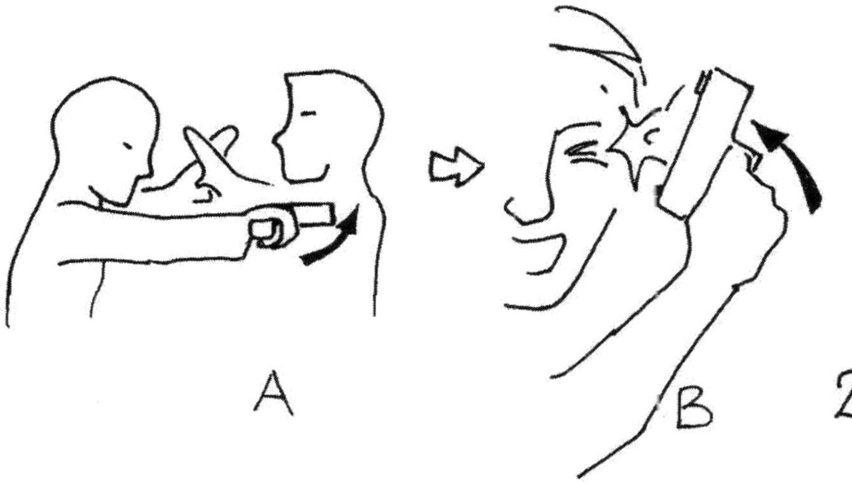

A B 2.

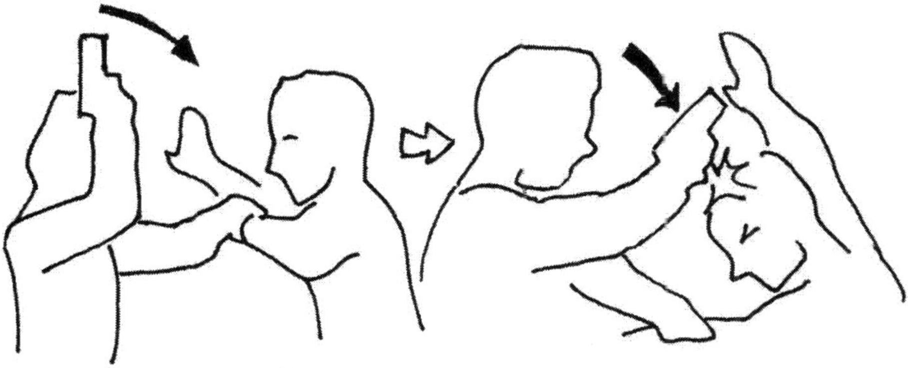

A B 3.

Firearms Training

There's no replacement for professional firearms training. You wouldn't buy a car and just take it for a spin without knowing how to drive. Just going to the range on your own and trying to hit the target will only reinforce bad habits and poor technique. Once you receive proper firearms training, frequent practice is needed to sustain and improve the level acquired. Getting involved in practical shooting is a good way to do that, supplementing your defensive shooting training.

1) Train like you fight so that when the day comes you will fight like you trained. People sometimes get caught in looking "cool" and moving a certain way but not fully committing to putting themselves in the situation they are supposedly training for. The lateral head movement after shooting is not a formality, it's for looking for other attackers. Don't just move your head left and right, actually "look" and do so with intent, your gun following in those same directions. Also, don't just stand there like a sitting duck, get of the X. Move (even if just a little) so that you no longer are a stationary target.

2) When someone is shooting at you, you become a target in a two way shooting range. Expect to be hit center of mass as well. If you are shooting back in self defense, notice that with most stances your gun and hands will be at the center of your attacker's target. This is why hands and arms often get wounded during gunfights and why it is so important to practice shooting single handed, with both hands.

3) If you need to chamber a round or clear a malfunction single handed, use your rear sight to catch against you belt and firmly push down to rack the slide. A sturdy belt and square angle metal sights are ideal for this. Tables, chairs, boots, jean's pocket, any firm material can be used.

4) "Tap" the magazine to make sure it is properly seated, "rack" the slide by pulling it back and letting it fly forward. Tilt the gun towards the right when pulling the slide back so as to facilitate the extraction of a round or stuck case. Now you can "shoot" as need. "Tap, Rack, Bang" usually works well for clearing most malfunctions in most auto pistols in the market today.

5) A "stovepipe" occurs when and empty case gets stuck in the ejection port. With the palm of your hand in front of the stuck case, quickly bring the hand back towards you in a reverse "karate chop". This will send the case flying away. If the gun failed to feed a round properly you want to rack the slide so as to put a round in the chamber.

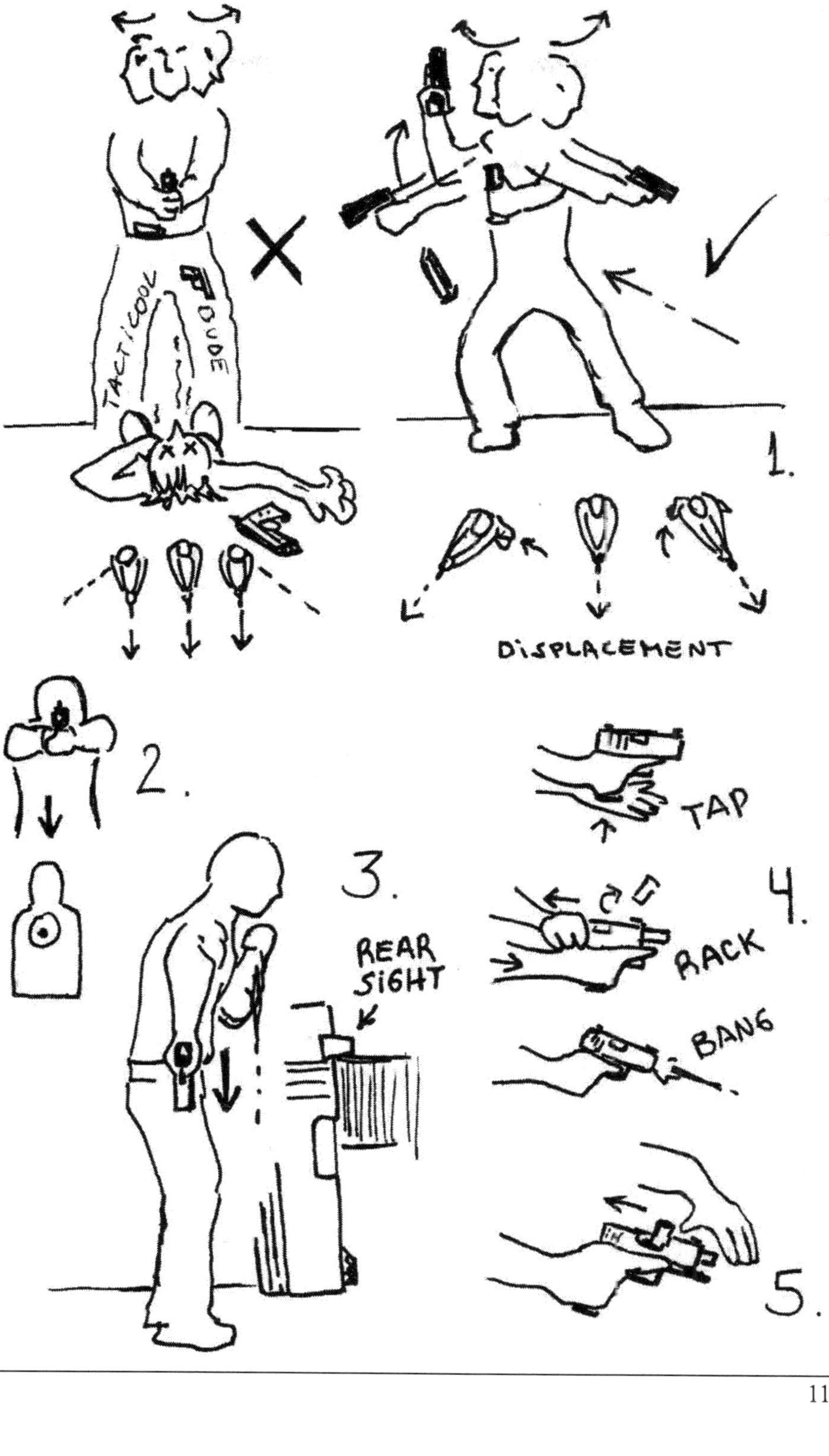
TACTICOOL
DUDE
1.
DISPLACEMENT
2.
3.
REAR SIGHT
TAP
4.
RACK
BANG
5.

Firearms Training Tips

1) Fold an A4 or Letter page in half. That's roughly the size of an IPSC target "Alpha" area. That's also about the area where your center of mass shots should group on an attacker's chest so as to have the best chances of incapacitation.

Cardboard paper plates 6" wide also make for good cheap targets. It's about the same size as the eight point black center area of a 25 yard bullseye target. They are more rigid than paper, making it easier to staple to sticks or wooden frames.

Always keep a stapler and a couple rolls of paper tape in your range bag. The stapler is needed to set up targets. The paper tape has hundreds of uses. It can be used for setting up targets too but its main use is covering holes on your paper target after shooting.

2) Know your gun and how the sights are intended to be used. Most combat pistols come with sights set to shoot at the point of aim but it is not uncommon to come across guns used for target shooting that will hit the bullseye when aiming at the bottom of the target's black area. Target guns are set that way because the black area of the target makes it harder to distinguish the sights.

3) The "poor man's holosight" is a technique that allows fast shooting with good enough practical accuracy for a man-sized target. Rather than using the front and rear sight as you normally would, use the protective hood or ears of the front sight and put your target within that frame. Some AK platform rifles have front sights with a circular shaped protection that works well for this technique. As long as you have a correct cheek weld, if you see your target within that front sight "box" or "circle", you will be reasonably accurate at short to medium distances.

4) Black sights are intended for target shooting. For combat shooting you want better visibility and faster acquisition. Paint the front sight with three layers of white nail polish (let it dry between coats) and one final coat of bright orange. If you are happy with the results spread a drop of cyanoacrylate super glue with a toothpick so as to have a layer that both protects the paint underneath and makes it easier to clean.

5) If you are grouping away from your point of aim, simply adjust accordingly to the opposite windage and elevation. "Kentucky windage" allows you to quickly get on target without having to adjust the sights.

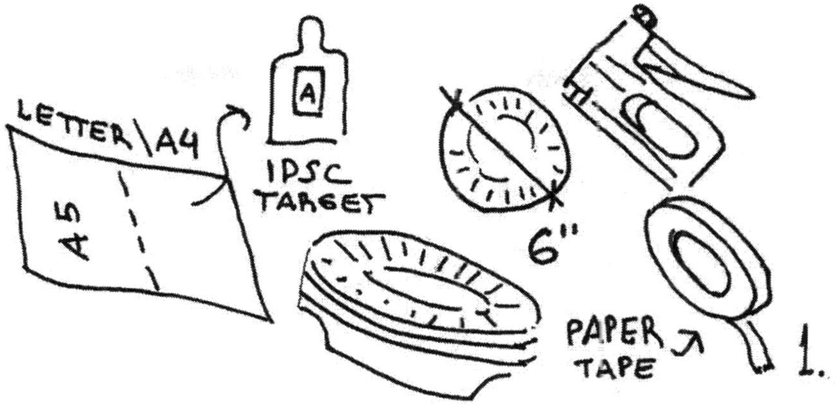
LETTER\A4
A5
IPSC TARGET
A
6"
PAPER TAPE
1.

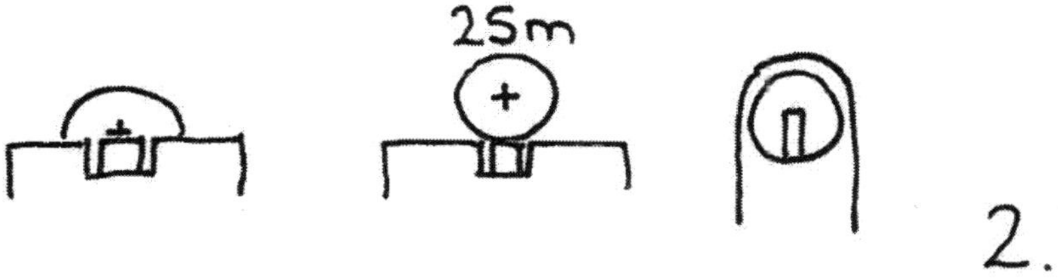
25m
2.

POOR MAN'S HOLOSIGHT
3.

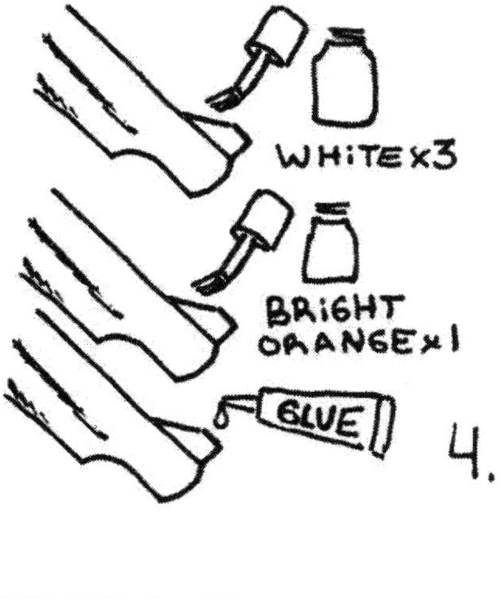
WHITEx3
BRIGHT ORANGEx1
GLUE
4.

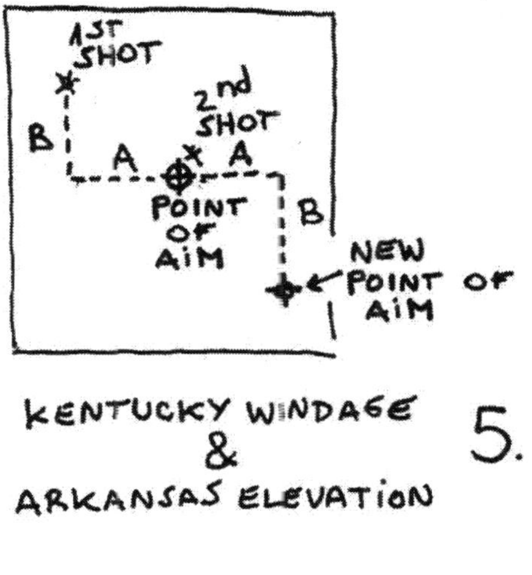
1ST SHOT
2nd SHOT
B
A
A
B
POINT OF AIM
NEW POINT OF AIM
KENTUCKY WINDAGE & ARKANSAS ELEVATION
5.

6) Dry fire is the process of going through the motion of shooting but without having ammunition loaded in the firearm. This is safe and does not damage most modern firearms (except for most rimfire firearms such as 22LR) but get snap caps to play it safe for extended dry fire sessions. Dry fire practice is essential to develop shooting skills. Dry fire allows repetition of movement, reloads, draw, stance, sight alignment, target acquisition, pulling the trigger while keeping the gun steady, clearing malfunctions, etc. Professional shooters will dry fire for hours every week, sometimes every day.

Safety is the number one priority. Make sure the gun is empty. Better yet, keep the ammunition in a separate room. Don't get distracted and don't have people nearby when dry firing. Expect the gun to fire when pulling the trigger, meaning find a place to practice where even if somehow a round does end up in the gun, you won't destroy anything you can't afford to lose. A large closet or bookcase backstop would work well.

7) Be honest with yourself. Your time spent on practical shooting won't translate well to the street if you compete with a big fancy race gun and carry the smallest pocket gun you can find for self-defense.

8) Train with the same type of clothes and gun you use for EDC. If you wish to develop skills for self-defense, then the gun you take to defensive shooting classes, practical shooting competition and for carry should be the same gun or as close to it as possible. Even the clothes, protective eyewear, belt and shoes, everything should remain as similar as possible.

9) Double action pistols and revolvers are ideal for dry fire practice but striker fired guns such as the Glock where the trigger is not double action need to be cocked manually by racking the slide for each shot. This can be disruptive for some dry fire drills where you want continuity and to keep working the trigger as you go from one target to the next in your dry fire practice session.

There are commercial gadgets available but a nice trick is to unload the gun, pull the slide back, slip a small plastic zip tie into the barrel and let the slide go forward. The zip tie will prevent the barrel from locking into place, keeping it out of battery. You can now move the trigger with your finger. It won't have the same trigger pull but it is still far more responsive and the finger movement is very similar to actually firing.

You can cut the tip of the zip tie and move it closer down the ejection port so that is doesn't get in the way of your sights. A small zip tie works best and you can put a couple drops of red paint to make it more visible so as to not forget it in your gun after you're done practicing.

6.

7.

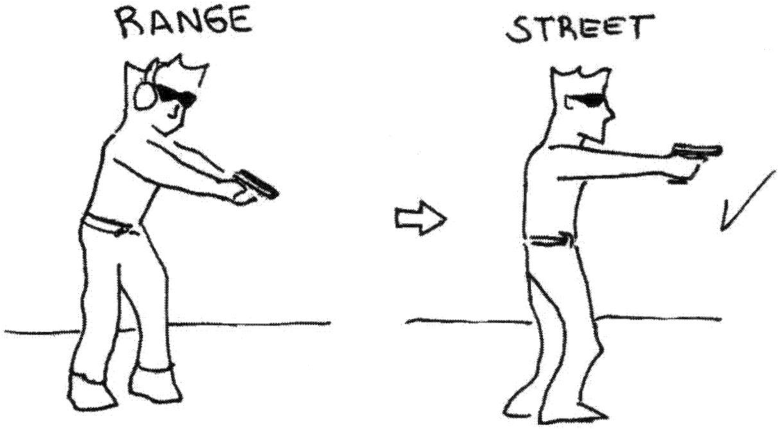

8.

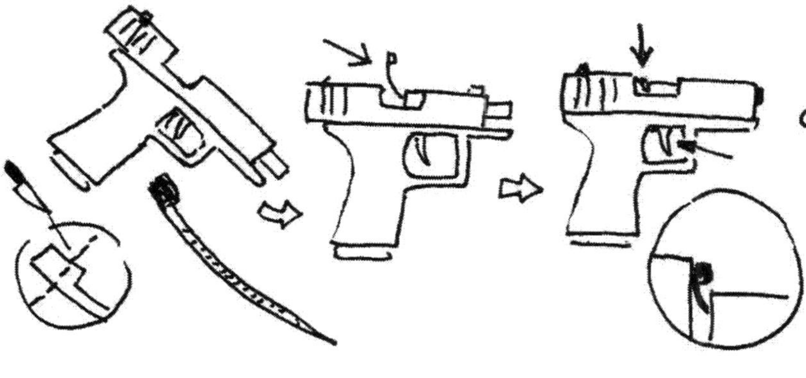

9.

NOTES:

Chapter 6
Bare Hand and Knife Fighting

"Everyone has a plan until they get punched in the face"
- "Iron" Mike Tyson

Bare Hand Fighting

Any kind of weapon is better than no weapon, even if it's just a solid metal pen, but you still need to know how to defend yourself and fight with your bare hands.

Few aspects of self-defense involve as much mysticism as martial arts. For decades the amount of fantasy and misinformation regarding Asian martial arts has been overwhelming.

Fortunately Vale Tudo came along and set the record straight. The Gracie family gained popularity in the United States and in 1993 the Ultimate Fighting Championship (UFC) was created. All of a sudden, people started asking themselves why their old Kung Fu master didn't go into the octagon, beat everyone and claim a UFC title. The answer was quite simple: Because that ancient secret martial art the guy was teaching in a mall for 10 bucks an hour didn't work. It never did.

So, what does work? A good way to answer that question is by observing how much sparring against non-cooperative opponents is involved and how realistic the rules of engagement are. How close to a real street fight is it? Turns out classic judo is a great way to go, especially for small children. Kids develop good upper body strength and balance and can learn techniques that can effectively put a bully on the ground. This applies to adults as well. ITF Taekwondo and some forms of Karate also have their merits. Ironically, it was the old art of "hitting and not getting hit" that ruled all martial arts all along: The "sweet science" of boxing.

No other martial art compares to the brutal efficiency of accelerating a person's head and rattling his brain inside his cranium so that he drops unconscious before hitting the floor. In the real world, a welterweight boxer with a solid amateur career would have dropped Daniel LaRusso, Mr. Miyagi and Johnny Lawrence one after the other. It's not just about delivering knock out punches. It's about knowing how to defend yourself, keep your distance and move. A boxer isn't just capable of delivering hard, accurate punches. He's also very hard to land on as well. In spite of what you may have seen in movies, when it comes to brawls involving multiple people boxing is without a doubt the martial art that allows you to both defend yourself from attacks and land punches on multiple adversaries fast. Unlike most feel-good self-defense schools, you don't feel good when you first walk into a boxing gym. As soon as you start sparring you get punched, a lot. And there's no way around that, you have to fight to learn. That's the point. Eventually you learn how to not get hit and you learn how to land punches yourself.

Later, when the new guy comes in, you see how easy it is to slap around those that don't know how to box. That was my experience and it's been somewhat similar for most people that ever practiced boxing.

But before you run looking for the nearest boxing gym, know this: No other martial art, no other sport asks so much of you. It's not about the time. It's not about the money. Boxing asks more of you than that. My coach was a guy that loved boxing. He worked in a factory, taught a bit of boxing three nights a week and then fought for money on weekends. He moved well, threw punches well, but he also giggled like a child when he laughed, had a slurred speech and needed a second or two to find the words he wanted to say at times. A young man that wasn't even thirty, with clear signs of brain damage. Ask yourself how much of a badass you want to be. Ask yourself if you are willing to pay such a high price.

Even if you do boxing you need to know at least some wrestling and grappling, at least enough to know how to defend yourself from them.

Wrestling is another traditional combat sport that didn't get enough recognition until UFC. It's effective in real fights, especially one on one, but even if it doesn't involve striking to the head like boxing does, injuries are also very common. Both judo and wresting are recognized Olympic sports and may get you college scholarships. Brazilian jiu-jitsu (BJJ) has proven to be very effective in combat, but like wrestling, the disadvantage is that on a street fight you never want to end up on the floor. On the floor is where you get stomped and kicked in the head. BJJ is the kind of martial art that is legitimate for self-defense and since there's no striking a person can keep on practicing it over time. With a responsible teacher, it's safe even for young kids.

For people of all ages, and especially for children, judo is a great martial arts foundation. BJJ is also very useful for self-defense since it teaches you how to take someone to the ground and defeat him there, but since you don't want to go to the floor in a street fight you are better off throwing someone to the ground like in judo but not going there yourself. Boxing, and to a great degree other striking combat sports like kickboxing, those are without a doubt very valuable for street fighting. I would try to practice them yet be careful with how much sparring you do. It may not seem like it, but every single punch to the head counts. You need to make up your mind about how much of your brain, how much of yourself, you are willing to sacrifice so as to gain that ability.

At the end of the day, you need to find which of these is available to you, get involved, and decide how far you want to take each one.

Having said this, here are a few points to keep in mind about fighting:

1) When in a fight, mind your distance and **keep your hands up**. This prevents most knock outs, not only in street fights but in sports as well. Hands up, feet apart about shoulder length, head tilted forward, one foot slightly forward (left foot for right handed, orthodox stance) while the one on the back is at a comfortable angle.

2) Don't forget about your guard just because you throw a punch. The other hand stays up covering you and you bring your punching arm's shoulder up to cover as much of your chin and face as possible.

3) Kicks require frequent training and even then stick to low kicks (under the waist). A kick to the head can deliver an instant KO but the risk of falling or getting the leg caught is too high to risk it in a street fight. Kicks should be quick and powerful. A sweep kick that drops a person may end the fight if the opponent hurts himself when he drops on the pavement or similar hard surface rather than a mat or rubberized floor.

4) At short range, elbows can be quite effective. A blow with the elbow is not just powerful, it is also likely to break bones or cut your opponent.

5) Going straight up against the chin of a taller attacker or coming down from above, smashing your forehead against his nose, head butts are often used successfully in street fights, especially against unexperienced attackers that rely on greater strength alone. Someone holding your arms using both his hands presents and ideal situation to use your head.

6) Knees generate a lot of power as well. Like kicks, hitting with your knees requires a greater degree of dexterity and regular practice but against someone trying to tackle you, lowering his head, it would present an ideal target. When using your knees, use your hands to keep your opponent from moving way. Putting your hands over his head (not interlocking finger but one over the other) gives you more control and momentum for using your knees as you lower your attacker's head.

Boxing, street fight or a gunfight, there are four elements (**ATAC**) in winning any fight: **Awareness**. Know what's happening around you. **Timing**. Know when it's your time to make a move. **Action**. Make that move with aggression and decisiveness. **Continuity**. Keep going, keep moving forward and keep the blows pouring until there's no doubt in your mind that your enemy has been defeated.

Even Jorge Masvidal landed two "super necessary" additional punches on Ben Askren after knocking him out cold in 3 seconds flat at UFC 239.

Punch, shoot and strike generously when the situation demands it.

1.
2.
3.
4.
5.
6.

7) Striking with the heel of the hand can be very effective and is less likely to cause injuries to your own hand. Blows can be thrown, just like normal punches. A blow to an attacker's face, smashing his nose with the heel of your hand, can break the bone and prove very effective.

8) It is very hard to land accurate blows in real fights. No one sits waiting to be hit. When smashing someone's face, dig your fingers into your attacker's eyes if the opportunity presents itself. Injuries to the eye can be painful, dissuading your attacker. Women with longer nails can use these to their advantage increasing the odds of hurting an attacker's eyes.

9) Palm strikes can be used to deliver powerful blows to the head, even knock a person down when done with enough force.

10) Slaps to the back of the head can be particularly debilitating. Known as a "Rabbit Punch" (trappers used it to kill rabbits) blows to the back of the head are the closest thing to a real-world "touch of death" punch. When a person gets knocked out with a punch to the face, it is usually the impact from hitting the floor the one that causes serious damage or even death. But with a Rabbit Punch, the blow itself can damage the cervical vertebrae and spinal cord. This is the reason why Rabbit Punches are banned in both boxing and mixed martial arts. Having said that, during boxing matches boxers can often be seen slapping or even punching the back of the adversary's head when clinching. Even a slight slap to the base of the skull can stun or slow down an opponent. Boxers will get warnings when doing this but rarely will they punch with full force given that if the opponent can't continue due to a Rabbit Punch they would be disqualified from the bout. In a street fight, consider this a blow that can kill or paralyze a person for life. Keep in mind the legal implications of doing such a thing.

11) When forming a fist, curl your fingers inwards and fold your thumb underneath, pressed against the fingers. Punch keeping your wrist locked and connect with your two large knuckles.

12) Slapping the ear can rupture the eardrum, but this is easier said than done. More likely and still useful, a solid palm to the ear can stun your attacker and affect his balance.

13) Keysi Fighting Method (KFM) has one technique that can be useful in brawls involving numerous attackers. It consists of keeping a traditional guard up but using it to strike with the elbows at the same time it is used for defense. Some of these KFM techniques have been used in movies such as "The Dark Knight" and "Jack Reacher". For chaotic brawls involving multiple attackers the technique has its merits.

7.

8.

9.

10.

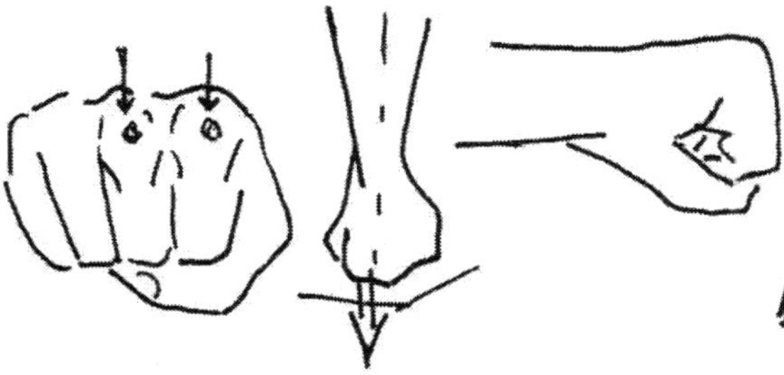

11.

12.

13.

Self-Defense with a Knife

There's a reason why cops shoot suspects with a knife if they don't keep their distance or refuse to immediately drop the weapon. The Tueller Drill shows that the average person can cover 21 feet in 1.5 seconds, stabbing an officer before he manages to draw and fire his sidearm. Knives are ubiquitous tools but they can also be formidable weapons. There are several martial arts that specialize on the use of edges weapons. Some people spend a lifetime mastering the use of knives but some basic knowledge and a couple tips can significantly improve your proficiency if you ever need to use one for self-defense.

1) Adopt a boxer/fighter stance. Different disciplines have different stances but a comfortable, athletic stance will do the job. This stance applies to boxing, but also to sticks, pens and other improvised weapons with slight variations depending on the weapon used. In the case of the knife, it makes more sense to lower your knife hand a bit.

2) Keeping the knife back improves your weapon retention. If facing a larger, skilled hand to hand fighter, keep your other hand (often called sacrifice hand) forward. If your attacker grabs your hand, that leaves an opening for stabbing quickly and repeatedly like a sewing machine.

3) Sometimes you want to keep the knife in front of you. Here you are using the weapon's range, keeping the action away from you and allowing for offensive strikes. It also increases the chance of a fast opponent grabbing your arm, wrapping himself around it and disarming you.

4) Most martial arts traditionally recognize eight angles of attack.

5) These aren't just theoretical and should be applied to specific body parts you plan on attacking. A knife fight is a bloody, violent and in many ways unpredictable event. Know where to slash, where to stab and mentally prepare yourself to adapt as circumstances change.

6) Blade up or blade down, keep a full hammer grip on the knife at all times. Different experts have different theories on what grip works best but sparring with rubber knives proves that there is a high probability of dropping the knife during the fight. Leaving an opening through which the handle can slip through during the heat of the fight is unacceptable. The best way to reduce the possibility of this happening is to wrap your fingers around the handle and lock your thumb on top of them as reinforcement. Your thumb is your strongest finger and will greatly improve your weapon retention if a firm grip is applied in such a manner.

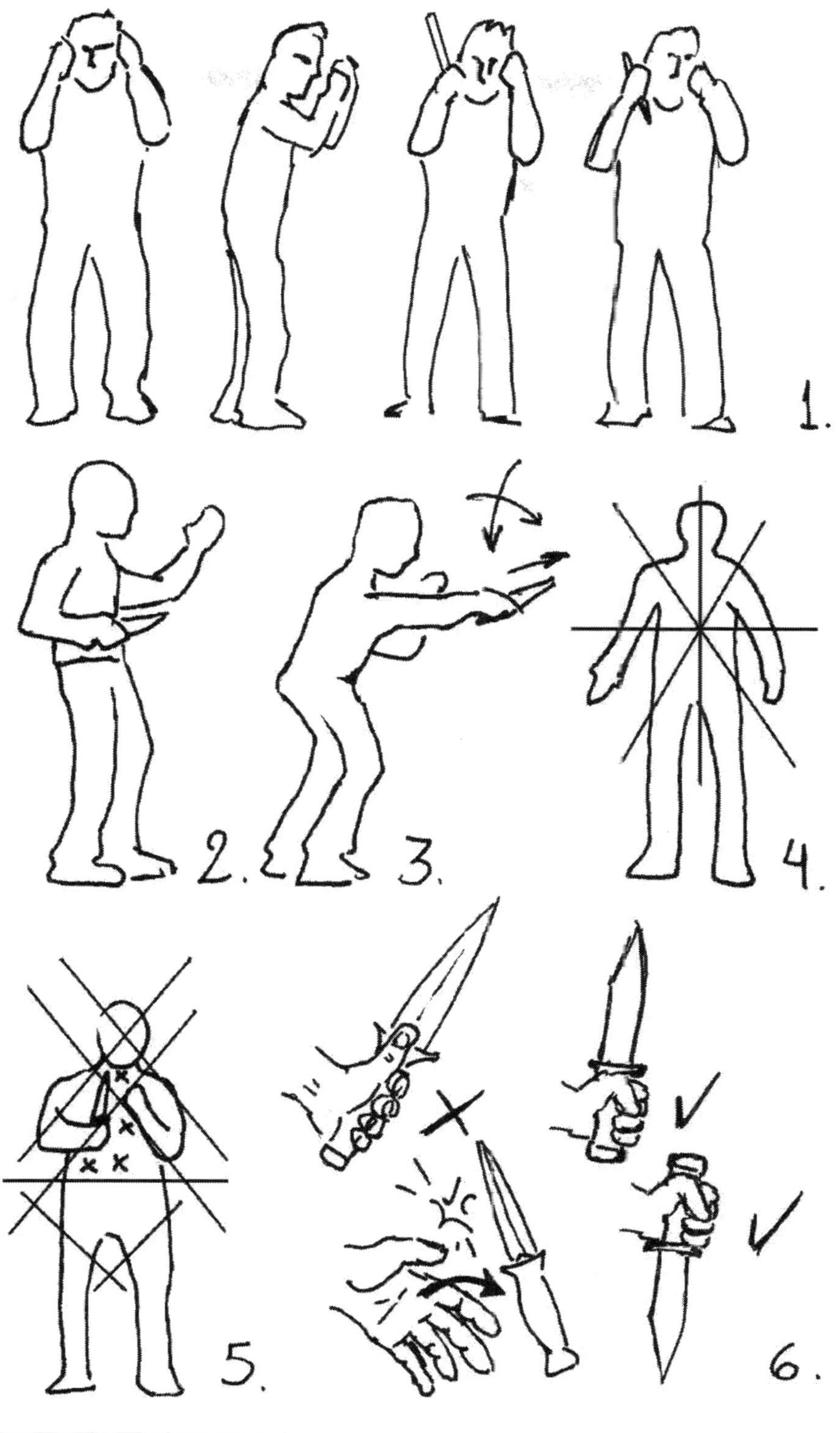
1.
2.
3.
4.
5.
6.

7) For a reliable defensive stance, adopt a reverse grip, tip down, edge forward. Keep the knife close to your body but in front of your other hand. With the edge facing forward, anyone that suddenly bum-rushes you will get cut. The blade can also be rotated to avoid this from happening if you believe innocent people may be bumping into you.

8) If someone suddenly attacks you, rotating the wrist vertically 90 degrees will bring the tip of the knife straight in line with anyone charging you, stabbing your attacker in the chest. From this position it's also easy to throw quick short stabs with the knife. It doesn't offer the most reach, but it does offer greater weapon retention from anyone trying to disarm you. This stance is ideal for when moving around a house and you believe someone may have broken in, trying to catch you by surprise. It applies well to large pointy chef knives found in most kitchens.

9) For larger blades you may want to adopt a different stance. Keeping the blade in front of you between any potential threads and yourself, the blade at a 45 degree angle offers you a couple options.

10) The blade can be brought up to block an attack, perpendicular to the floor, covering your upper body.

11) Or it can be brought down, parallel to the floor, ready to stab forward or slash. Unlike stick fighting, little momentum is needed for a heavy sharp blade to do a lot of damage so it is unnecessary to bright it back more to deliver powerful blows.

12) Whenever possible, when going against someone armed with a knife, get a coat, jacket or sweater to use in your other hand. Numerous knife and sword fighting manuals across hundreds of years and from different countries around the world take note of how important this is. The coat can be used to parry strikes away from you without getting cut. It can be used as a whip to strike an attacker's face. It can be whipped across your attackers hand to try to disarm him or move his weapon away from you as you attack. If it has some heavy contents in the pockets it can be thrown at your attacker's feet to tangle him. It can be thrown at his head to block his vision. These are all tricks used hundreds of years ago for "sword and cape" fighting. Gauchos in South America used their ponchos in a similar manner. These are people that fought for real, with frequency, using these techniques.

13) Keep your guard up with your other hand but make sure the palm of your hand is facing you and not your opponent. You want to keep your veins and tendons from getting cut.

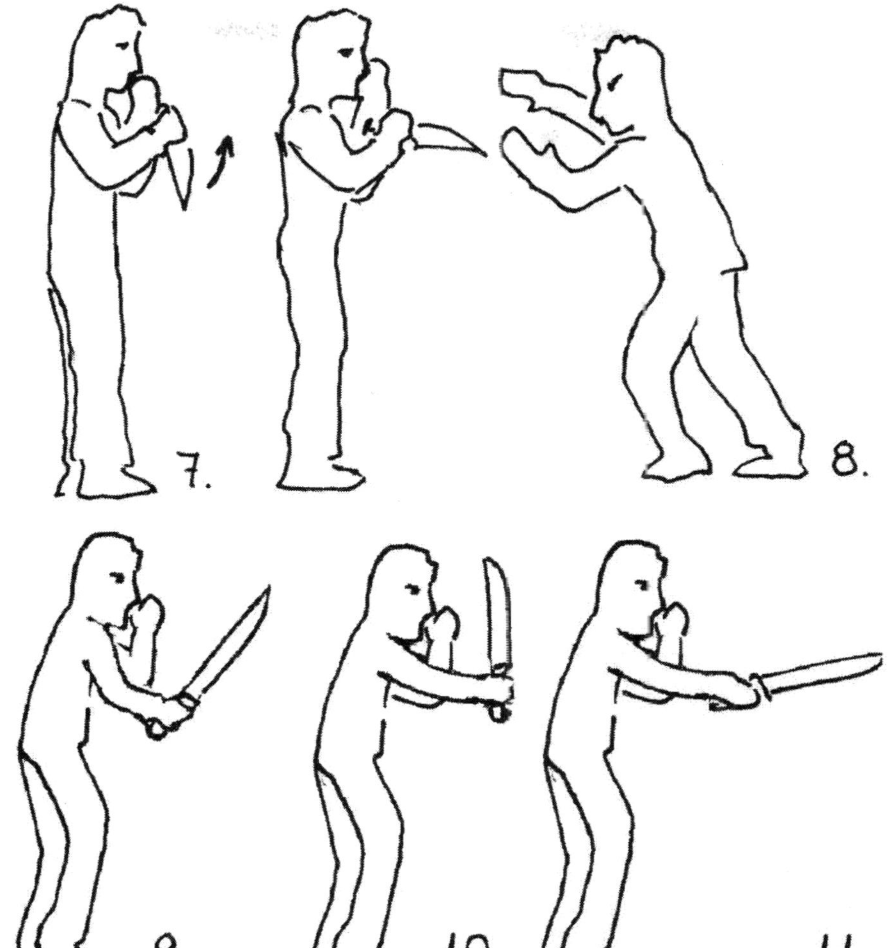
7.
8.
9.
10.
11.
12.
VEINS
TENDONS
13.

Where to Strike

Having a basic understanding of the human body allows you to more effectively disable an attacker. No one stands still in a fight waiting for you to strike. The more you know about human anatomy, the easier it will be to have a strategy regarding where you want to attack and take advantage of targets of opportunity that present themselves as the fight progresses.

1) The heart is a highly prized target. Damage to that vital organ is among the most effective attacks when it comes to incapacitation, second only to the central nervous system. The liver is another vital organ that can be targeted. In boxing, a "liver shot" can KO an elite fighter. A stab wound would be even more effective.

2) Kidneys are another prime target. They are located on the lower back, just above the hips. Punches to the kidneys are illegal in boxing. They are full of nerve receptors and a punch can be as effective as a blow to the liver. A stab to the kidneys would be excruciatingly painful.

3) So as to stab the heart, strike between the 4th and 5th rib, left of the sternum at about the height of the nipple. Angle the stab inwards given that most of the heart is behind the sternum. Keep the blade horizontal so as to slip through the ribs. Since people rarely walk around naked and nipples can be in different places given the different body types, a good tip is to use the armpit as a reference point. Left of the sternum, armpit high should be accurate enough in a fight.

4) Slashes to the brachial and femoral artery will cause a person to bleed out fast. Slashing across the lower abdomen can disembowel a person. It will not kill an attacker immediately, it may take hours, but few things are as shocking as literally spilling your guts all over the floor.

5) A stab with a long blade so as to reach the aorta would be even more effective, with a person bleeding out in seconds.

6) The carotid artery in another valuable target given how much blood flows through it, supplying the brain. Strike low on the side of the neck and go deep so as to cut through all the neck muscles and fat.

7) An attacker being on the floor does not mean he's no longer a threat. A quick way to disable someone on the floor is by stomping him. Stomp the articulations for pain and compliancy. Stomp the middle of the bone to break arms and legs. A stomp to an attacker's neck can cause spinal cord damage and immediate incapacitation. Both are brutal, but kicking the head like a ball is often faster and more effective than stomping.

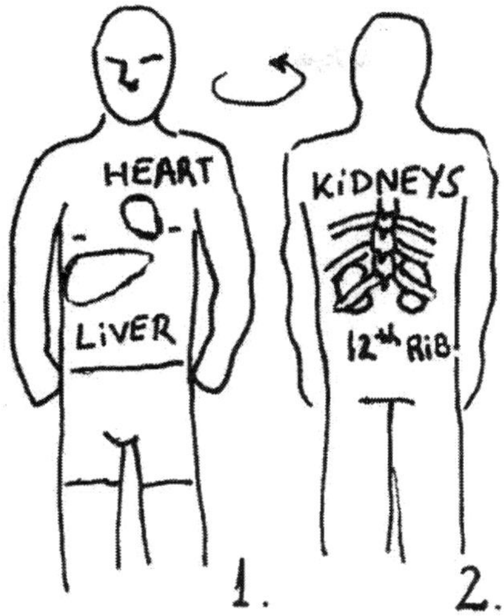
HEART
LIVER
KIDNEYS
12th RIB

1. 2.

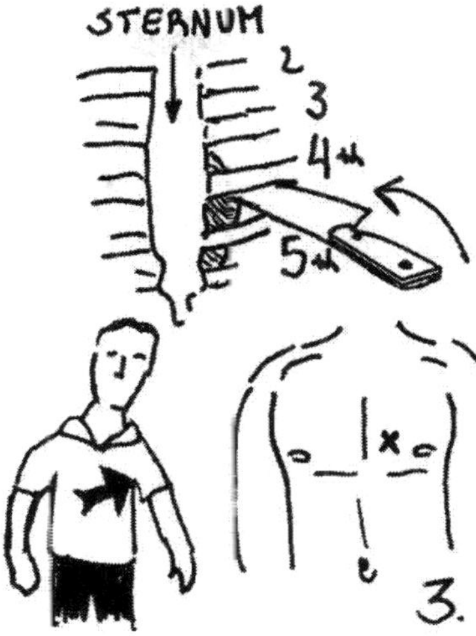
STERNUM
2
3
4th
5th

3.

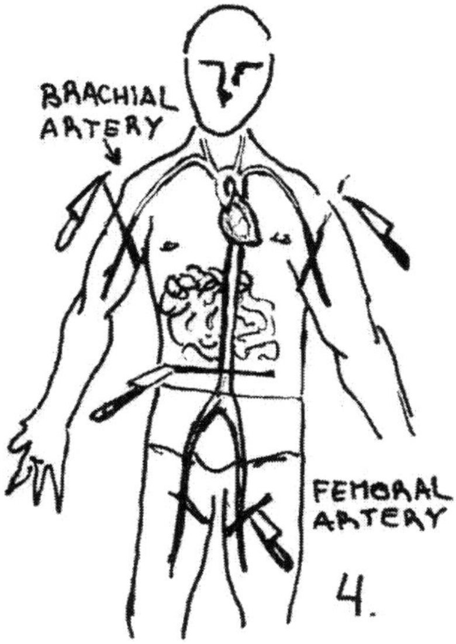
BRACHIAL ARTERY
FEMORAL ARTERY

4.

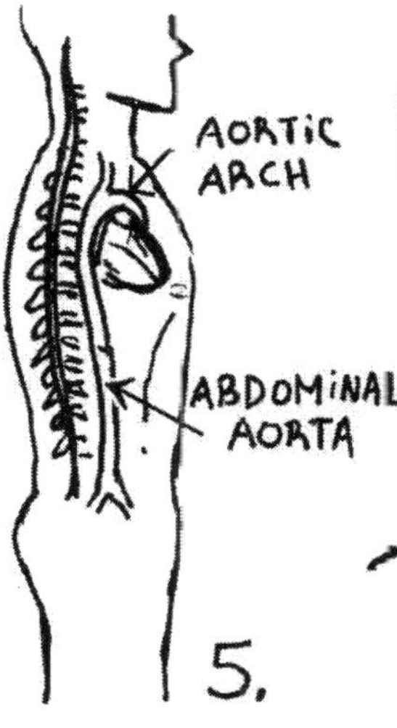
AORTIC ARCH
ABDOMINAL AORTA

5.

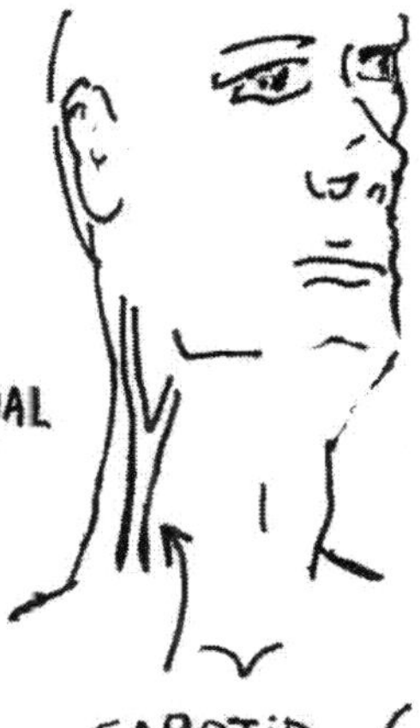
CAROTID ARTERY

6.

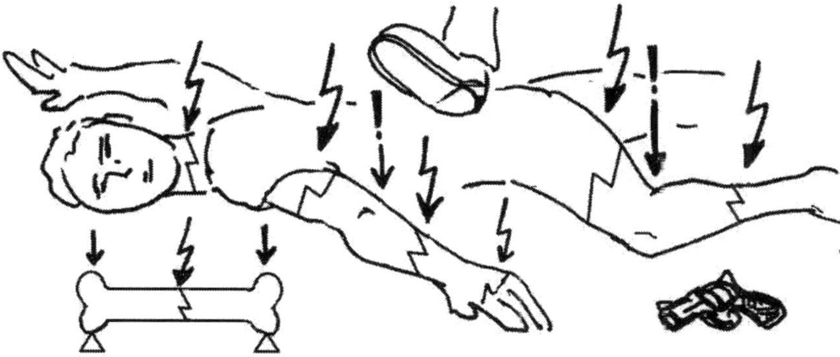

7.

How to Defend Against a Knife Attack

Confrontations are to be avoided whenever possible but this is particularly true when lethal weapons such as knives are involved. Knife attacks are bloody, messy affairs but they can also be unassumingly dangerous too. A single stab wound in the wrong place can be fatal, leaving behind just a few drops of blood and a hole poked in the chest.

1) As soon someone comes at you with a knife move to create as much distance as possible while trying to defuse the situation. Put any object you can between you and the attacker. Chairs, tables, trees, cars or moving to different rooms and closing doors behind you.

2) When you can't get away and turning and running will just get you stabbed in the back you need to fight. A person wielding a knife can be disarmed, but it will depend on a number of factors such as your training, speed, strength and timing as well as your attacker's. Use any object you can as a weapon or shield. A large jacket is ideal. A sweater is ok and even taking off your t-shirt is better than nothing. This can be used in a number of ways. A sudden slap with it can catch the blade and disarm your attacker. Bring the jacket down diagonally from the opposite side of the hand in which the knife is held, pushing the handle through the fingers rather than through the palm. This means going down diagonally from left to right when your attacker is right handed.

3) Even if this fails the first time, give it a strong tug to try to disarm him. Entangling the blade alone means you are now able to redirect the knife away from your body, close in and attack or disarm your opponent.

4) Old navaja fighting manuals describe using hats as a shield to catch and parry attacks. You can throw a cap (or t-shirt) before closing in as a distraction and to block your attacker's vision. Even if it doesn't, as harmless as it may seem, your opponent's eyes will still acknowledge the object and unconsciously calculate its trajectory.

5) Grab the attacker's wrist and twist it away from you. Depending on the knife you may be able to grab parts of the handle or hilt for leverage.

6) For attacks to the abdomen grab the wrist, lock your arms to keep the blade away from your body.

7) Wrap your arm around the attacker's locking it under your armpit.

8) Twist the arm and push down on the elbow. From this position you can use your knee or simply drop with your weight on the arm to cause additional damage and neutralize your attacker's arm.

1.
2.
3.
4.
5.
6.
7.
8.

Handgun Disarm Technique

Trying to disarm a gunman is extremely dangerous. Only attempt it as a last resort. Action is indeed faster than reaction and when moving fast there is a good chance of catching the gunman by surprise, redirecting the firearm away from you so as to avoid getting shot. Being held at gunpoint is stressful and there's no second chances. Once you make your move, keep moving towards the gunman and don't let him use the gun. Guro Marc "Crafty Dog" Denny from Dog Brothers Martial Arts calls this "stinking" your opponent, meaning keep moving, stay on top of him.

1) Stay calm and step as close to the gunman as possible.
2) Raise your hands and adopt a compliant tone of voice and body language as you get closer to the attacker. Raising your hands is perceived as a surrender and submissive gesture. It also puts your hands closer to the gun you will try to take away from your attacker.
3) Quickly grab the wrist with your closest hand while moving the gun away from your body and moving your torso out of the line of fire.
4) Grab the muzzle of the gun with your other hand from underneath and twist the gun up and towards the gunman.
5) Aim for the wrist when grabbing the gunman's arm.
6) Twisting the gun up forces the grip of the gunman to open up.
7) Slip your hand from the wrist towards the back of the gun.
8) Pull the back of the gun towards you and the muzzle towards the attacker, ripping the gun away from his grip. Once you have control of the weapon, if it's an auto pistol "tap, rack, bang". (see page 118)

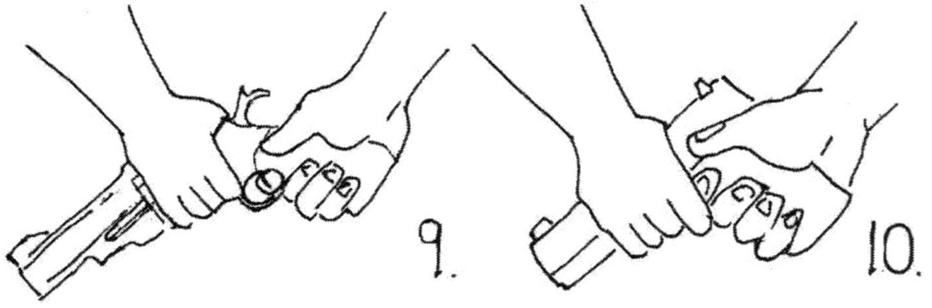

9) A firm grip over a revolver keeps the cylinder from turning and firing. A thumb over the hammer keeps it from dropping if already cocked.
10) A firm grip over the slide and frame of a pistol will cause the gun to jam after firing once since it can't eject the spent case. This does not hurt your hand in any way. The slide cannot move when held firmly.

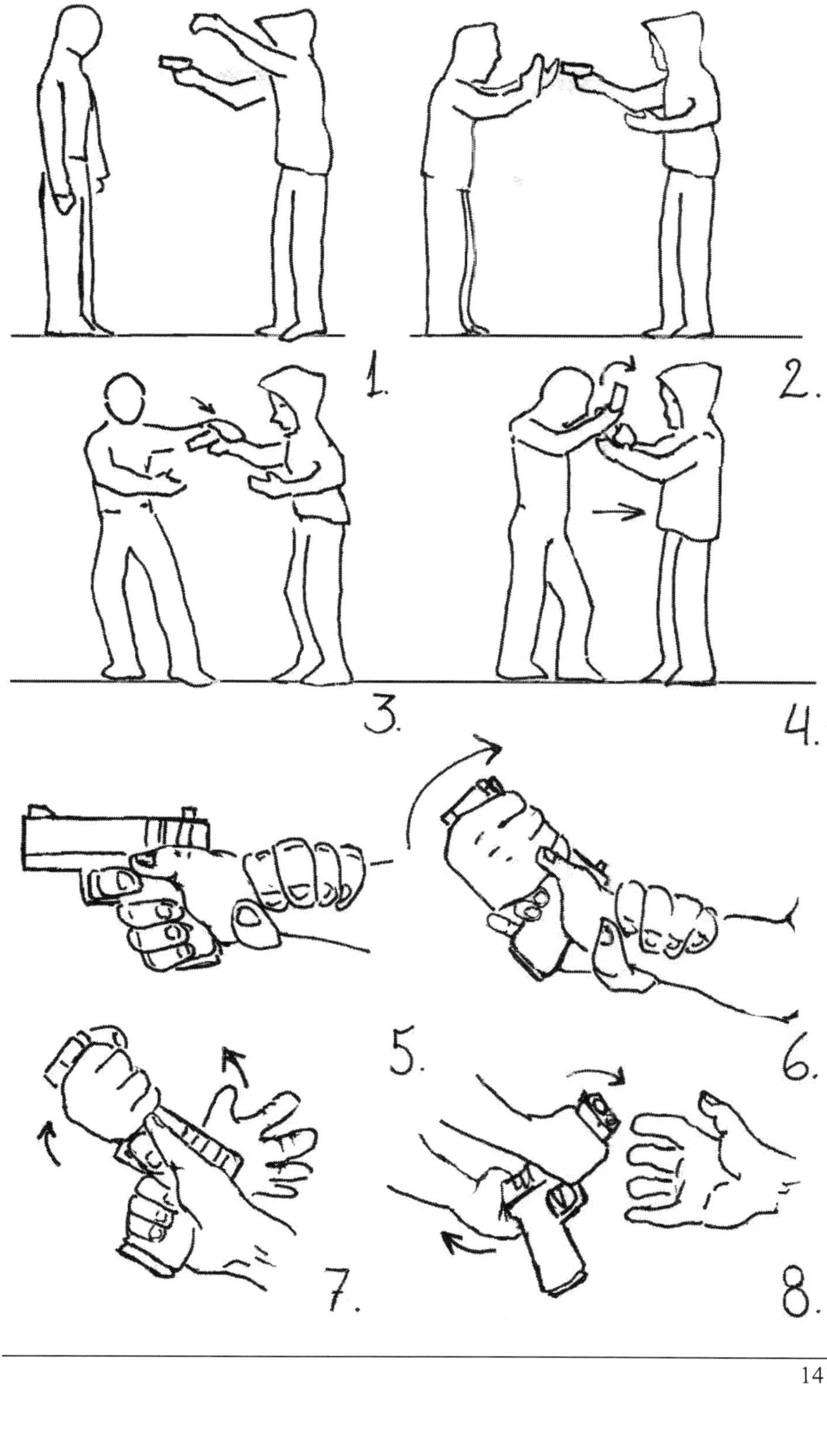
1.
2.
3.
4.
5.
6.
7.
8.

NOTES:

Chapter 7

Improvised Weapons and Armor

"Among the many misdeeds of British rule in India, history will look upon the Act which deprived a whole nation of arms as the blackest."
- Mahatma Gandhi

Improvised Body Armor

During desperate times desperate measures may be taken. If an active shooter or terrorist attack occurs in a school, shopping mall or workplace then stacking any odds in your favor can be the difference between life and death.

One of those desperate measures is improvising body armor, something you should only do as a last resort.

1) If time allows, improvising some ballistic protection is better than nothing. A small backpack covering your front can be used as an improvised plate carrier.

2) Although dangerous and far from ideal, a 500 page ream of printer paper (found in most offices) is likely to stop most common handgun rounds. The more paper you have the more protection it provides, but too much may become bulky and slow you down while trying to escape. Two 500 page reams of paper or two large books of similar size have a good chance of stopping handgun rounds such as 9mm, 40 S&W or 45 ACP. More paper doesn't necessarily make sense since even 10 reams won't stop most rifle rounds and they wouldn't fit in a backpack anyway.

Some commercial bullet proof backpacks are available. They have a Kevlar insert that will stop most handguns rounds. A ceramic SAPI rifle plate can be placed in the laptop holder of most backpacks and bags. A rifle plate is a bit heavy but will also protect you from high power rifle rounds and is far better insurance than running around looking for reams of paper during a mass shooting.

3) The backpack can be worn as you normally would so as to cover your back while escaping the shooter. Place it in front of you if you need to move towards the shooter for whatever reason (not recommended).

4) Depending on the situation, the backpack can be used as a shield, putting your arms across the straps. This will at least provide some protection from threats in front of you.

5) When using the backpack as a shield cover as much of your head and upper torso as you can while trying to escape. Either using it while escaping or for rushing the attacker, the best course of action depends on the situation you are presented with. If caught without any possible escape, then fighting back is your only choice. You could use your improvised shield in one hand and an improvised weapon in the other. Again, this is a desperate, last resort action. Escaping the areas is always the smartest thing to do whenever possible.

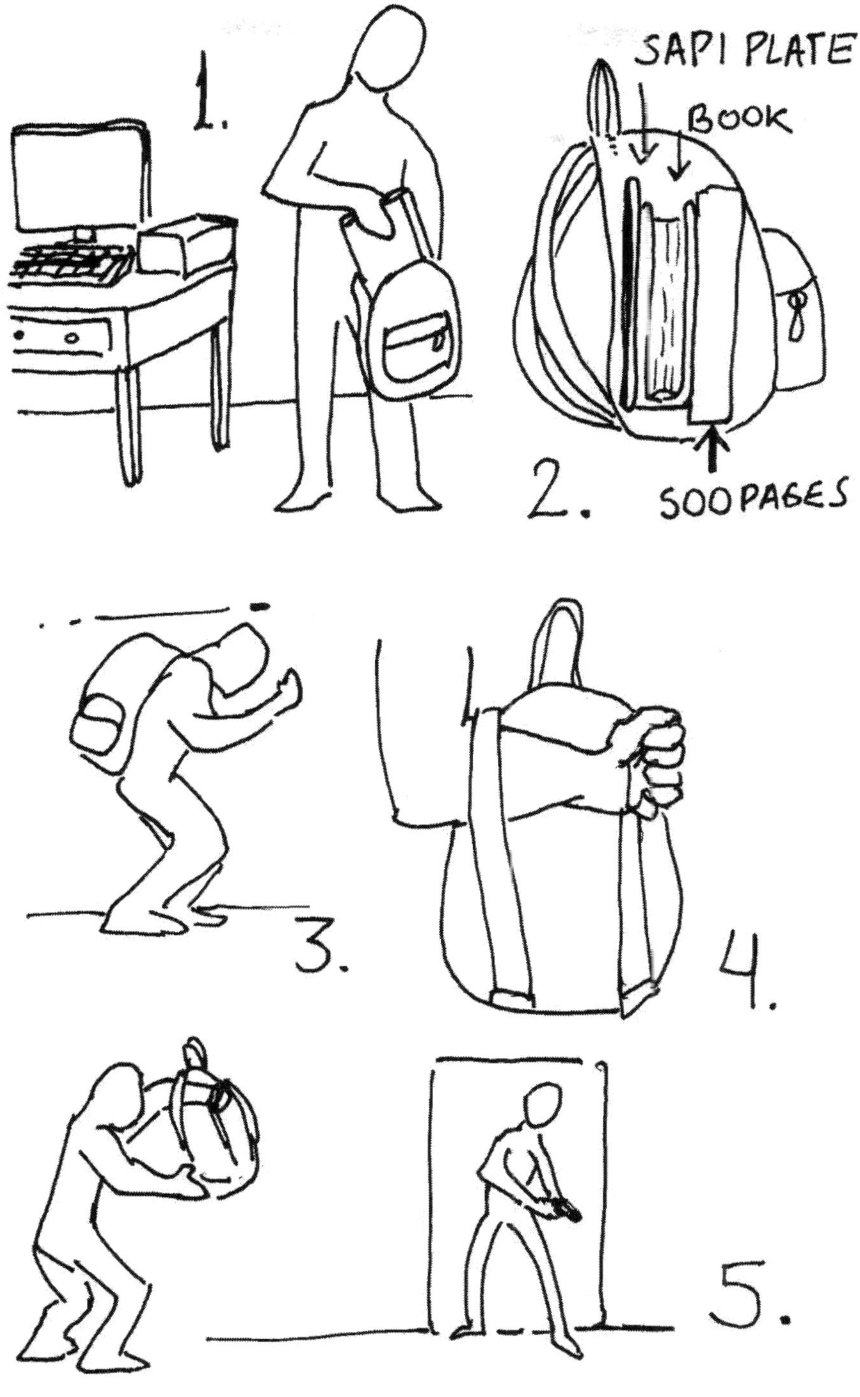
1.
SAPI PLATE
BOOK
500 PAGES
2.
3.
4.
5.

Improvised Weapons

It is often the case that people don't carry weapons for self-defense. Sometimes it is lack of commitment or due to local legal restrictions. In other cases it is due to policy at the workplace, when traveling or regulations in federal buildings.

In any case, it is important to identify potential improvised weapons that you may come across or carry yourself. The difference between improvised and hidden weapons can be hard to distinguish but it is an important one. A "tactical" pen is a weapon intended to pass along as a pen. This may get you in trouble with security at the airport or at other security checkpoints. A beefy, solid metal pen is simply that and no one can argue it is anything else.

1) Bottles are common around places such as bars, parties, places where there may be trouble and an improvised weapon is more likely to be needed. A large glass bottle can be used as an impact weapon on its own but a broken bottle can cause even more damage and be more dissuasive. Just smashing a bottle won't work. You will be left with the broken bottle neck in your hand and little else. Hit the bottom of the bottle at a 90° angle, preferably against granite, metal or some other hard surface.

2) For home defense a simple sharp stick can be tremendously effective. Spears have been used since man walked the earth for a good reason. The reach puts you at a much safer distance than using a knife. Considerable force can be applied in a two-handed grip thrust and impaling someone with a stick is pretty dissuasive. Products such as oven cleaners (not all) or spray bottles with sulfuric acid or water with caustic soda (Sodium hydroxide) can cause serious chemical burns. Warning! Chemical attacks leave horrible wounds and are a serious crime in most countries, even when used for legitimate self-defense.

3) Umbrellas, pens, flashlights, even keys can be used if there's nothing better. When using keys, hold the largest pointy one between your thumb and index while firmly holding the rest of the keychain in your hand.

4) A watch, preferably a metal watch can be used as an improvised weapon. It can be used as brass knuckles but the lack of support means it is likely to injure your hand. A better method is to grip the watch and have the sharp edges of the metal buckle on top of the hand. These sharp metal edges can be used to lacerate your attacker's face. The watch itself supports your grip and can work as a loaded fist making your hand heavier and giving you some extra punching power.

HIT AT A STRAIGHT ANGLE
Just the bottom

1.

OVEN CLEAN
ACID

2.

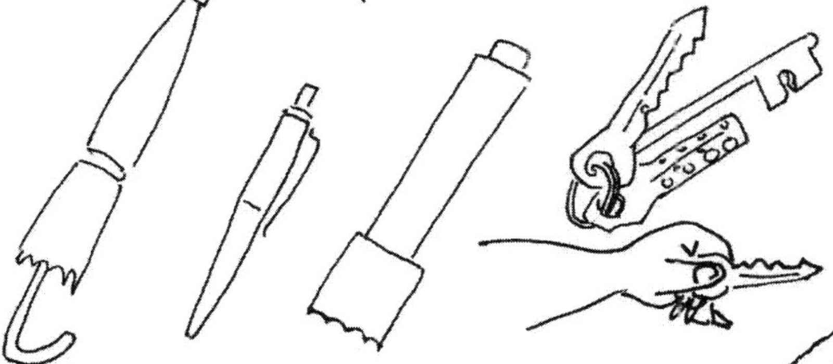

3.

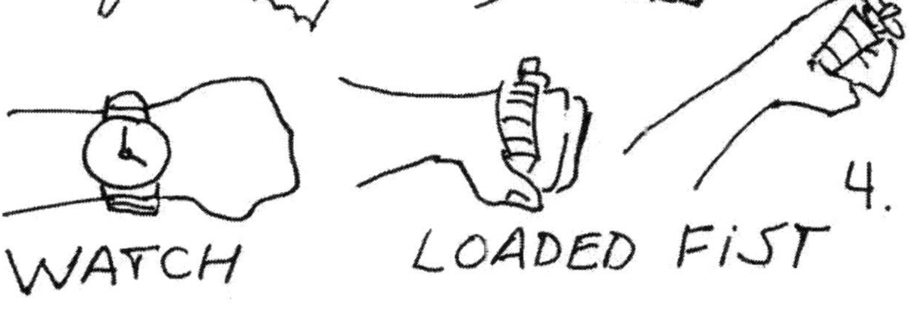
WATCH
LOADED FIST

4.

Belt as a Weapon

Belts are ordinary apparels most people wear daily. But a belt can be used as an effective improvised weapon. Choose the right one for you and practice with it so as to understand better its capabilities.

1) You want a solid, sturdy belt with a heavy buckle. Belts that are more flexible are better for swinging around. Rigger's Belt like the ones used as gun belts have a solid steel buckle and the stiff material makes them better improvised saps. Choose a belt that can be easily removed.

2) When quickly removed, the belt can be used as a whip in a surprise attack. Although unlikely to be all that effective, it can be used to keep someone away and can be quite painful when used correctly.

3) When space and opportunity allows, keep the belt moving, either in circles or figures of eight like it's done in different martial arts. When your attacker gets within range strike, hit him with the buckle.

4) Just like a flail, the advantage of using a belt is that when used accurately it is very hard to block. When an arm or hand is held to block a swing, the nature of the weapon makes it wrap around the arm and continue its path, striking whatever is in its way. This was how flails were intended to be used against someone wielding a shield.

5) Held with both hands and applying tension, the belt can be used to block attacks, fists or weapons. Some martial artists practice wrapping the belt around the hand or weapon during the block or around the neck to choke the opponent. This is easier said than done, especially on the streets with someone trying to stab you.

6)What can be done is, keeping the belt in this position, luring your opponent into testing your belt defense, only to let go with one hand and send the buckle flying towards his head when he least expects it.

7) Wrap the tail of the belt around your hand and wrist. This gives you greater retention and protects some of the most vulnerable parts of the hand from knife attacks. Wrapped a couple times around your hand and wrist, a Riggers Belt becomes a sturdy sap or blackjack.

8) This allows you to use the weapon at much closer range, even when fighting with someone on top of you. The striking is similar to stick fighting, hitting with the narrow part of the buckle. This is ideal for when the attacker closes in, neutralizing the techniques mentioned earlier in which the belt needs more range to be put to use.

1.
2.
3.
4.
5.
6.
7.
8.

Flashlight as a Weapon

Some flashlights can be effectively used as weapons.

Many tactical models include strobe modes intended to disorient attackers with the flashing bright light. Although its effectiveness may be exaggerated at times, high intensity light can disorient a person, especially at night. At the very least it makes it harder for your attacker to see you clearly as his eyes suddenly need to adapt to a brighter light.

Larger flashlights can be used as batons. Many tactical flashlight models come with a sharp crown or strike bezel so as to improve its utility as a striking weapon. The more aggressive the strike bezel is the more damage it tends to do although discrete models can be quite effective too.

1) Hold the flashlight in a reverse grip, hands up similar to the boxer's stance with the reflector facing forward. If an attacker grabs your wrist, bring it down applying pressure with the strike bezel to his wrist.

2) When attacked, simply intercept the blows with the strike bezel, catching the incoming blows in the same manner you would use your gloves to stop punches in boxing. The difference here is that the sharp metal is very likely to lacerate your attacker's hand or break the small finger bones.

3) Still using boxing techniques throw a jab like you normally would but striking with the strike bezel.

4) Throw an overhand punch, or hammer down over your attacker's head with the flashlight. Remember that the steel or hard aluminium in the strike bezel can cause serious damage, especially against the skull. Use these techniques when in fear for your life, in the same way you would use any other lethal weapon.

5) Normal jabs can be thrown as well but with the intention of contacting with the strike bezel rather than with your knuckles.

6) The idea here is to skip past the target and lacerate with the sharp edges of the strike bezel.

7) Larger flashlights can be used with the body extending over the shoulder when in use, keeping them ready to strike. This can be done while holding a firearm in the other hand. Kept in this position, it is rather similar to a stick fighting stance. The flashlight can be used to strike using its metal body. Simply bring it down like you would with a stick in one of the angles of attack.

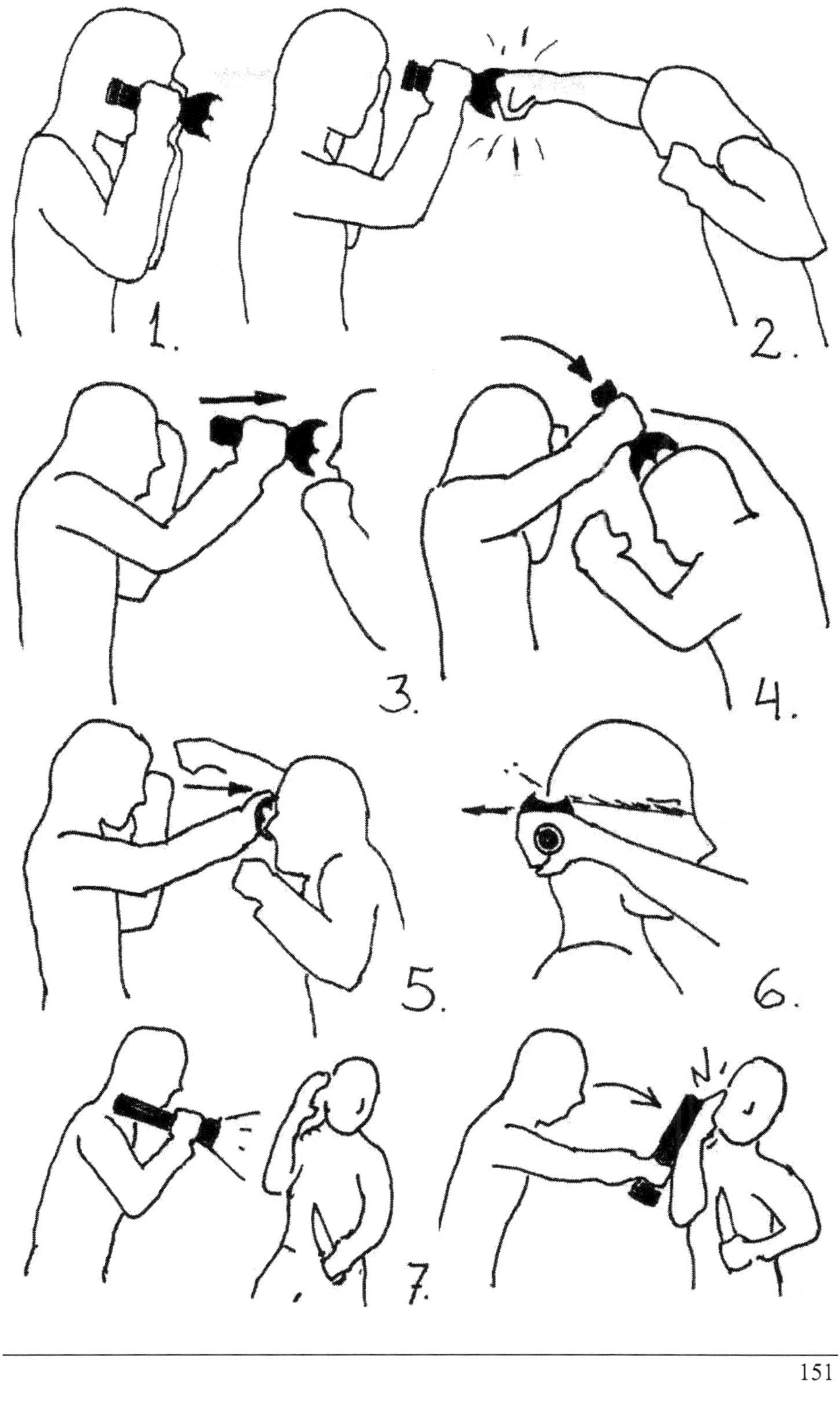
1.
2.
3.
4.
5.
6.
7.

Umbrella as a Weapon

Umbrellas have the advantage of being ubiquitous objects that are considered harmless and no one gives them much consideration. At the same time, this is a long staff with a metal tip that you are already holding in your hand as you walk down the street. It is true that, in certain parts of the world where it doesn't rain much, carrying one around seems a bit odd but still, most people won't give it much thought beyond that.

Also, keep in mind that not all umbrellas are made equal. Some cheap ones will break right away when you strike someone with them. Some of them are far sturdier, especially made for self-defense. Those are the ones you want if you plan on carrying an umbrella for defensive use.

1) Carrying an umbrella in a certain way allows you to instantly use it to defend yourself. Rather than using it like a walking stick holding it by the handle, hold it by the middle. This balances well as you walk around and it is better suited for quickly using it to block or strike.

2) Simply bringing the umbrella up shields you from a number of incoming attacks. It may not seem like it, but held this way the umbrella covers a significant area. It allows you to block punches, kicks or even attacks with blunt or edged weapons much better.

3) Carrying an umbrella this way also allows you to quickly retaliate any attack by simply bringing the tip forward. Holding it by the middle not only balances better, but it makes the length shorter, better for those close range surprise attacks. This also works well when defending yourself in tighter quarters such as corridors, elevators or crowded places.

4) If your awareness allowed you to detect the threat in time, you can use the greater reach of the umbrella to your advantage. In this case the umbrella would be used like a stick and the striking techniques would be similar to the ones used in stick fighting. You want a sturdy umbrella for this type of technique because a more fragile one will break right away.

5) You can use the umbrella like a spear, thrusting with the tip as you would with a staff. A lot of energy can be delivered by striking this way with a two-handed grip. This is also more forgiving structurally speaking, with a normal umbrella being less likely to break given that the force is applied along the length of the shaft. Aim for the face and throat.

In general, thrust attacks will be the best choice. They are faster, require less skill and strength, deliver more energy in a smaller area and are less likely to break or compromise the integrity of the umbrella.

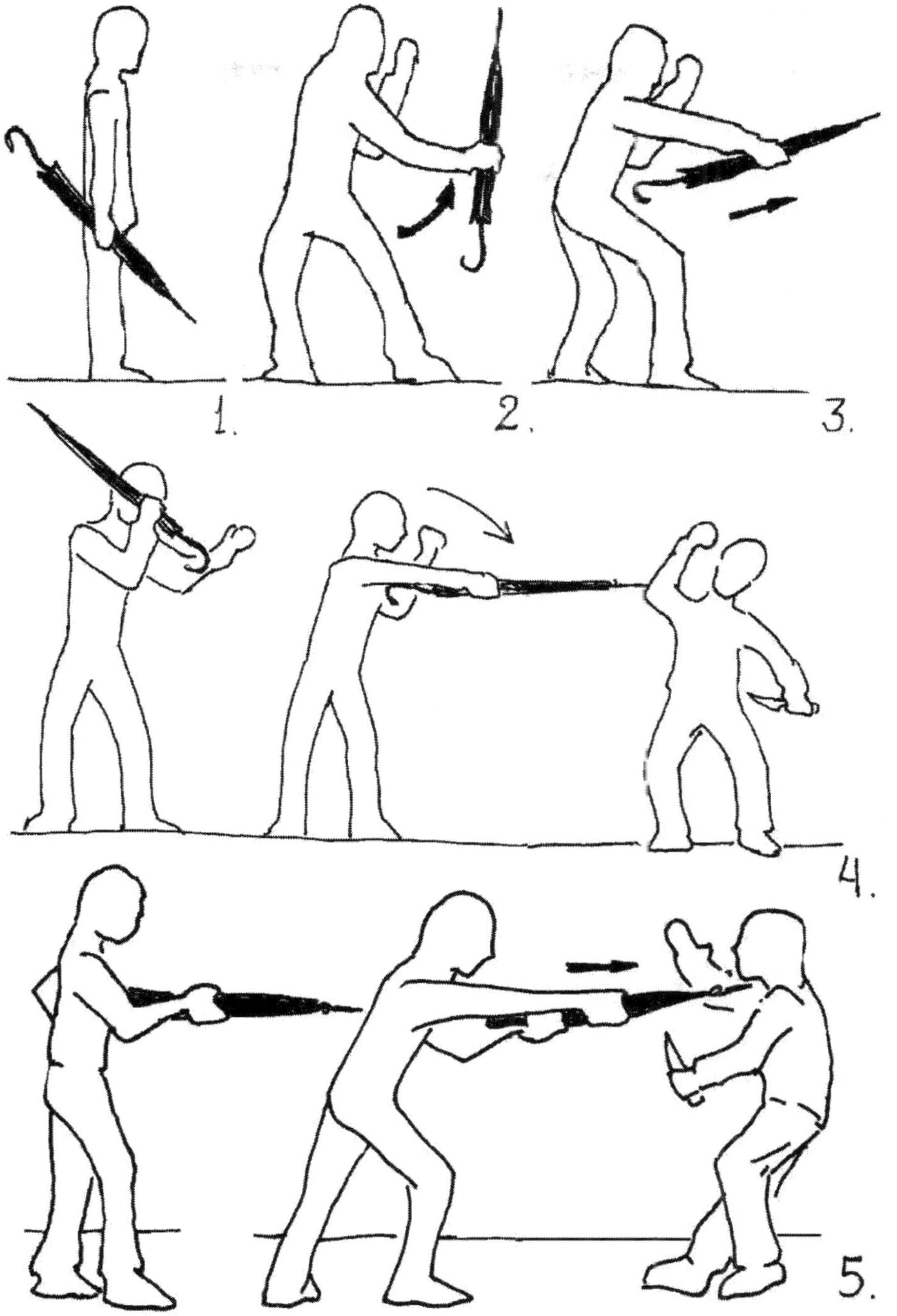
1.
2.
3.
4.
5.

Chair as a Weapon

In a perfect world you would be adequately armed for every threat you could potentially encounter. Although having a CCW (concealed carry weapon) whenever possible is highly recommended, sometimes you need to improvise and make do with ordinary objects you happen to have within reach.

Chairs are all over the place, particularly in places where you are likely to need them. Bars and dinners are places in which fights often break out. Mass shootings or terror attacks often take place in schools or universities. That means classrooms full of chairs. Keep these tips in mind if you ever end up using a chair to defend yourself.

1) Pick up the chair, holding it by the seat. This is the fastest, most effective way to wield most chairs.

2) Grabbing a chair by the seat with both hands also allows you to use the backrest, either to shield yourself or to strike with it with a push-pull motion on the seat which can catch an adversary by surprise.

3) Use the chair to keep an attacker away. Especially against edged weapons, a chair can provide much needed range to shield you from stabs and keep the attacker at bay. Use forward motions to strike with the legs of the chair.

4) Depending on the situation, you can just grab the back rest and swing the chair. No reason why you shouldn't throw chairs at an attacker if there's plenty around to pick. With a bit of luck, the chair hurts your attacker to some extent.

If it doesn't, at the very least it works as a distraction and gives your attacker some pause, something to think about. Be smart about it too. Just throwing a chair at someone during a mass shooting may only get you shot next. What to do depends on the specifics of the situation. It will be up to you to make that call when the time comes.

5) Another alternative is grabbing the seat with one hand and the backrest with the other. This gives you a bit more range if you need it but it is also a bit slower to wield.

6) Use it in the same way, arms pumping in quick forward motions to thrust with the legs. This focuses more energy in a smaller area. It is also quick and keeps the chair between you and the attacker providing some protection. Some light chairs can be held grabbing only the backrest. This gives you more range but is also slower and the arms get tired faster.

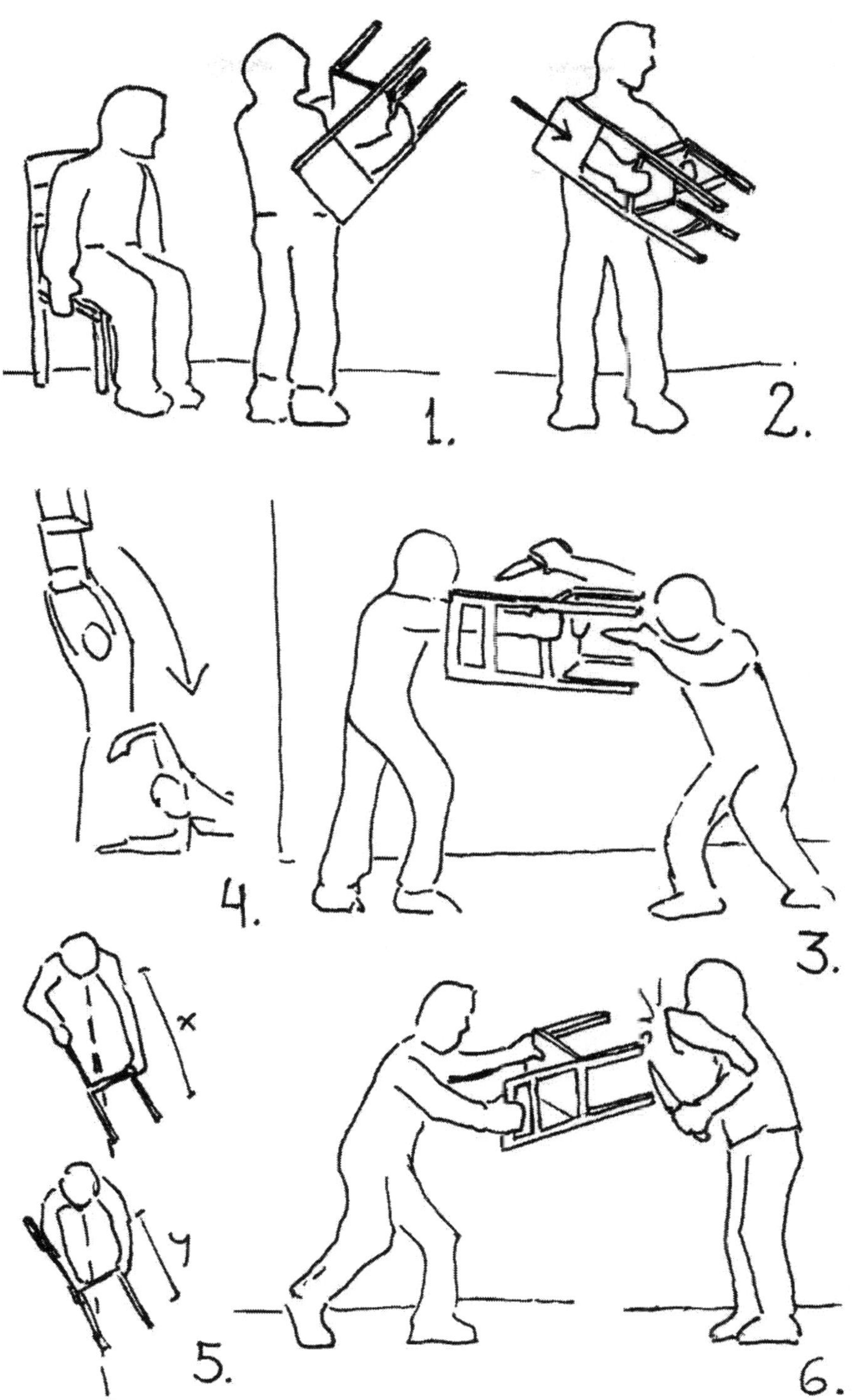
1.
2.
4.
3.
x
y
5.
6.

Making a Leather coin Pouch

A leather coin pouch is a handy accessory. You can of course keep change there, a few coins, some bills, use it as a wallet. But a leather pouch with a handful of coins is also an effective improvised weapon. One of the biggest advantages is that a leather coin pouch is legal in every country and in most places, including airplanes. Still, it works like any other blackjack or sap. Saps are leather impact weapons full of lead shot. These were favoured for decades by police officers because of how effective they were while being compact and easy to carry in the pocket.

1) Start with a square of supple leather about 20cm x 20cm (8"x8"). Cut two straps of leather, 4mm wide (0.15")

2) Fold the rectangle in half. This may still be a bit too long for a practical pocket pouch although it would make a better sap. Cut whatever length works best for you but leave enough so as to grip it firmly and have a handful of coins at the bottom of the pouch for weight.

Keep the nice finished side on the inside, it will be folded inside out when you're done.

3) Stitch a semi-circle at the bottom and close the open side to form the pouch. Cut the excess but leave a bit for the stiches to hold firm on impact. Use good strong nylon thread. Cut four vertical lines to thread the strap for closing the pouch.

4) Turn it inside out and thread the strap. Put a knot on the end and the job is done.

5) Keep a handful of coins in the pouch but don't overfill it. Try swinging it a few times and see how it feels. Adjust the amount of coins to suit your grip and strength.

6) Give your new leather pouch a go. Try hitting various objects to get a feel of how sturdy it is and the kind of damage it is capable of.

Saps are still fairly popular weapons among old school police officers and some still carry them in police departments that allow them. They are simple, easy to carry and very effective. In fact they were so effective, that's the reason why they were banned in most police departments. A police officer would take a swing with it to restrain a suspect and even when not meaning to it would easily crack a person's skull, causing serious injury or death.

Keep that in mind before putting it to use.

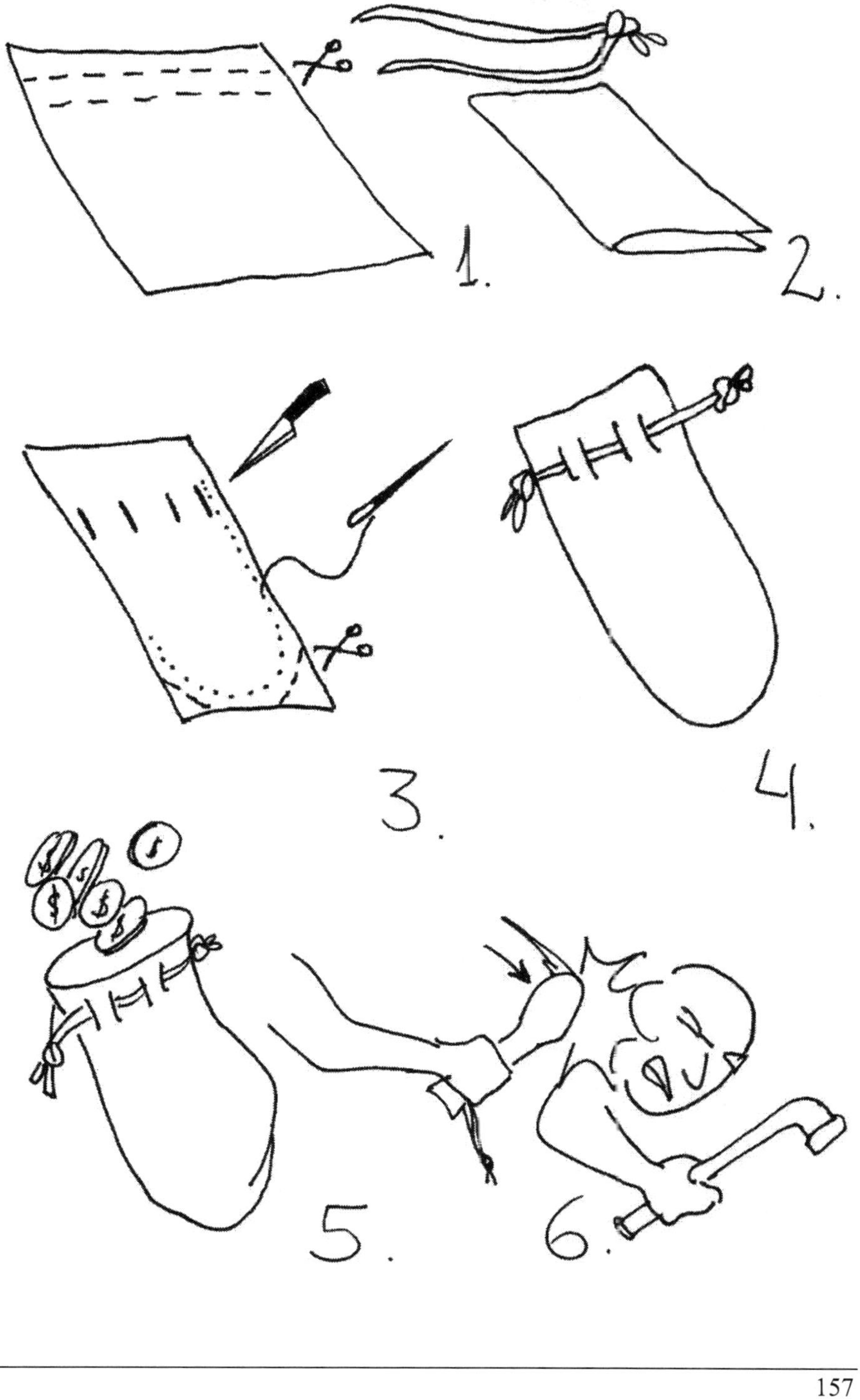
1.
2.
3.
4.
5.
6.

NOTES:

Chapter 8
Defensive Driving

You are the weapon.

Everything else is just tools and accessories.

Awareness in Vehicles

Just like when on foot, situational awareness is important when in a vehicle as well. In order to respond accordingly, you need to know what is happening around you. This takes a bit more effort given that the vehicle itself blocks your surroundings to an extent. Get used to looking not only the road like you normally would but further down, quickly scanning the horizon. Get used to checking your surroundings beyond what is immediately around you.

Learning to look for what's out of place and just doesn't look right will allow you to detect potential threats in advance so as to react in time.

A) 7 in 2. It takes about two seconds to quickly scan 360°. Visualizing the 7 sectors, from left to right, you can tell what's happening around you. Frequently scan these sectors when parked, especially in areas of high crime where a mugger of carjacker may attempt to sneak up on you and catch you by surprise.

B) Make sure not to box yourself in when driving. Always keep your distance, leaving about the length of your vehicle worth of maneuvering space in front. This will give you some wiggle room to use and maneuver your way out of that spot. In the event of a chain collision, the more room you have the less likely you are to be crushed against the vehicle in front of you.

When stuck in traffic, always mind your surroundings and manage how much distance you leave when considering potential escape routes. A few more feet may mean leaving a potential opening between two light posts or trees in case you need to go over the sidewalk and access an alternative route. Always move around and stop your vehicle in ways that give you the most options available in case you need them.

C) If you believe you are being followed, make three turns in the same direction, drive around the block. If the car is still there then it's fairly certain that you are being followed. If so, keep driving looking for more populated areas, maybe drive to your local police station. Flash your lights or honk at a police vehicle to get his attention or call 911.

This same strategy can be taken when suspicious vehicles are noticed when approaching your home. Do not stop and certainly do not get off your car or open the garage with a suspicious vehicle or people nearby. Keep driving and go around the block. Keep your distance and call the police if the suspicious people are still waiting.

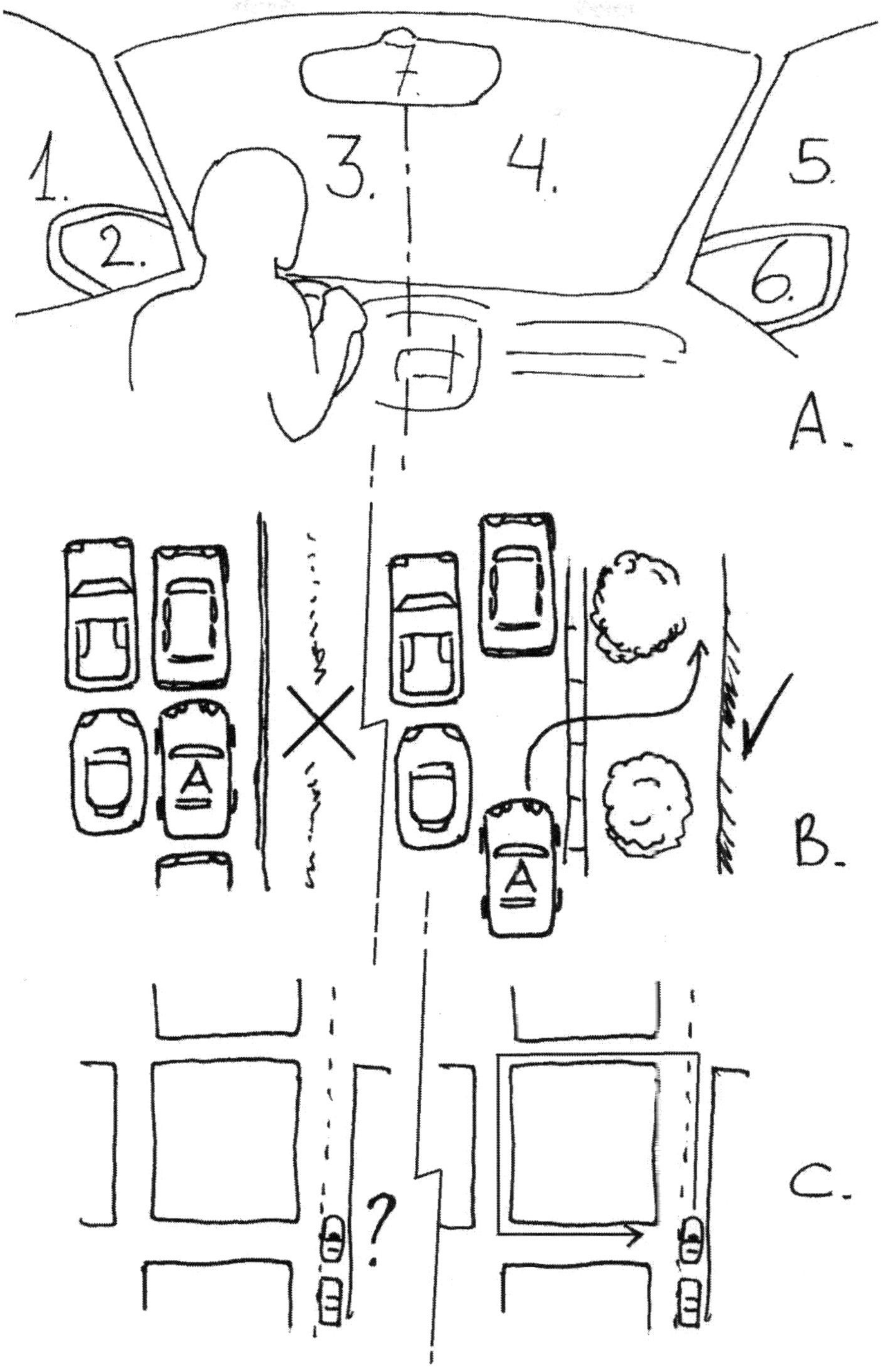
1.
2.
3.
4.
5.
6.
7.
A.
A
B.
A
C.
?

Many violent crimes take place in parking lots or when in or near to your vehicle. Road rage can quickly escalate into a life threatening situation. In dangerous areas, entering or leaving your house presents criminals with a window of opportunity they can exploit. Bring up your awareness level a notch or two during those moments.

1) Park so as to be able to make a quick exit if needed. Car "A" is close to the store you are at. It's also well positioned so as to leave fast in an emergency. Cars parked close to the windows of stores were people inside have a clear view are less likely to be broken into or vandalized.

Car "B" is also well position so as to make an emergency exit by going over the sidewalk. In this case, a 4x4 or SUV with good ground clearance may be required so as to go over the curb undamaged. The parking space right next to it isn't as good because it has a tree blocking the exit.

2) Quickly moving the stirring wheel in short right and left turns driving in a tight "S" makes other drivers move away. Especially during the first few seconds, it catches most people by surprise and they tend to give way or put more distance between yourself and them if they are tailgating you.

3) Stickers with political slogans or about firearm manufacturers say more about you than you may want to let people know. A gun sticker says you probably keep a gun in your vehicle. Anyone looking for a gun is more likely to break into yours looking for one. Certain political commentary stickers will do that as well. Political stickers in general can trigger reactions from people that belong to opposite parties. It may escalate incidents of road rage or fights at a parking lot that would otherwise be avoided. A sticker with a stick family showing how many family members you have, names, pets and more is also a terrible idea.

4) Keep your car door locked at all times. The easiest thing for a criminal to do is to just open your door at a red light and threaten your with a weapon or directly attack you. Seatbelts should be used at all times. The chances of not wearing a seatbelt saving your life (jumping out of the car when being shot at) pale in comparison to common traffic accidents.

5) Keep an anti-theft bar for your vehicle and use it when parking on the street. These sometimes come in formats that allow them to be used as impact weapon which adds another valuable use for the tool. Some even have a glass breaker tip which can be very handy for escaping a burning or sinking vehicle after an accident or help someone else.

Anti-theft bars can be cut with a saw easily enough, but criminals looking to quickly steal a car will go looking for an easier target.

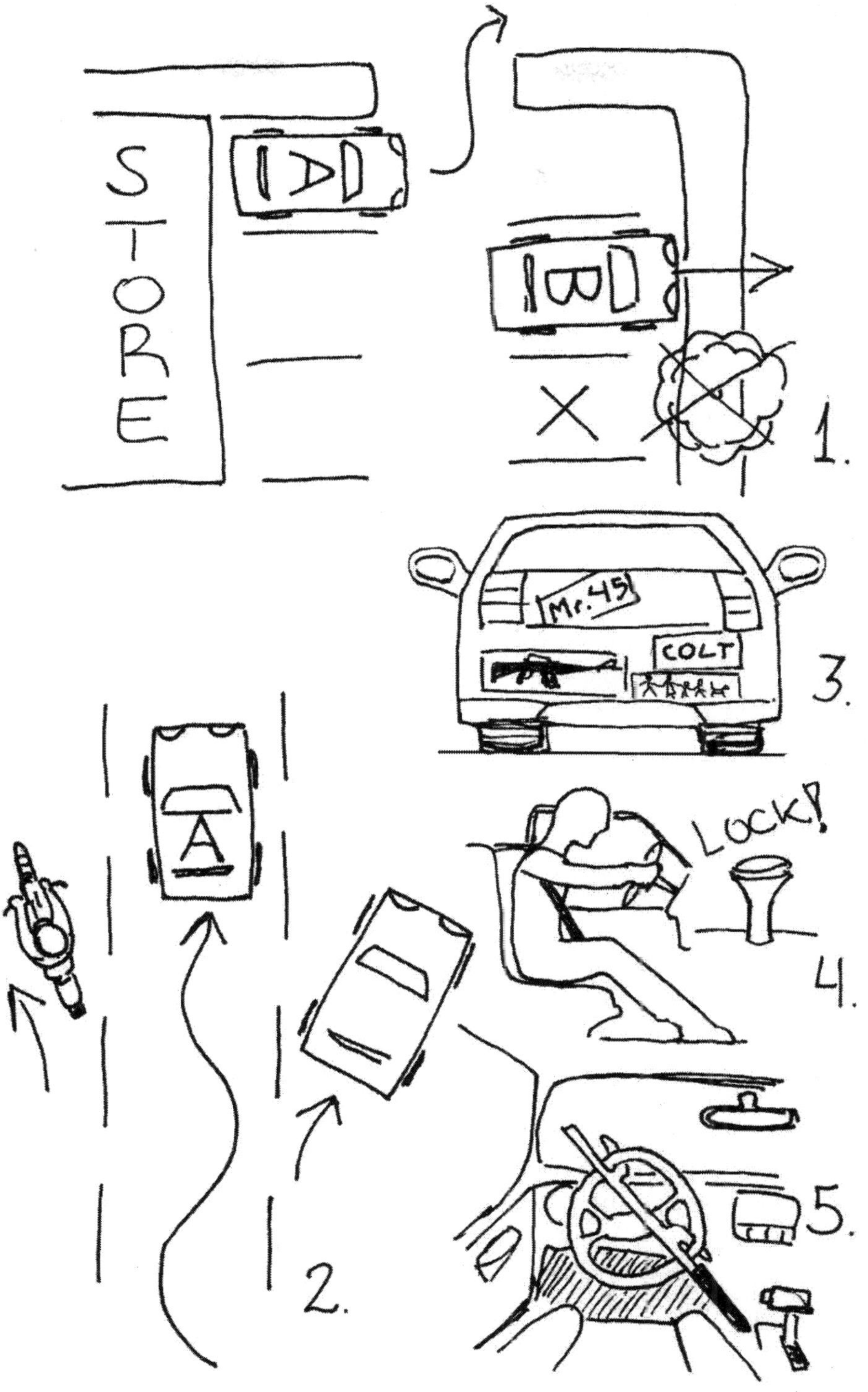
STORE
A
B
1.
Mr.45
COLT
3.
A
2.
LOCK!
4.
5.

6) Projectiles going through glass will deviate from their original trajectory towards the one that is perpendicular to the plane of the glass. This means that a round shot from a car inside out will shoot high, therefore you have to aim about a foot low for targets within a ten yard range or so. Shoot at the lower torso for a center of mass shot. When shooting from the outside into a vehicle, it will go low in relation to the point of aim. A head shot will probably hit the upper chest. Adjust your point of aim accordingly if you ever have to shoot through a windshield either way.

Keep in mind that the heavier and bigger the projectile, the less it will deviate from its original trajectory as it goes through the glass.

The deviation will be more noticeable for the first shot. After the glass shatters it won't present the same kind of resistance and as the glass breaks completely there may be little or no deviation at all.

7) Many kidnap victims have escaped simply by jumping out of the moving vehicle when they had the chance.

Express kidnappings usually don't include handcuffs or zip ties. The victim is generally just forced into a vehicle at gunpoint in a hurry. For most express kidnaps in populated areas, kidnappers want to be as fast about it as possible to avoid any unwanted attention.

When the moment presents itself, jump. It is better to be smart about it. Wait for your opportunity and don't jump into oncoming traffic or where you have signs or posts that guarantee certain death. As you jump, cover your head like you would when adoption a crash position as explained by stewardesses when flying. You are after all crashing into the pavement and it is crucial to protect your head as well as you can. Jump away from the vehicle. You do NOT want get dragged or caught under the tires. Don't try to break the fall. Land on your shoulder if you can and let yourself roll so as to minimize the damage received.

8) You want to cover your head as much as possible as you jump. Your elbows cover the front, the forearms the sides and your hands on the back of your head. Avoiding serious head injuries is your priority.

9) Express kidnaps are often fast and improvised. The perpetrators aren't always all that smart about it. If forced into a car at gun point, do your best so as to not end up between two kidnapers.

Ending up seated by a door is your best shot at escaping by jumping from the vehicle.

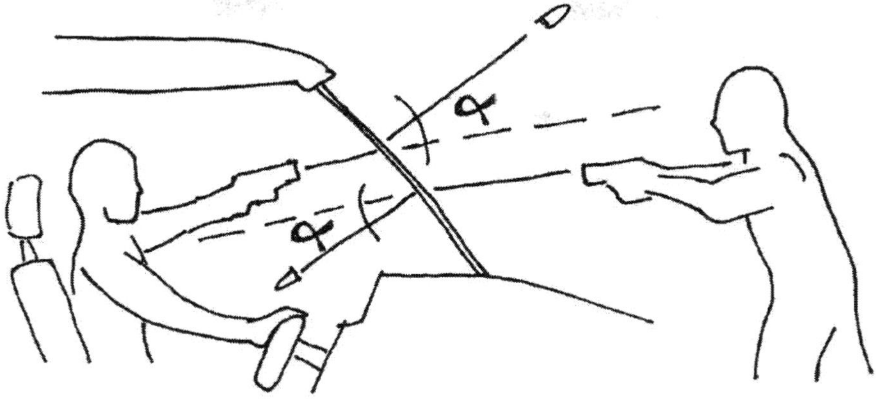

6.

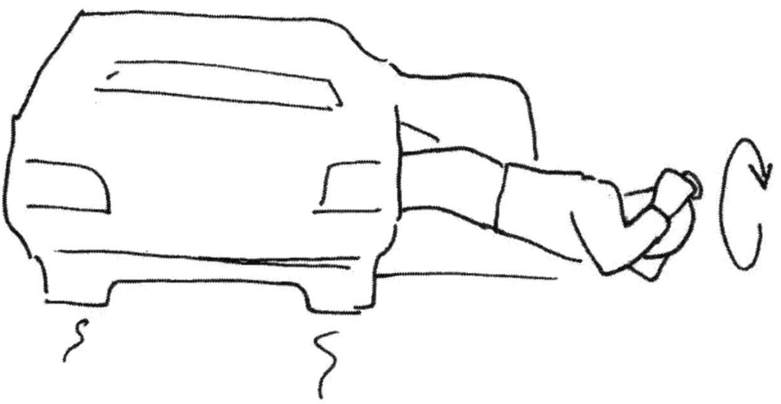

7.

8.

ROLL INSTEAD OF BREAKING THE FALL

9.

Ram a Vehicular Roadblock

Drive around roadblocks whenever possible. The risk of damaging your own car is too high. Having said that, know how to ram one if you are ever left with no choice.

1) Approach at less than 20 mph and brake before impacting the car.

You want to stop before crashing and PUSH the car rather than crash your way through.

This is important so as to not damage your vehicle and keep it from running (which you need to escape) but also so as to keep the airbags from deploying. Airbags are likely to deploy when crashing a stationary vehicle at speeds of over 15 mph.

2) Aim for the rear axle of the blocking vehicle. This is the easiest side to push. With the engine on top of the front axle, that's where most of the weight is and where the most friction will occur between the tires and the pavement. On gravel and especially on ice, the friction will be considerably less but on pavement the difference is noticeable.

3) Approach the vehicle slowly and remember to hit the brake to minimize speed before making contact.

4) Once you make contact with the rear axle, accelerate.

5) Because of the weight distribution on most vehicles, as you accelerate pushing the rear, the car will pivot on the front axle. The greater the speed, the faster the car will turn as you push it.

6) Accelerate and drive away.

Some experts advice to disable the airbags in the vehicle. This does not make a lot of sense for most people since the chances of the average person dying or getting seriously injured in a collision because of the lack or airbags is much greater than the need of ramming other vehicles, especially when you take into account that you can ram/push vehicles out of the way as long as you follow the precautions mentioned earlier.

Disabling such an important built-in safety feature in a car will no doubt cause a number of legal complications. Car insurance and life insurance companies will most likely have an issue with this, likely voiding their contractual obligations.

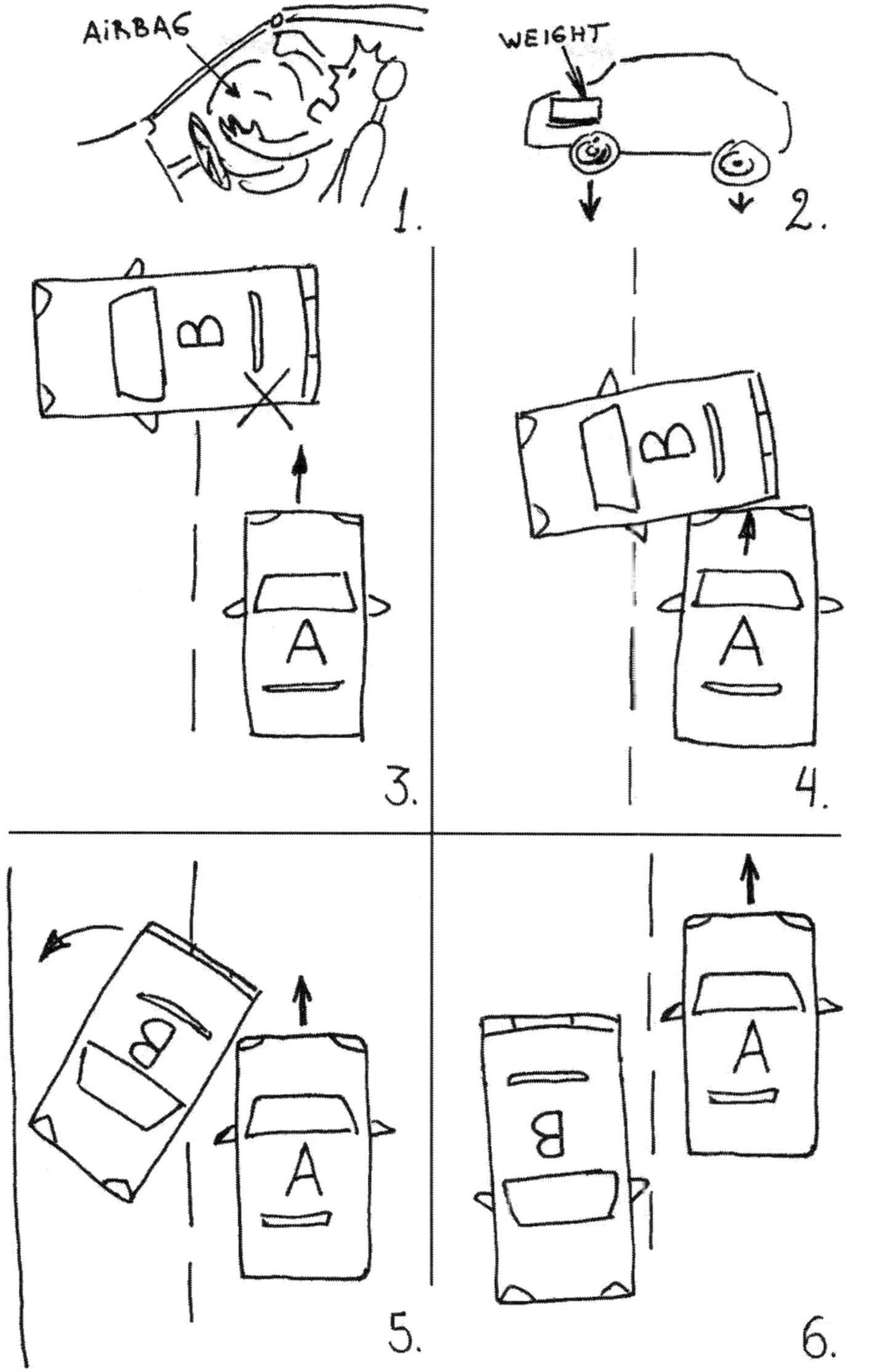
AIRBAG
1.
WEIGHT
2.
B
A
3.
B
A
4.
B
A
5.
B
A
6.

How to do a Bootleg Turn and Handbrake Turn

A bootleg turn is the quickest way to turn around 180 degrees and go back the way you came.

It is not hard to perform but it can be dangerous and it will depend on the type of vehicle, speed and type of road you are in. Awareness while driving is key so that the bootleg turn is of actual use when trying to avoid ambushes, roadblocks or carjack attempts.

A classic bootleg turn requires a manual transmission car:

1) While traveling forward, put the car into second gear. You don't want to go too fast. About 35-40 MPH will do for most cars, but it will depend on the specific vehicle and type of road.

2) Turn the wheel quickly in the direction of the opposite lane.

3) When doing so, the rear end of the car will skid as it turns.

4) Once the turn is complete accelerate away.

Handbrake turns are similar but easier to perform. They work on both manual and automatic transmission vehicles where the handbrake locks the rear wheels.

1) While driving forward pull the handbrake. On manual transmission cars you want to press the clutch before you do this.

2) As soon as you pull the handbrake and feel the car skid, turn the wheel in the direction of the opposite lane while keeping the handbrake engaged.

3) You want to use the handbrake to regulate the turn and bring it down when you have turned enough. Remember that it is the handbrake the one that is making the car skid as it turns.

4) Fully let go of the handbrake and accelerate away from danger. On manual transmission cars let go of the clutch before you accelerate.

Tip: Although the handbrake turn is a legitimate skill and I have used it many times before, it can be dangerous, it's tough on tires and more modern vehicles have systems specifically intended to keep your car from skidding. More often than not, awareness and a controlled U-turn is the safest, most reasonable course of action when looking to avoid dangerous situations on the road.

1.
2.
3.
4.

How to do a J Turn

Like the Bootleg turn, the J-Turn is another useful driving maneuver.

In some ways the J-turn is even easier, less dangerous and more likely to be used since its done when the vehicle has stopped and is moving backwards.

1) Put your car in reverse and driver backwards. Accelerate to 30 or 40 MPH. How fast you need to go will depend on the type of vehicle, weight distribution and the type of road.

Like with bootleg turns, dirt roads have less traction and cars skid easier on them. An icy road or snow is even easier although the lack of friction could be downright dangerous, sending the car spinning out of control so even more caution is advised.

2) Position your hands on the wheel for a quick half turn. Take your foot off the gas and quickly turn the steering wheel.

3) The car will turn sharply 180 degrees given the weight of the car mostly being on the front where the engine is. Once the turn is complete, quickly steer the wheel in the opposite direction to keep the car straight.

4) Put the car on drive, press the accelerator and drive away.

The steps are mostly the same with a manual transmission vehicle.

1) Press the clutch and shift to reverse. Accelerate driving backwards.

2) Press the clutch, position your hands and give the steering wheel a quick turn.

3) The car will complete the 180 degree turn. When it does, quickly steer the wheel in the opposite direction to keep the car straight.

4) Shift into 1st speed (sometimes 2nd is best) and lift your foot from the clutch pedal. Accelerate to drive away.

Although J-turns are safer and often easier to perform than Handbrake turns, just like in the case of the U-turn, a slow and more controlled J-turn is also advised if there's not that much urgency.

Tip: Keep a can of pepper spray in the glove compartment, within easy reach. This can be a very useful tool during confrontations on the road where lethal force is uncalled for.

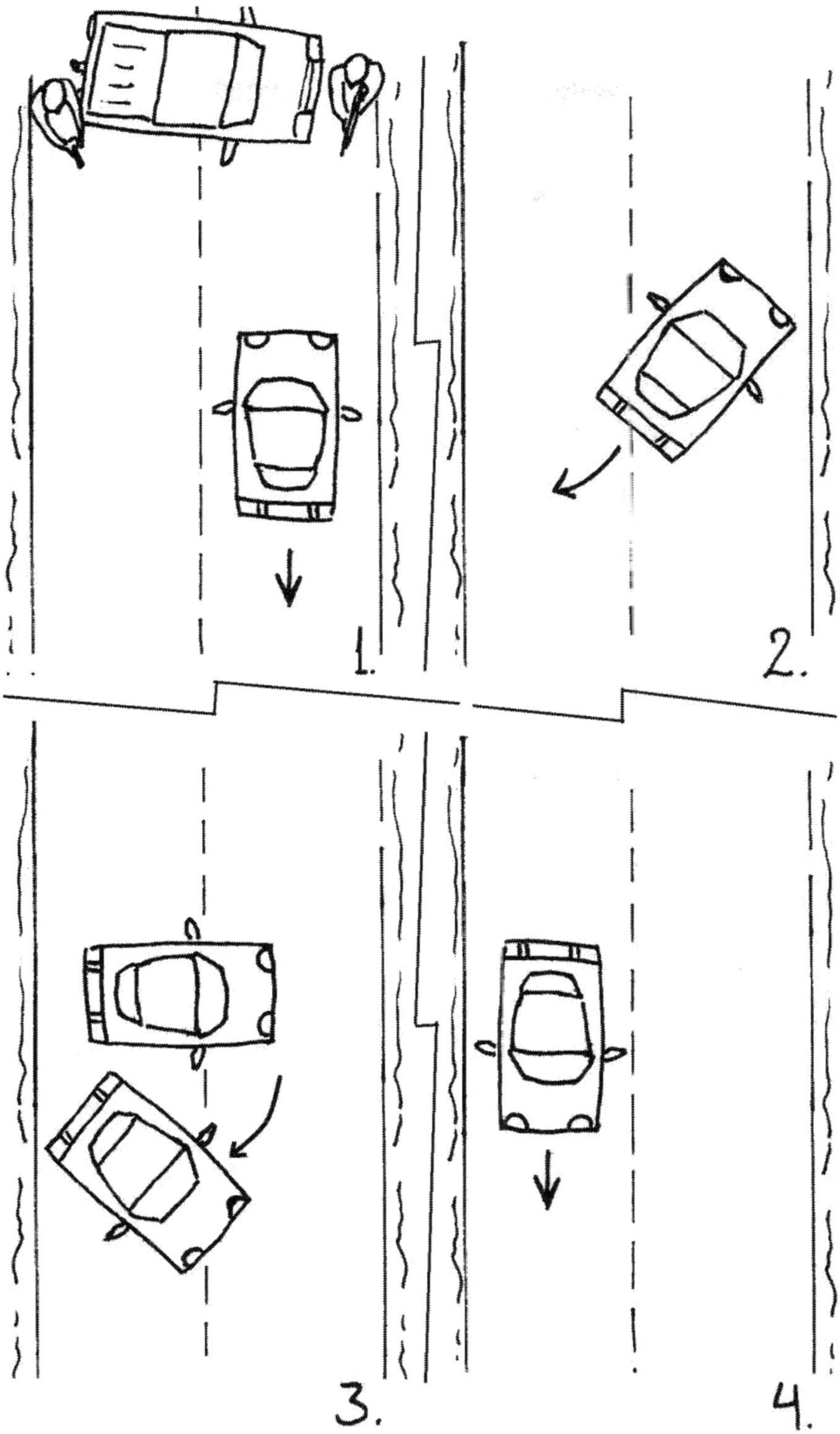
1.
2.
3.
4.

PIT Maneuver

The PIT maneuver, (Pursuit Intervention Technique) is a technique used to cause vehicles to lose control, turn sideways and force them to stop. The PIT maneuver must be used with care. At speeds under 35MPH, it is considered a less than lethal maneuver. The car will lose control, skid laterally, end up looking in the opposite direction, turned 180 degrees. At speeds greater than 35MPH vehicles are likely to roll over, crashing and injuring the occupants.

To perform the PIT maneuver:

1) Match the speed of car "B" with your car "A" and approach it from the side. Both cars need to be moving at the same speed.

2) Align the front of your car "A" with the read of car "B". Do not touch with your tires, only the part of your vehicle in front of the front axis. Steer to the right until you make contact, leaning on car "B". Do not crash into the vehicle. Done correctly, there's should be hardly any paint chipping in your front bumper. Once you make contact, push the rear of car "B" to the right, as if committing to change lanes.

3) When this happens, Car "B" will rotate. Continue pushing in a straight line as you accelerate, causing car "B" to turn 180 degrees. Do not steer in the direction of car "B" as it turns.

4) Push car "B" out of the way as you escape.

Performing a PIT maneuver is considered a serious crime in the United States and most other countries. It will also be very hard to prove a need to perform a PIT maneuver given that it needs to be performed by the chasing vehicle. If you are in fear of your life, it could be argued that not chasing the car in front of you would have been the right thing to do.

Just as important as knowing how to do a PIT maneuver is knowing how to counter one. The obvious first reaction should be to rapidly slow down your speed, below 30 MPH. Once your vehicle start rotating, rather than fighting it let the car turn 180. You can now drive away in the opposite direction. You can also continue turning past the 180 and make a full circle or perform a J-turn so as to continue going in the same direction. You could hit the brakes as they close in. Brake "checking" is likely to send you forward out of control if the chasing vehicle crashes you. This works better with larger, heavier cars but it does damage the front of car "A" in exchange for damage to your rear.

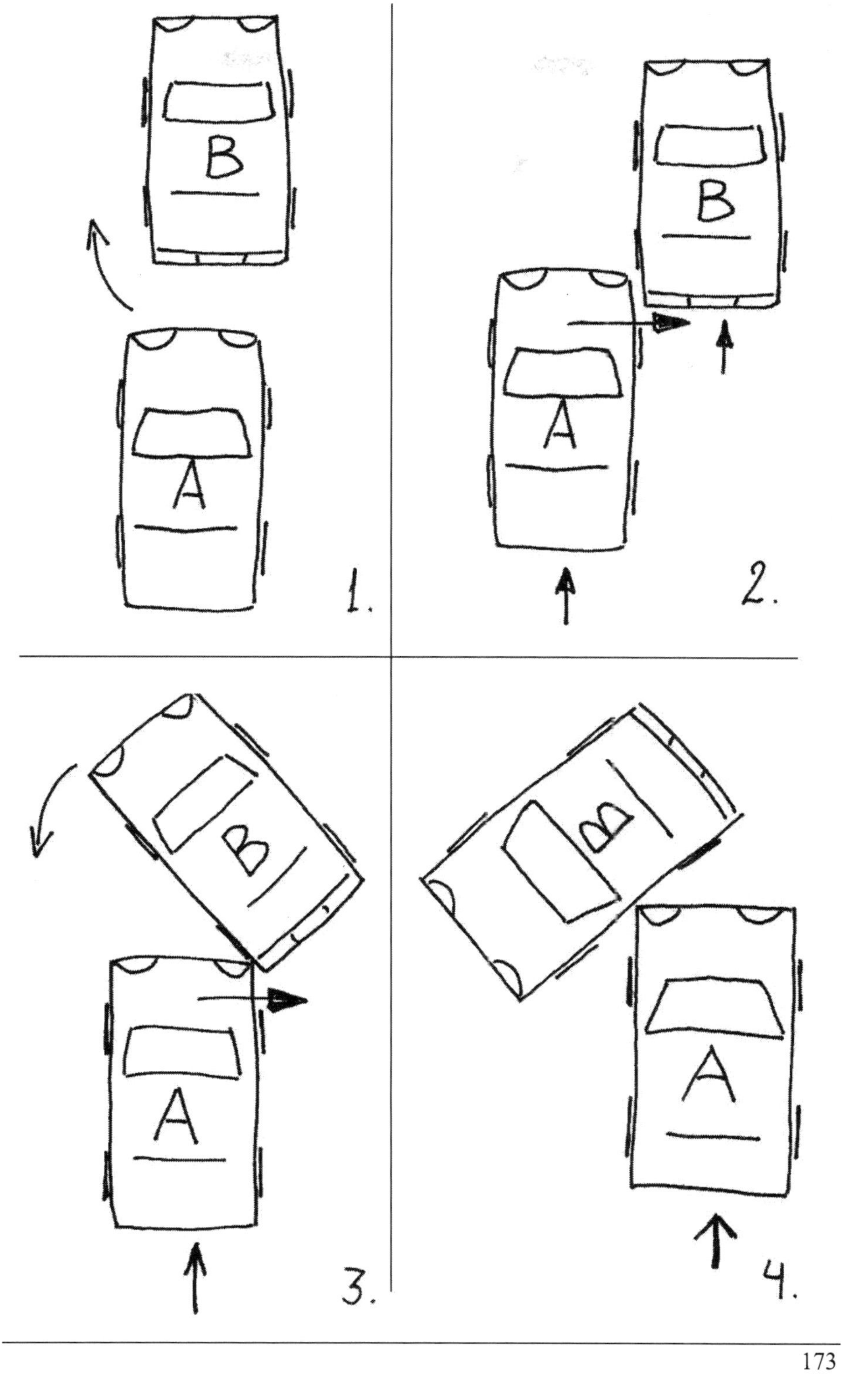
B
A
1.
B
A
2.
B
A
3.
B
A
4.

Using a Car against an Armed Attacker

Carjacks are a common occurrences in cities with serious crime problems. They can also be a problem in smaller towns considered "safe" by the local community. In some cases road rage incidents may leave you in a somewhat similar scenario, facing an armed attacker while sitting in your vehicle.

Cars pack some serious power. Even modest ones are a few thousand pounds of steel and over a hundred horsepower engine. For any attacker standing in front of it, the best tactic is to get as low as possible in the seat (the engine provides the best cover) and accelerate so as to hit your attacker.

There are times though when such a straightforward tactic is ill-advised.

1) When an attacker isn't in front of your car but to the side, against cars or a wall, crushing him head first means we are also immobilized and while the attacker's lower body will be pinned, we are still exposed if he opens fire. Car "A" could drive into the carjacker but risk getting shot and rendering his car inoperable, vulnerable to other attackers.

It is a common tactic for carjackers to simply step out of a car and just point a gun at their victim demanding them to get off the vehicle. In this case "A" is the victim and "B" is the support car from which the carjacker got off. A possible variation is car "B" stopping in front of "A" in an attempt to block its escape. If "A" is capable of maneuvering around it, the situation will still be similar with the carjacker still caught somewhere between "A" and "B" so the same tactic still applies.

2) Rolling the person between cars "A" and "B" is a better, more effective strategy. You are able to accelerate away, remaining a moving (harder to hit) target. This method is also immediately effective in that the brute force of the vehicle quickly sends the person spinning. When done properly, any attempt to take an accurate shot by the carjacker is futile as he is violently rolled and is unable to stay on target.

Of course, there's a chance of causing severe injuries. A person crushed by a car will likely end up with broken bones, internal bleeding and other injuries even if you are attempting to roll them rather than directly crush them. Like in any other use of lethal force, only do it when under attack by armed criminals and when in clear fear for your life.

3) Being caught in such a manner between cars or against a wall, the violent spinning will cause the attacker to fall, most likely drop any weapon he may have been holding in the process.

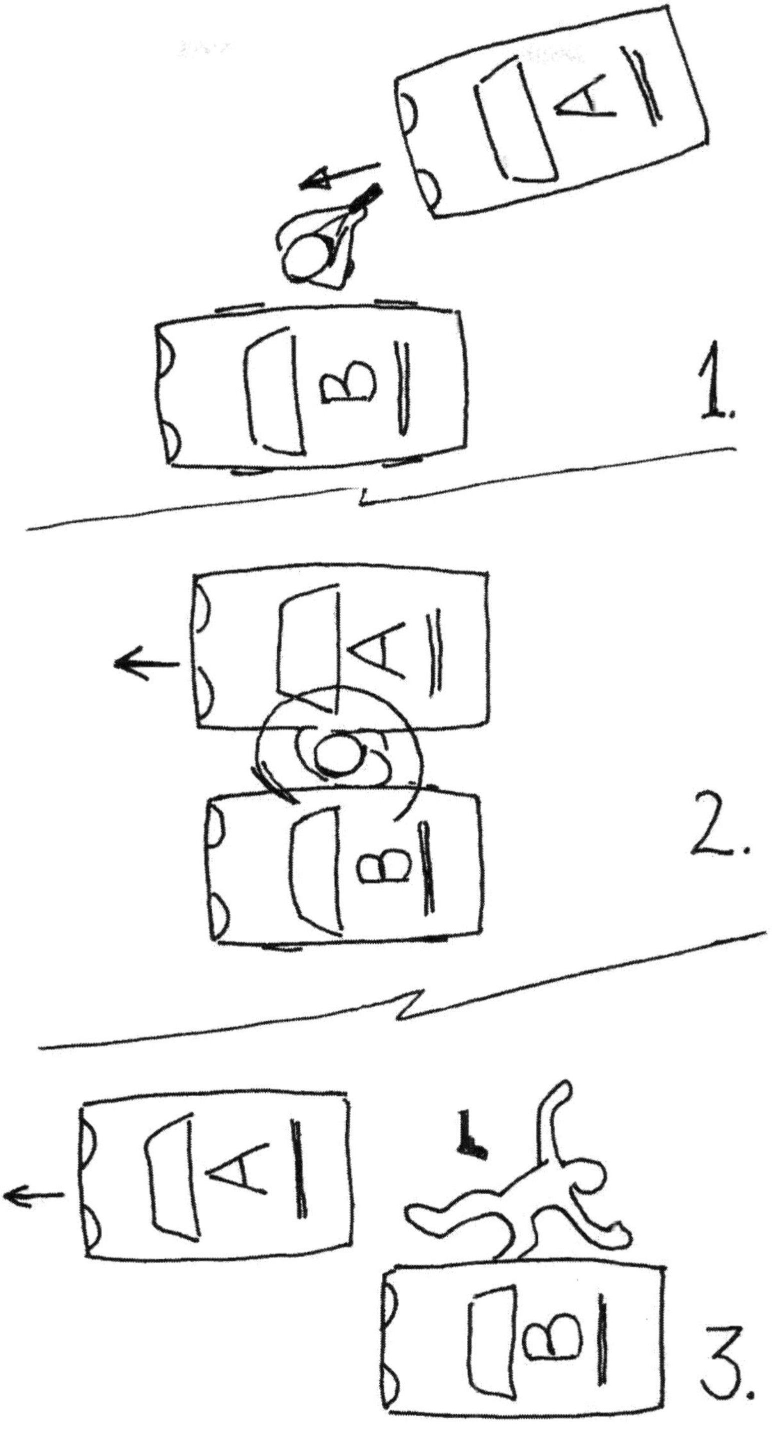
A
B
1.
A
B
2.
A
B
3.

Car Ambush

If you realize you are driving into an ambush, then the logical thing to do is to drive away using one of the 180 degree turn techniques and get the hell out of there. But sometimes, for whatever reason, running just isn't an option and some other plan is called for.

1) Detecting the ambush in time is key. Sometimes criminals place nails on the road to puncture your tires and force you to stop, sometimes they simply place large rocks people end up hitting with their car. Be careful of bridges from were rocks, pipes and other objects can be thrown into your windshield. If you notice a car barricade, then stop immediately, turn around and leave.

2) If leaving isn't an option then you don't want to stay sitting in the car. Cars offer very little ballistic protection. You want to move out of there as soon as possible. During night time, turn on your main beams (high). This will help cover your movement. Open the door, get out and move to the back of the vehicle.

3) From here you have different options depending on the specific situation, the number of attackers, geography around you and what your priorities are. You can continue moving back, retreating while using the car as cover. If you have a Bug out Bag or Get Home Bag in your trunk (which you should) then pop it open before exiting the car. It is not a bad idea to keep a rifle in there as well. This would be the perfect time to put it to good use. If you have trees, a ditch, tall vegetation or some kind of structure at the side of the road it can be used to cover your retreat. It could also be used to cover your movement as you flank your attackers.

4) If you have other people with you a similar strategy can be used to attack those ambushing you. Drive in reverse, getting close to the side of the road. Stop for a moment so your friends can get out. Remember to keep your high beams on. Get as close to the side of the road as you can to cover the movement. Once they get off the car you can keep driving on reverse, make a "J" turn and drive away.

On the meantime the friends you left behind can move into position, flank them and catch them completely by surprise. These strategies go way beyond what a person would normally do in a self-defense scenario. 99% of the time you are clearly better off in every aspect just driving away. Sometimes though, if family is in danger, if police aren't responding and you simply don't have a choice, it's a good idea to know how to act in these kind of situations.

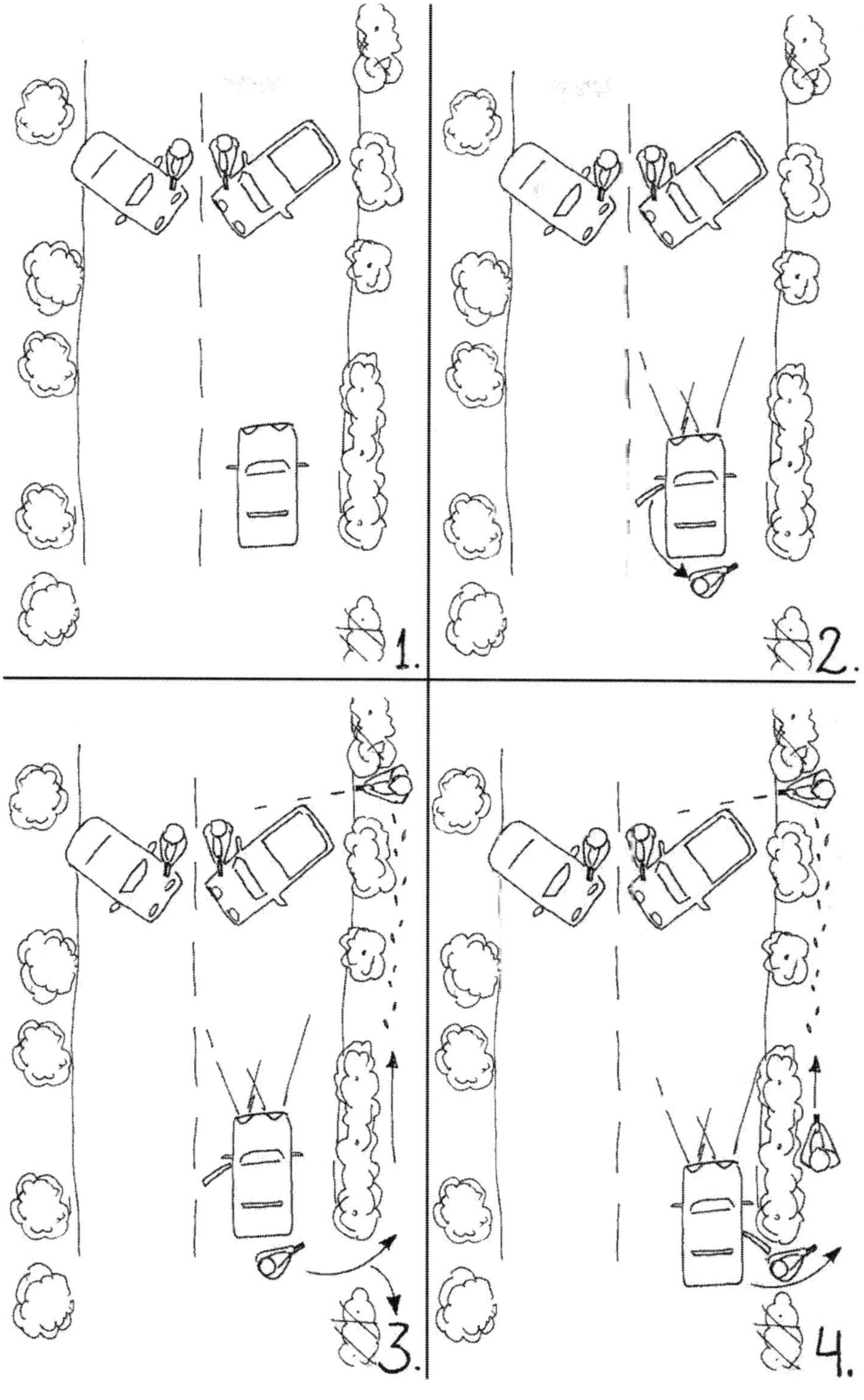
1.
2.
3.
4.

Using a Car for Cover

Cars are all around us and because of the nature of violent social interaction, we are often either inside a car or near one when these unfortunate events occur. Being mugged in a parking lot, hit when parking our car when going home, attacked during a road rage or active shooter incident, you need to know what to expect from a car and how to use it properly for either cover or concealment.

1) Cars are not the bullet proof wall we often see in movies. Cars are made of relatively thin metal and the best part to take cover is behind the engine. After the engine, axels and wheels present another good option for cover. The rest of the car, it is literally hit and miss. If a round hits a mechanism inside the door, a beam or folded metal, then it MAY stop the round, but if it hits most areas where it's just thin metal and plastic it will zip right through. Especially with rifles rounds, it's very likely to go right through the trunk or doors with enough force to kill you.

2) While taking cover, keep your distance from the car and your head down, making sure the top of your head isn't exposed.

3) You can return fire shooting over the hood, then go down behind cover again. Shooting over the hood you are exposing most of your head. Depending on the type of vehicle, especially SUVS and trucks with robust metal bumpers, shooting around the front of the car may provide a lot more cover.

4) Because the engine provides the best cover, if someone opens fire right in from of you, steer a bit before exiting the car so that the front of the vehicle covers you as you exit.

5) Projectiles don't bounce like rubber balls when they hit a hard surface, instead they deform and follow a trajectory parallel to the surface they impact. This means it's relatively easy to shoot someone's feet by shooting under the car without having to go all the way down and taking a direct shot. Use the wheels to protect yourself when taking cover.

6) This also applies to rounds that make contact with the hood of the car. If the angle and power of the projectile isn't enough to penetrate, the round may just skid over the hood, hitting anyone taking a peep.

7) You can take cover by opening the car's door, going low on your seat and positing yourself behind the "A" pillar. Open the door but keep it as closed as possible given that the angle greatly improves the protection it provides. Keep your feet inside and change your gun to your left hand if you must (regularly practice shooting with both).

engine
engine
1.
2.
3.
engine
A
4.
5.
6.
7.

NOTES:

Chapter 9

Moving, Barricade and Gaining Entry

"The past is an illusion. You must learn to live in the present and accept yourself for what you are now. What you lack in flexibility and agility you must make up with knowledge and constant practice."

-Bruce Lee

Safety Roll

Some parkour moves are relatively easy and safe when not looking to perform fancy stunts. They are a great way to train your balance and flexibility while practicing a skill that can come in handy in a number of situations such as breaking a fall after a jump or avoiding injury when you fall. Tripping and falling are common causes of injury.

If attacked and pushed, knowing how to roll means you can avoid injury and be back on your feet almost instantly. While the safety roll requires a bit of dexterity, most people can learn how to do it and maintain the ability if they practice it every now and then.

1) Start by practicing from a crouching position. One knee up and the arm from that same side placed across, palms against the floor next to one another. Your torso must be at a 45° angle from the direction in which you are going to roll. The blade of the hand in front should be pointing out while the thumb points towards you.

2) Unlike a traditional gymnastic roll, you want to avoid your head making contact with the floor given that you will do this on hard surfaces. If doing the roll over wet paint, it should leave a line starting at the blade of your hand, shoulder and across your back.

3) From this position, bring your torso forward and bring the shoulder down. When you reach the tipping point commit to it and roll forwards doing your best to keep the contact along the line described earlier.

4) Your head should be to the side, chin to your chest. Tuck your legs as they go over you as you roll.

5) As you roll, prepare yourself for your foot to contact the ground when you find yourself vertical again. You should be in somewhat of the same stance you started with, that same leg and shoulder forward. The momentum will carry you and as the foot contacts the floor use your hands to stabilize yourself.

6) Push against the floor with your leg to bring yourself up and continue the motion, running forward. With practice you will become more fluid and the motion becomes more natural.

Tip: Some time ago while out for a stroll with my wife I slipped on the curb and fell. Before I knew it I was rolling downhill, my wife laughing uncontrollably. It was the clumsiest, most awkward roll any human being ever performed but I got right up without a scratch on me. Practice it enough and it will come naturally when you need it.

1.

2.

3.

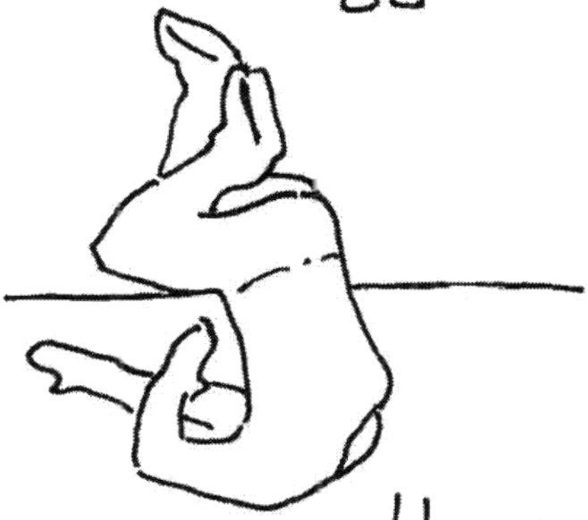

4.

5.

6.

Step Vault

The Step vault, sometimes called safety vault, is one of the most simple yet one of the most useful skills learned in parkour. Most people have done something similar at some point in their lives but it's useful to understand the mechanics involved so as to do it correctly. Occasionally practicing the step vault will allow you to quickly overcome low walls, rails, benches and other common urban obstacles. This means you can move faster from point A to B, put an obstacle between you and an attacker or allow you to quickly duck behind effective cover when shot at, when a second or two may be difference between life and death. If the opportunity presents itself, don't miss the chance to practice it.

1) Understand the obstacle you are working with. You don't want to start with a wall that is higher than your waist. Start with lower walls until you become comfortable and have a better idea of what you are capable of.

2) Approach at speed so as to have enough momentum.

3) Place your hand on top of the wall with the fingers pointing forward while you also bring the opposite leg up.

4) Your hand should be just under your shoulder, your leg should not be fully extended nor curled beneath you but at a comfortable middle point. When done correctly, both contact the top of the wall at the same time.

5) As you make contact, bring your other foot over the wall between your hand and foot. Bring it all the way up so as to not catch it on the wall. The lower the wall, the easier it is to perform this move until you have a better understanding of the mechanics involved.

6) The foot you just brought over the wall is the one that continues the movement. This is the foot you should land with on the other side.

You can practice by putting your hand and foot on top of the wall and bringing your other foot over the wall, stepping through back and forth. Do that a few times until you have a better idea of how far your foot should go up so as to not get caught when doing it at full speed.

Once you get the hang of it, step over the wall a few times putting your hand and foot in position and stepping through. Get comfortable doing this before attempting to do it at full speed.

This skill is simple but needs to be practiced. Once you do, it's surprisingly useful given the number of urban obstacles in which you can use it. Practice doing it both sides, stepping through with the left and right foot.

WAIST
HIGH
1.
2.
3.
4.
5.
6.

Jump Landing

Jumping from a certain height seems simple enough but there is a proper technique so as to do it the right way and minimize the impact. Eventually a roll can be added to the jump, further dissipating the energy of the impact. The two techniques combined allow some parkour practitioners to safely jump from heights that would otherwise be very dangerous. Even if you have zero interest in parkour, you never know when you will have to jump to escape danger, anything from a fire, terror attack or a shooter at your workplace.

The ability to not only jump but to do so in a way you can continue running away from danger is key.

1) Start by identifying your landing area. Softer surfaces such as grass or sand are preferable whenever possible.

2) Jump projecting yourself forward rather than up. Stay vertical and don't tilt your upper body forwards or backwards. Keep your legs slightly bent so as to minimize the impact to your knees.

3) You want to keep your feet angled down so as to avoid landing on your heels. Stay relaxed but firm enough for your toes, ankles and knees to absorb the impact.

4) Touch the ground with the balls of your feet, both at the same time. Bend your legs a bit, your body working like a coil to absorb the impact.

5) Drop forwards and allow your hands to contact the ground. Slapping the floor with your hands dissipates energy. Use your hands to avoid bending your knees beyond 90 degrees, which could strain your tendons. Make sure not to bend your back forward too much either.

6) Push yourself forward with your hands and legs to continue running, using the momentum to redirect the energy of impact.

When practicing, try landing as quietly as possible. Landing quietly and softly means you're doing it right.

Step 5 would be the start of your roll should you incorporate it to the landing. It is important to be comfortable with your safety roll before incorporating to your jumps and to do it from a safe, reasonable height.

The idea here is not to jump off buildings like a stunt double but to learn and occasionally practice a couple basic techniques that allow you to work on your balance and agility and that may come in handy on certain occasions.

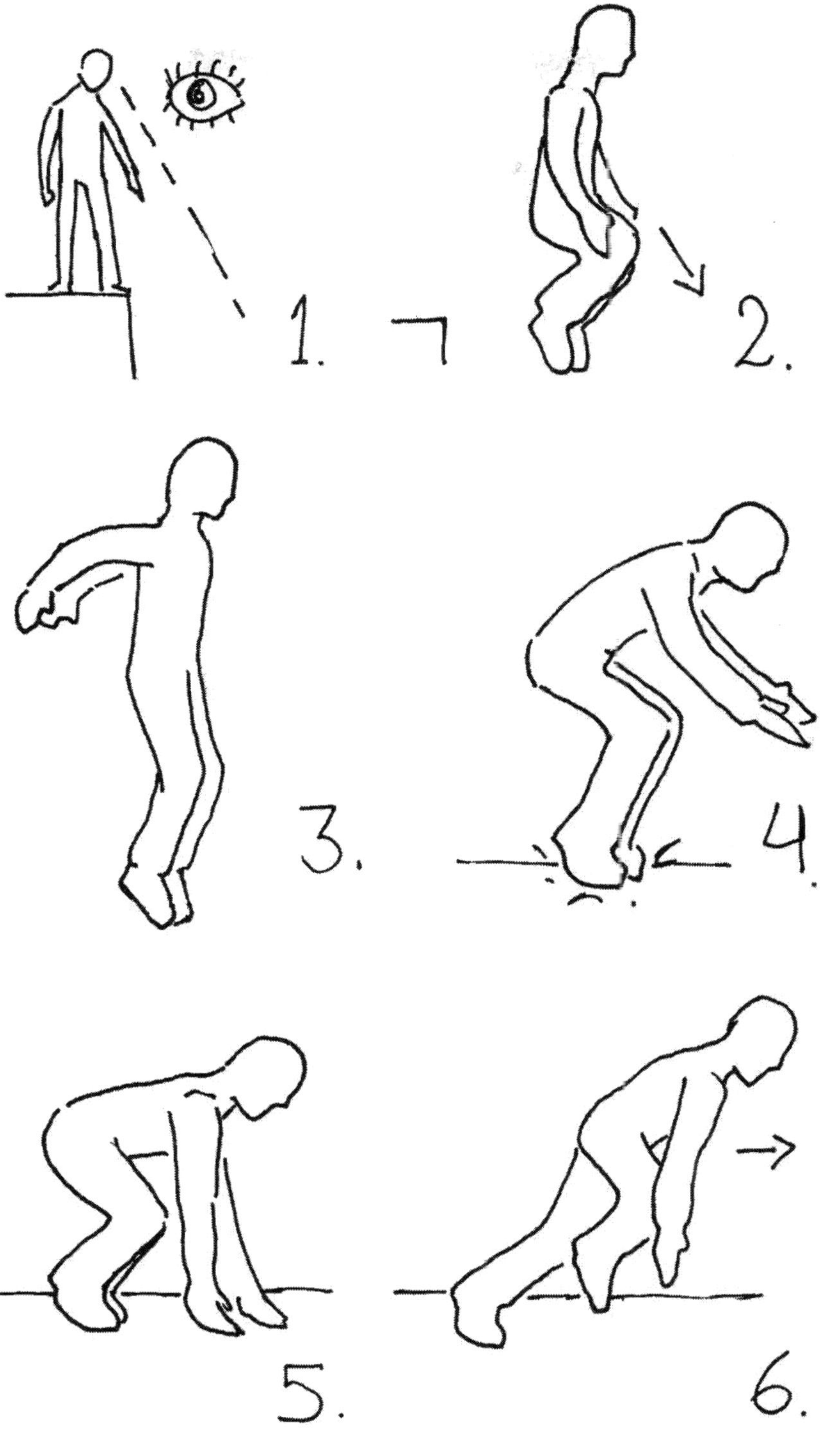
1.
2.
3.
4.
5.
6.

Dropping

During dangerous situations it is easy to panic and just jump or fall from heights. It is better to use the proper technique for it. Dropping from heights correctly significantly increases your chances of not getting hurt in the process, allowing you to either reduce the severity of the injuries received or to continue moving so as to escape.

1) Visualize your landing area. Make sure there are no objects that could injure you when dropping. Choose clear areas, preferably softer ones such as grass, barkdust or sand.

2) Get on your knees and bring one leg over the edge at a time. Keep a firm grip so as to not fall before you get into position.

3) Use your forearms to hold yourself. It is easier to support yourself this way. The objective here is to minimize the height from which you drop. Now you can lower yourself further, using your hands for support. This will require about the same amount of strength as the one used when doing pull ups.

4) Try putting your feet against the wall so as to create some distance.

5) When dropping facing a wall at very close distance there's a risk of hurting yourself, either by falling forwards against the wall or falling backwards. Try using your feet and hands to push yourself so as to put some more distance between you and the wall as you fall.

6) Drop in a vertical position, back straight, legs slighting bent and feet pointing down so as to avoid landing on your heels, using instead the ball of your feet. You want your body to work like a coil spring absorbing the impact. Bring your hand down and touch the floor or slap it if needed to dissipate more energy. Use your hands to stabilize yourself and to keep yourself from falling forward as you drop.

7) With a bit more practice and agility, you can push yourself against the wall so as to turn 180 degrees and end up looking away from the wall as you drop.

8) Dropping away from the wall, a roll can be used to dissipate the energy of the fall. This kind of drop will not only require more agility and practice, but it can also be more dangerous, especially when used during an emergency in less than ideal circumstances.

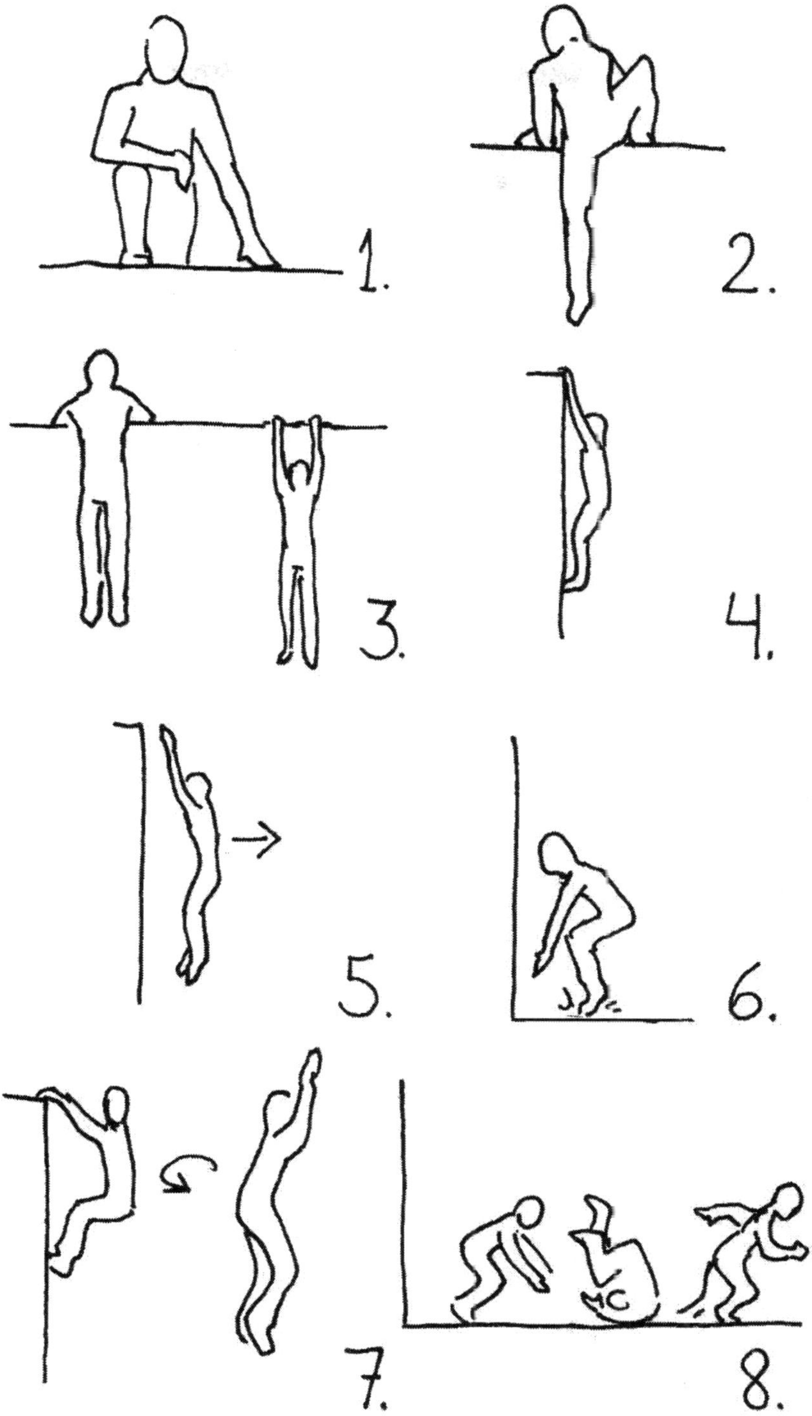
1.
2.
3.
4.
5.
6.
7.
8.

Going Over a Wall

Wall running is a parkour skill that allows you to run up a wall and climb it like a ninja. It is definitely a nice trick to practice but unlike the previous parkour skills explained, wall running does require a lot of dexterity. Having said that, climbing over walls can be a lot easier with a little help when working with other people.

1) One man places his back against the wall, knees at a 90 degree angle.

The other man steps on his thigh, close to the knee, grabbing his shoulder for support.

2) Continue climbing by stepping on the shoulder and placing your hands over the top of the wall for support. Put your forearms and elbows on top of the wall for better leverage as you pull yourself up.

3) Put one leg and arm over the wall. At this point, and depending on the situation you are in, you may want to keep your torso and head against the top of the wall so as to minimize your profile.

4) Holding yourself with one arm and hooking one leg, slowly lower yourself on the other side of the wall.

5) Unhook your leg and hang from the wall with one or two hands.

6) Let yourself go and drop on the other side of the wall.

Of course this entire operation can be done using both hands but it can be done easy enough using one hand while keeping a gun in the other if needed.

When working as a team, as people keep dropping on the other side of the wall they continue to position themselves to secure the area. Front, left, right, forming a semi-circle around the place where people cross the wall.

Two guys stay on top of the wall to help the last man cross without having anyone to step on. Each man holds one arm and helps him up over the wall.

With a bit of practice, a team can get over a wall using this method surprisingly fast.

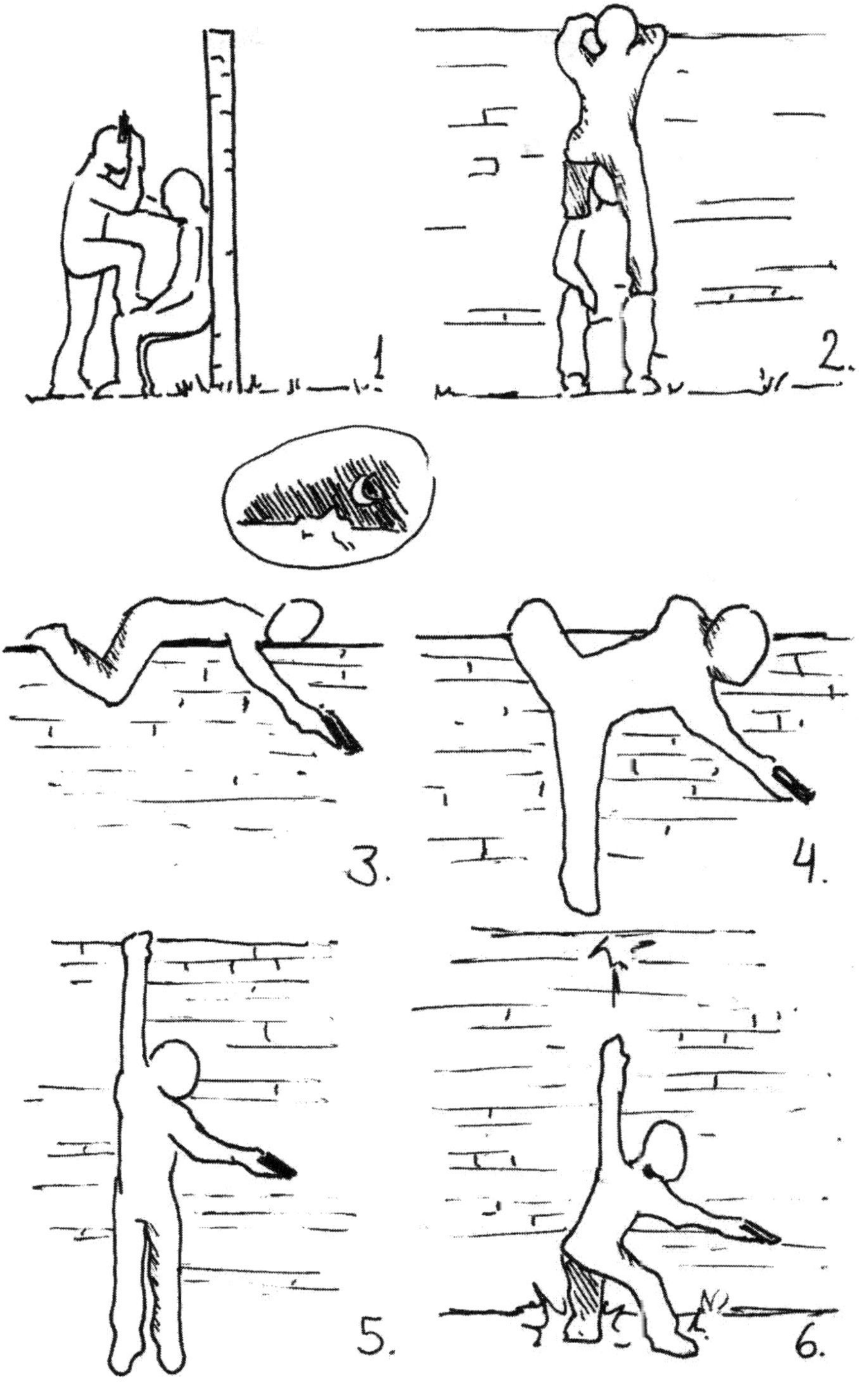
1.
2.
3.
4.
5.
6.

Lock Picking

Lock picking can be a valuable skill in a number of situations. The difficulty depends on the quality and complexity of the lock. Simple locks are easy enough to pick with a little practice. Lock picking tools are legal in most countries. A basic pick set and torsion wrench is enough to get started. Bobby pins and paper clips can be bent with pliers to make lock picking tools. These work well enough for simple locks.

1) Start by inserting the torsion wrench (the double L tool with flat sides). Keeping it at the bottom of the keyway and apply light torque right or left so that the plug turns as you pick each pin.

2) While maintaining light pressure with the tension wrench, insert the pick. You want to feel each pin until you find the "weird" one and apply pressure to push it up until it reaches the shear line where it is no longer locking the plug from turning. Once you are done, move to the next pin that shows resistance and push that one up and so on. As you work each pin, the plug will keep moving because of the pressure applied with the torsion wrench until it fully turns and unlocks.

3) A lock pick gun as the one often seen in movies works in a similar manner. You still need to apply a bit of torque with the torsion wrench. Insert the pick of the gun all the way in and pull the trigger. The pick will snap with a sudden movement, pushing all the pins at the same time. Pull the trigger a few times until all the pins have been picked. It usually takes one or two trigger pulls but they do pick locks in a matter of seconds.

4) A "bump" key is another effective lock picking tool. Sets of bump keys can be purchased or made. These are keys that simply have all their peaks cut all the way down to the lowest grove. Insert the bump key all the way in, then pull it back slightly about one millimeter. While applying tension as if using a normal key to open the lock, the bump key is struck with a small hammer or screwdriver. This sends energy to the pins causing the driver pins to jump past the shear line and allowing the plug to turn.

The bump key can be made even more effective by adding a rubber o-ring that acts like a spacer. Insert it all the way in and strike the bump key while applying pressure. Give it a couple more hard taps if needed to unlock. Bump keys are fast and easy to use and require little skill compared to traditional lock picking methods.

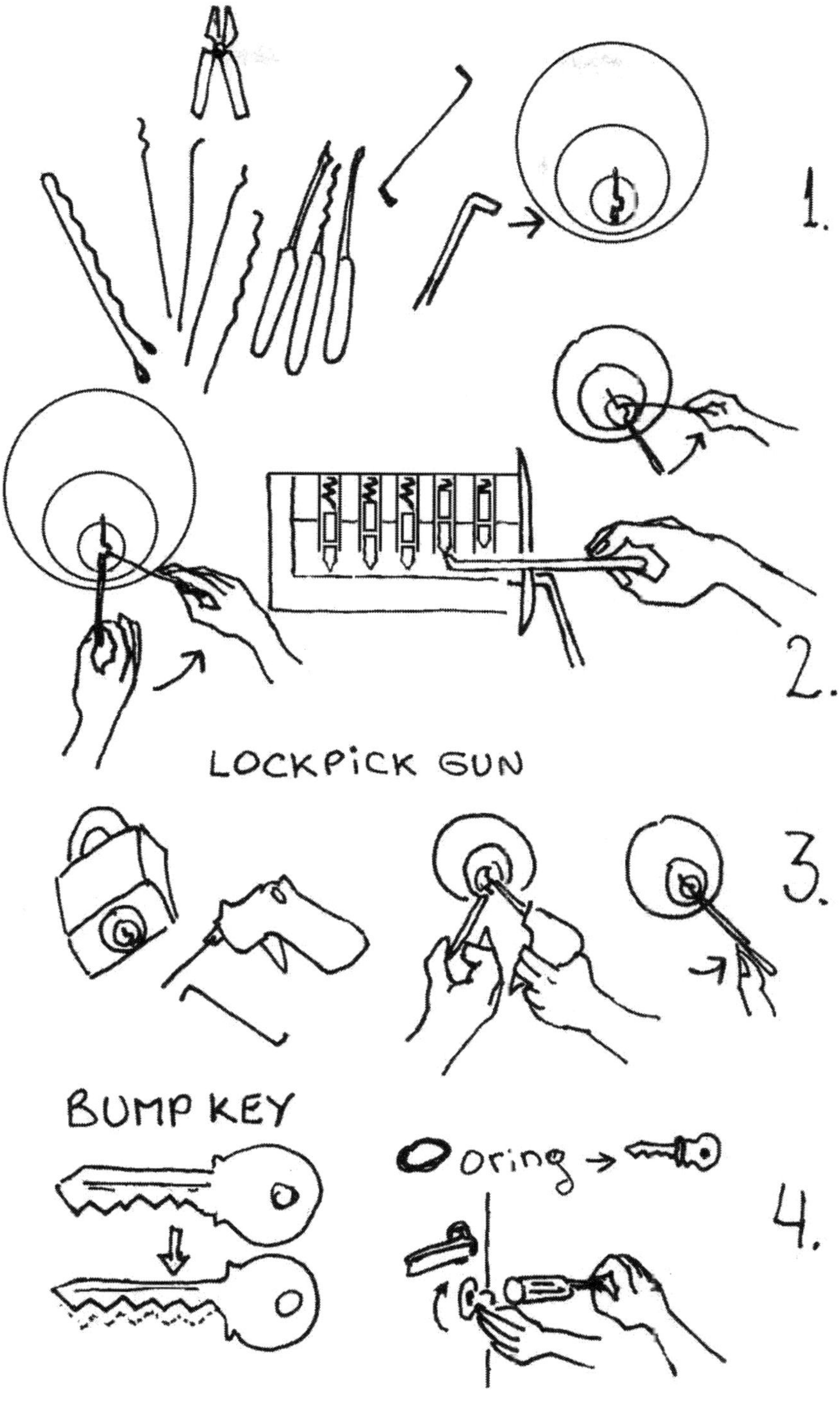
1.
2.
LOCKPICK GUN
3.
BUMP KEY
oring
4.

Door Breaching

There can be several instances in which you may have to breach a door. House fires or someone unconscious locked inside and in need of assistance are just two of the most common examples.

1) Bashing a door with your shoulder is unlikely to work on anything other than the weakest, most fragile doors on the market. Kicking a door is preferable. It's more effective and less likely to leave you injured.

2) Before attempting to kick a door open, check the hinges to see if it swings in or out. If you see the hinges, then it swings towards you and kicking it won't work. The door will have to be kicked to pieces to get through, something you will only archive with weak, thin doors.

3) Standing in front of the door, give it a powerful frontal kick, committing to it by putting as much of your weight into it as possible. Aim to the side or just below the door knob. Your goal here is to break the wooden frame which is usually the weakest part of the door. A solid wood door with three inch screws will present a challenge. A reinforced security door on a metal frame will be impossible to kick open. If expecting trouble from people on the inside don't just stand there. Right after you kick it open pivot away from the door to take cover.

4) Shotguns are often used to breach doors. These are loaded with door breaching frangible rounds made of compressed metal dust that disintegrates on impact preventing ricochet. Aim between the lock and doorjamb at a 45 degree angle, both vertical and horizontal.

5) If the shotgun has a breaching muzzle brake it can be placed directly against the door. If not give it an inch or two for gases to escape.

6) If the door won't open after shooting the lock, you may need to shoot the hinges.

7) Kicking backwards can work well on certain occasions. It is not as powerful as a frontal kick but it may be enough for weaker doors.

The advantage is that, as you kick it, you can do so while exposing a lot less of your body.

8) If there are bad guys inside, keep in mind that the moment you kick the door open, all eyes (and all guns) will be on you. You will be standing there in the "funnel of death", exposed to everyone on the inside, your profile perfectly outlined.

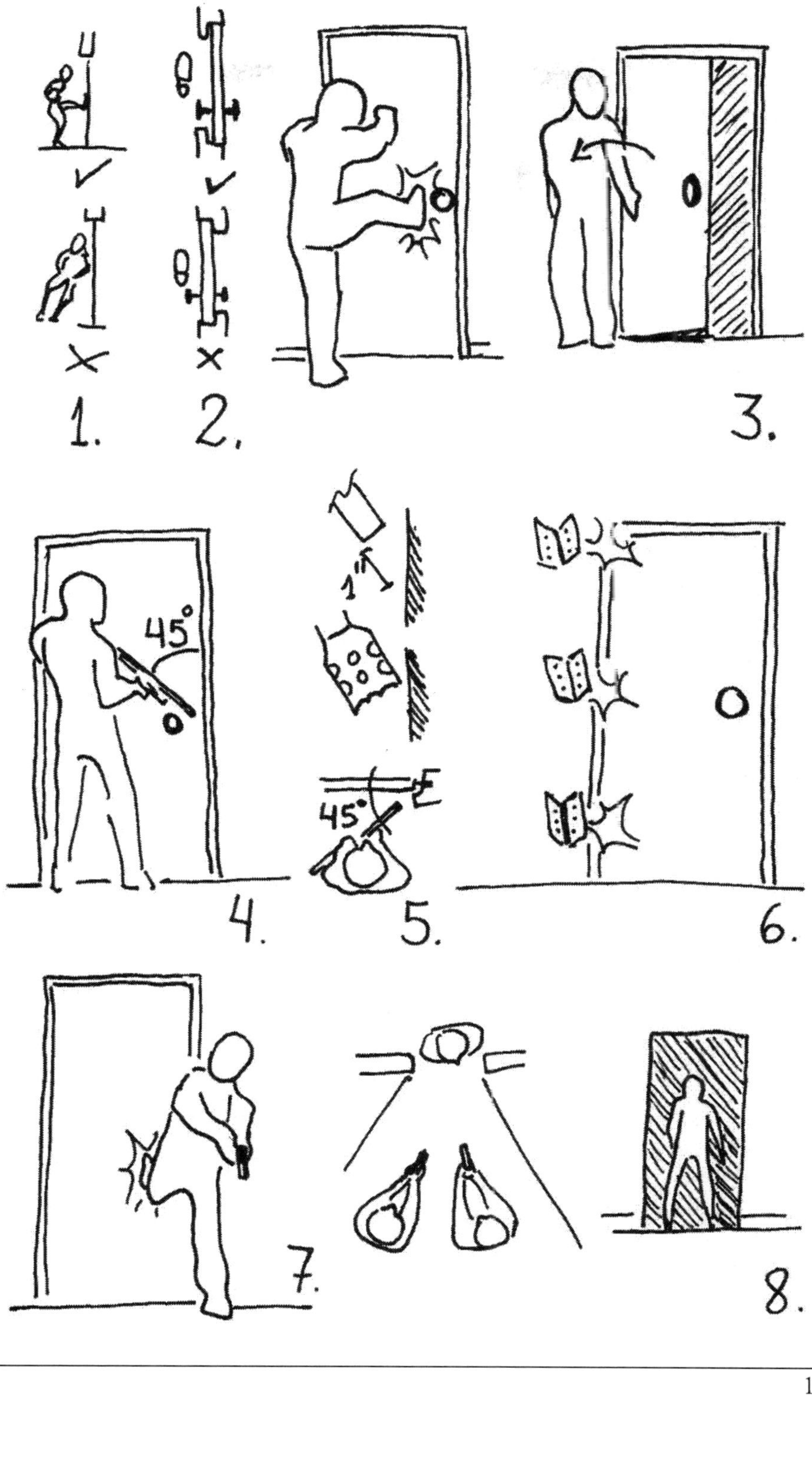
1.
2.
3.
45°
4.
1"
45°
5.
6.
7.
8.

Sometimes we can use tools we find lying around to gain access. There are few things the humble power grinder can't cut through but even simple toolbox contents and hardware supplies can be used.

9) Paint rollers are fairly common in job sites. They can also be found in stores and there's a good chance to come across one in workshops and garages. Remove the screw or nut that keeps the roller in place. Pull the roller out, leaving you with just the hook and handle.

You now have a hook that can be used to open certain double exit doors[8] from the outside.

This is just one possible way in which the paint roller can be used. The hook can be bent so as to adapt it to different needs and different type of locking mechanisms.

10) A padlock can be busted using two wrenches.

Pick the largest wrenches you can find that will still fit inside the shackle.

Place each wrench against the side of the shackle, with the back of the spanners making contact. This contact area will be your pivot point. The larger the wrench and the longer the shaft, the more force you will be able to apply using leverage.

Make sure you look away as you bust the shackle. A lot of force goes in breaking a padlock and small pieces may fly in all directions.

This is the most widely known method of busting a padlock using wrenches but it is not the most efficient.

11) A better use of force would be to pull the shackle up, rather than busting it sideways. Pulling up engages the weakest part of the shackle, requiring less force to break it. This may make a big difference if all you have are smaller wrenches or you need to improvise so as to apply leverage with tools of shorter length which apply less force.

Place one of the wrenches flat on the body within the shackle. Place the second wrench perpendicularly with the shackle inside the opening.

Press down on the wrench. The end of the wrench will push the shackle up, ripping it open.

Other tools can be used applying the same principle.

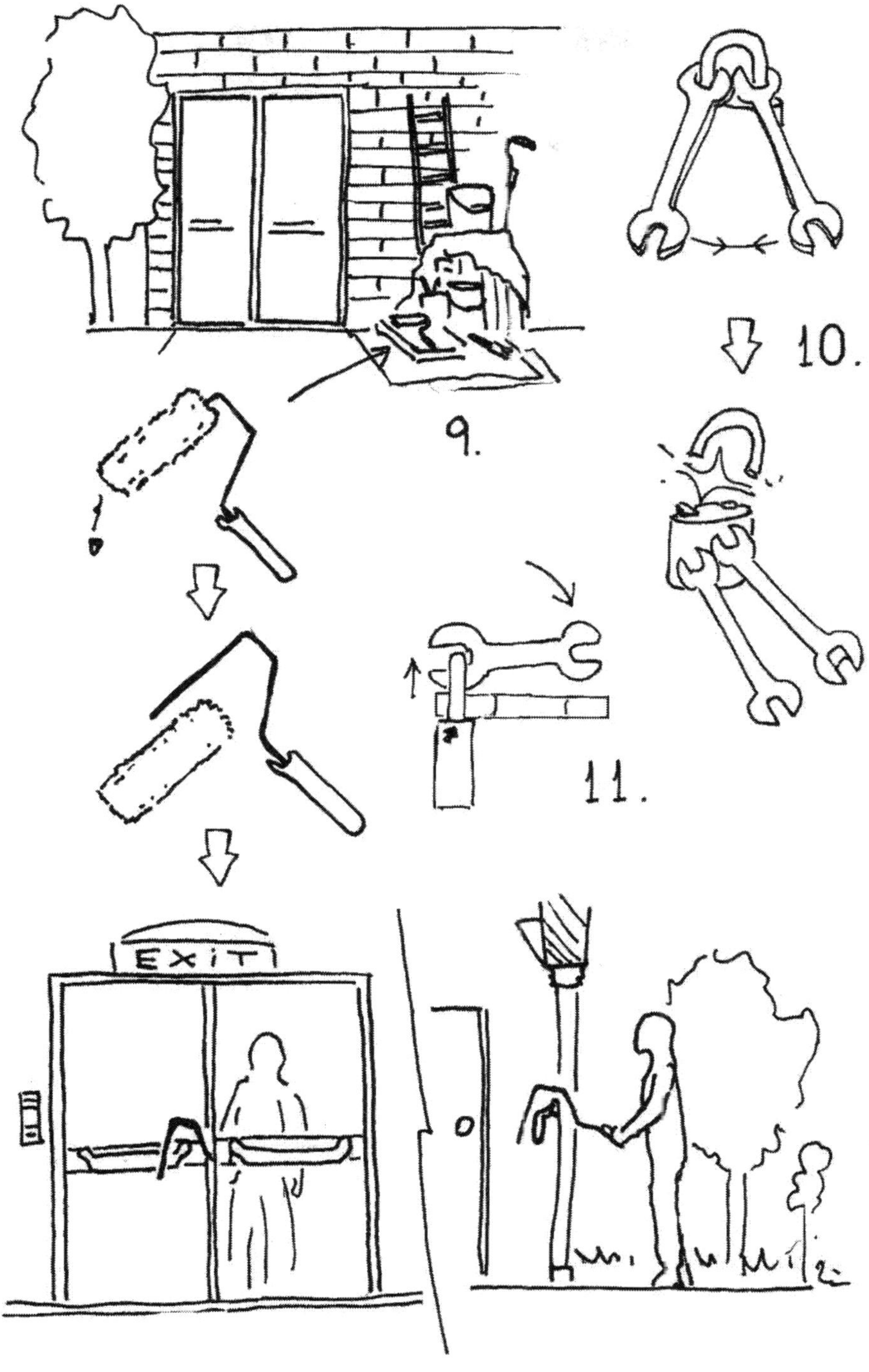
9.
10.
11.
EXIT

Barricade a Door

Knowing how to properly barricade a door is an important skill when it comes to surviving terrorist attacks and mass shooters. Attacks generally occur indoors. Knowing what to do and doing it fast greatly improves your chances of survival. While many of these techniques aren't perfect, a mad man looking to kill people will rarely waste much time trying to figure out how to open a door and will move to the next one once he isn't able to walk right in as he initially expected.

1) Know what kind of door you are working with. If you see the hinges, it means it swings into the room you are in. If you don't, it means it swings out. Look at the door handle. The most common type is a lever handle. These are easier to secure than rounded door knobs if you find a way to keep the lever from going down.

2) Using a rope, cable, belt or tie, simply fold it and use a cow hitch knot to quickly tie around the door handle. Tie the other end around any nearby object such as other door handles, pipes or handrail.

3) While other people look for ways to barricade the door, keep the attacker from opening the door by using a belt, tie, scarf, extension cord, purse or backpack sling or any other cordage you can improvise. Tie a knot around the handle and step aside in case he shoots through the door. Most common doors are not bullet proof.

4) Pile as much furniture as you can to barricade a door. If possible, align furniture against the opposite wall so that an inward swinging door cannot be opened. A large table or desk can be used to barricade the portal of an outward swinging door.

5) A common college prank, some inward swinging doors can be jammed by stack pennies (about 2 to 6) placed at the top and bottom of the door, jammed as tight as you can. This creates pressure between the door latch assembly and the striker plate.

6) A chair can be used to hold the door, giving you greater leverage.

7) In some double doors, chairs can be used to barricade the door and keep it from swinging open.

8) Large screwdrivers, knives and other tools can be wedged under the door on the same side as the handle, and kicked hard to jam the door shut. With enough pressure the door will not open, but this technique depends on the size of the tool used, how hard has it been kicked in and how much friction there is with the floor.

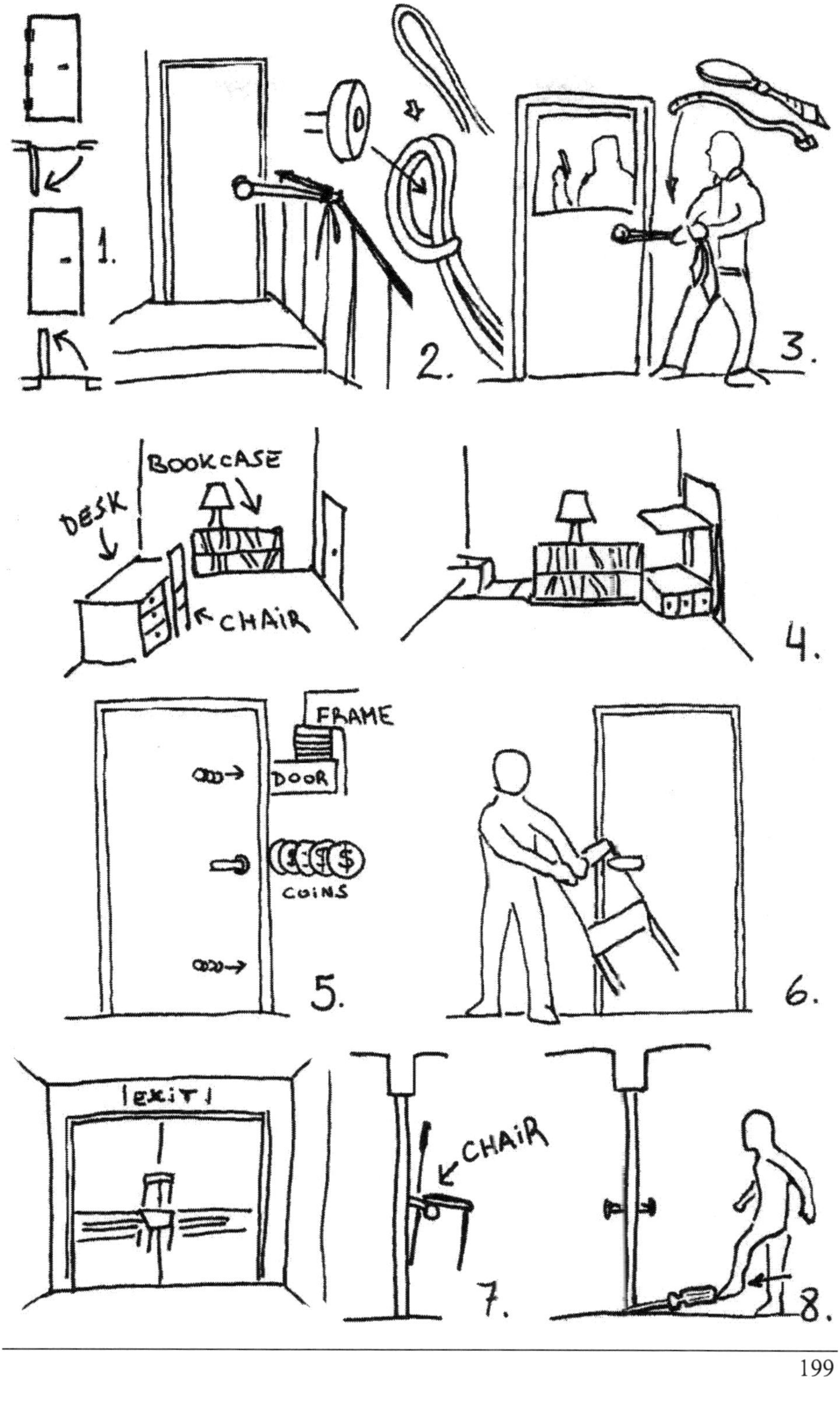
1.
2.
3.
BOOKCASE
DESK
CHAIR
4.
FRAME
DOOR
COINS
5.
6.
EXIT
CHAIR
7.
8.

9) Sometimes a screwdriver can be used to jam a door knob.

Shove the tip between the door and the frame. Jam the screwdriver under the door handle. With some door handles, the screwdriver will keep the handle from rotating and opening the door.

10) Look around your office. In many offices and classrooms there's a good chance of finding and adjustable swivel chair next to a desk.

Jamming a chair under the door knob rarely works as well as in the movies. The chair either easily slips when someone opens the door or the back just isn't the right height.

An adjustable desk chair has a lever underneath used to regulate the height to each person's needs. This can also be used to adjust the chain so as to perfectly jam a door lever.

11) Move the chair and place the back under the door lever. If it's too high step or sit on it and press the lever so as to lower the chair all the way down. Once it's under the door handle, press the adjustable lever on the chair so that it goes all the way up, adjusting perfectly so as to keep the door from opening. This will work well with some of the most common desk chairs typically found around the office.

The advantage is that it allows you to jam doors no matter if they swing in or out as long as the door has a lever handle.

Try this and other techniques ahead of time so as to know what to do during an emergency when every second counts.

12) Automatic door closers can be jammed shut with belts, ties or other cordage[9].

Take a moment to study the door closer and consider the best approach given the cordage you have at your disposal.

A possible solution is to tie the two pivot points, keeping them from moving apart. A tie, paracord or some other rope can be used for this. Remember that a lot of force goes into this mechanism when the door opens, so wrap as much cordage as you can.

13) A belt or shoulder strap can be used to keep the arms of the door closer from spreading when the door opens. Loop the belt on one of the arms, wrap the belt tight around both arms interweaving them before tying the tail of the belt.

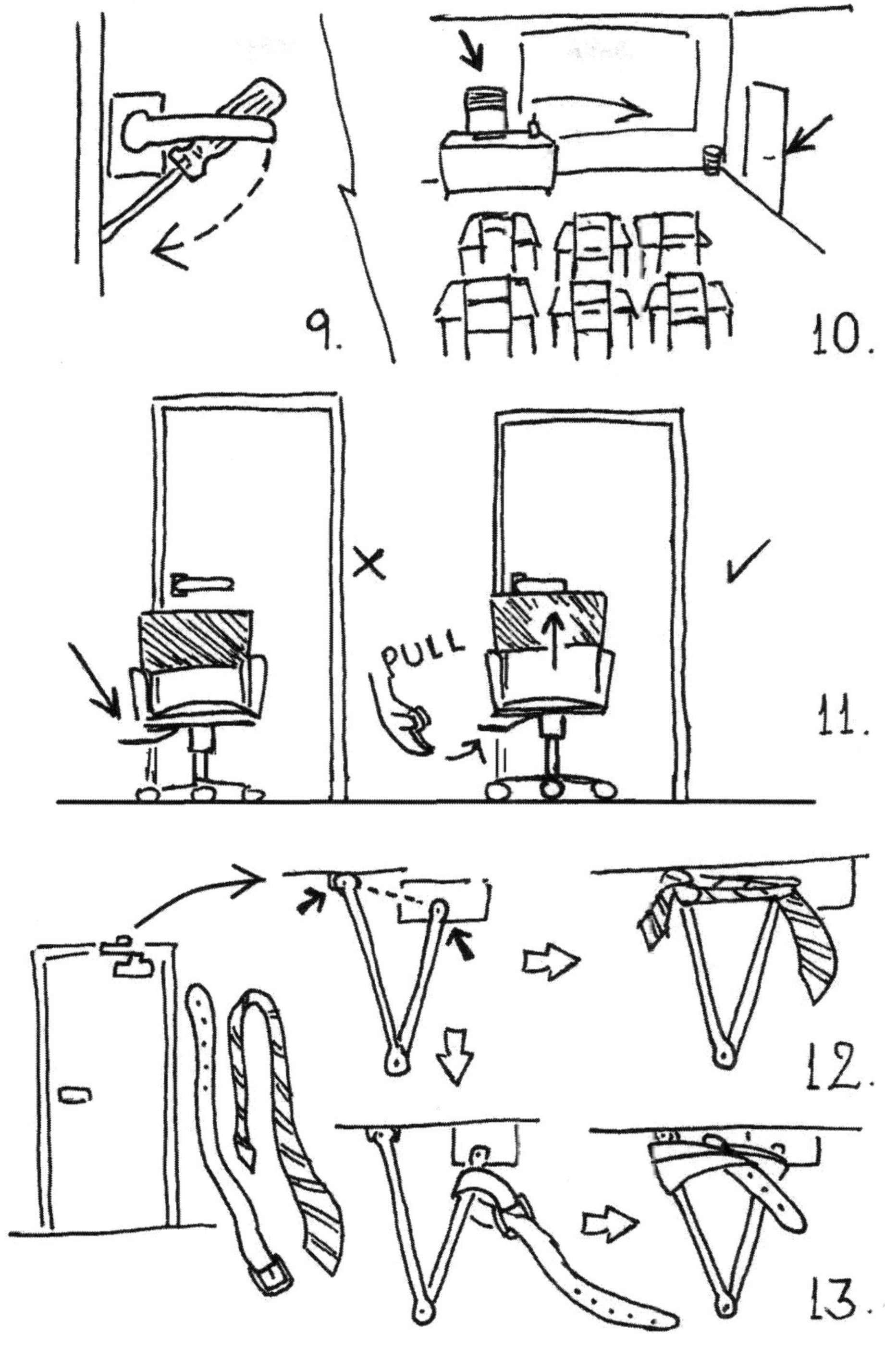
9.
10.
PULL
11.
12.
13.

NOTES:

Chapter 10
Food and Cooking

"To eat is a necessity, but to eat intelligently is an art."
- Francois de La Rochefoucauld

Start a Fire

Starting a fire is an elemental survival skill to develop. Fire can be used to keep us warm, cook food and as an important morale booster, everyone gathering around the campfire during tough times.

Matches, lighters and ferrocerium rods are plentiful but building a proper fire starting with tinder and larger pieces of wood is more challenging.

1) An effective fire starter can be made using typical household items. This works great for starting fireplaces, campfires or barbeques (I've been using it for decades). As a matter of fact, all you need is likely to be found on the table right next to the grill: Vegetable oil and some paper napkins. Toilet paper can be used as well. Grab a couple paper napkins and press them tight into a ball. Use two more to wrap around the ball you just made, like a cup. Pour some vegetable oil over the paper ball. The cup will keep it from spilling. Place the wood, lump charcoal or briquettes around the fire starter and light it up. The fire starter will burn for several minutes. The more oil you use the longer it burns.

2) Electricity can be used to create heat and get an actual flame going. You can use a AA battery (other batteries of similar voltage or greater will work too) and a gum, cigarette or candy wrap, the kind that has a metallic surface. Cut the wrap into strips in the shape of an hourglass. You can use scissors but it can be done with your fingers alone if careful. You want a fine strip about 2mm wide between the two wider ends.

Using the metal side of the wrap, connect the positive end of the battery with the negative end. Use paper or cardboard spacers so as to not burn your fingers. Have tinder ready next to the narrow area since this will instantly heat up and produce a tiny flame. If this doesn't work, try cutting the paper so that it's even narrower and more likely to ignite.

Fire can be started using a 9 volt battery (often found in smoke detectors) and steel wool. Just dragging the battery contacts across the steel wool will ignite it, burning the small strands of steel.

A cell phone battery can be used along with metal foil in a similar manner to start a fire. Simply stabbing a battery with a knife will cause a violent exothermic reaction but this is not a recommended method. Besides emitting toxic fumes, it can only be done once. A few small strips of gum wrap or metal foil along with the phone battery allows you to start multiple fires. The flame will likely be very small so have fine tinder such as cotton or similar fibers next to the foil before making contact. The battery also needs to be charged for this to work.

PAPER NAPKIN
VEG. OIL
PAPER BALL
VEG. OIL

1.

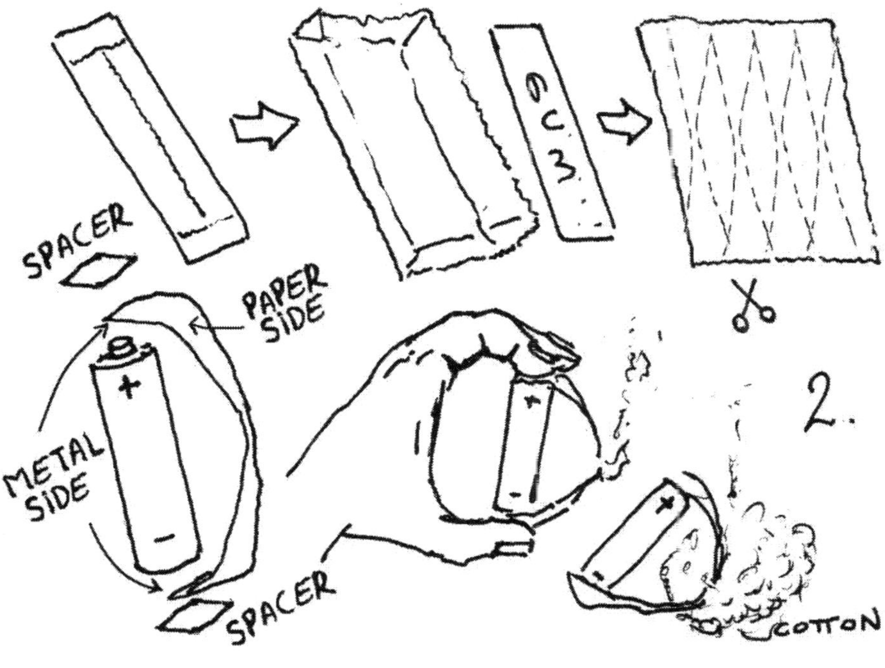
GUM
SPACER
PAPER SIDE
METAL SIDE
SPACER
COTTON

2.

Filtering and Purifying Water

Diseases cause the most deaths during large-scale disasters. This is strongly linked to the lack of clean, safe water.

1) One of the most effective ways of killing dangerous bacteria and make water safer to drink is by using pure household bleach. Filter the water with a cloth or coffee filter before treating. You want to use pure bleach, unscented with no additives. The Center of Diseases Control[10] (CDC) and United States Environmental Protection Agency[11] (EPA) recommend the following dosage: For 5-6% household liquid chlorine bleach add 8 drops to 1 gallon of water or 2 drops for 1 quart/liter. For 8.25% household liquid chlorine bleach - add 6 drops to 1 gallon of water or 2 drops for 1 quart/liter. A quart is not a liter, but it is close enough for the purposes of disinfecting water. If water is cloudy, double the dosage of bleach. Mix well and wait at least 30 minutes before using.

2) Bleach and other methods can be used to disinfect water, but they don't remove toxic chemicals and radioactive pollutants. One of the best methods to get rid of most contaminants is distillation. This can be achieved using specialized equipment. Improvised distillation units can be very effective as well if properly constructed.

3) Solar water disinfection (SODIS) can be a viable method under certain circumstances[12]. It uses both heat and UV light to disinfect water. SODIS requires clear water since turbidity reduces its effectiveness. PET soft drink bottles are well suited for this method. Fill soda bottles with low-turbidity water. Shake the bottles to oxygenate. Place the bottles on a roof or rack for 6 hours if sunny or for 2 days for cloudy weather.

4) Always use quality commercial water filters whenever possible. If you can't, an improvised filter can be made. Cut the bottom of a soda bottle. Place a coffee filter or cloth on the inside up against the neck of the bottle. You may need to place some large pebbles first to keep the cloth from going through the neck of the bottle. Stack layers of activated charcoal, fine sand, activated charcoal, fine sand and gravel. Place coffee filters or pieces of cloth between the layers.

5) A piece of cloth, two cups and gravity can be used to filter water. This does not purify water but the capillarity does remove particles and improves the clarity of the water. It's a slow process and may take up to an hour to fill a small cup.

6) Boiling is a proven method of water disinfection. Using a lid, boil the water for at least one minute or three minutes when above 6,500 feet.

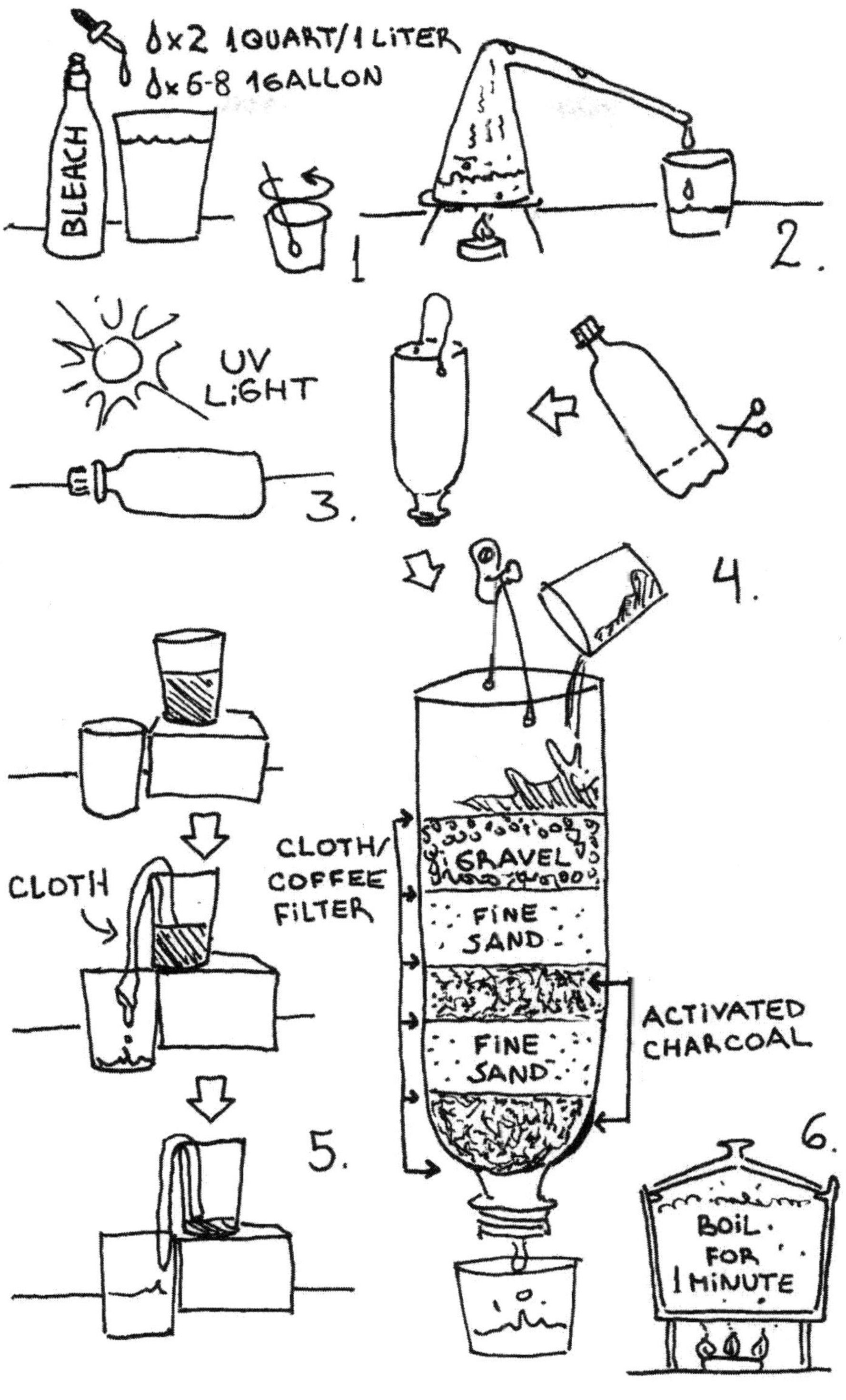
x2 1QUART/1 LITER
x 6-8 1GALLON
BLEACH
1
2.
UV
LIGHT
3.
4.
CLOTH/
COFFEE
FILTER
GRAVEL
FINE
SAND
ACTIVATED
CHARCOAL
FINE
SAND
CLOTH
5.
6.
BOIL
FOR
1 MINUTE

Food Storage

A reasonable stockpile of food should be procured. You should have no less than a month worth of food, ideally six to twelve months. Unlike other preps which you may never use, eating isn't optional. You will eat, no matter if a disaster occurs or not. Specialty long term rations such as MRE (meals ready to eat) or freeze dried "prepper" food can be expensive. Fortunately, your grocery store has everything you need. It's just a matter of knowing what to stockpile and how to store it. You should also consider your daily diet. You want to store what you eat, eat what you store, thus rotating your supplies and get used to cooking with the food you keep in the pantry.

1) Wheat, lentils, rice, beans and corn, these store well for up to two years if kept in a sealed bag in a cool dark place, but properly vacuum sealed, those same staples will last decades. Canned vegetables such as peas and carrots or canned tuna, these all have long term expiration dates and can be safely consumed well past those dates as well.

2) A cheap and simple method is to use plastic soda bottles. These must be properly cleaned and perfectly dried. The soda bottle alone is a far better container that the brittle bag most grocery staples come in. Introducing an oxygen absorber will allow them to store for many more years. Oxygen absorbers are used depending on the volume of the container you intend to use them in (CC). The volume of oxygen it can absorb isn't perfectly accurate. Don't hesitate to use an extra oxygen absorber or two, especially when sealing larger buckets of food. Keep in mind the volume of air in the food you store. Rice and lentils are small and leave fewer pockets of air, thus require less oxygen absorption. Beans or macaroni have much larger pockets of air between them.

3) Small and medium sized Mylar bags can be used to properly vacuum seal food. Fill them with food, add the oxygen absorbers needed leaving enough bag to seal correctly. Remove as much air as you can and seal the bag with a hair straightener. Verify that the oxygen has been removed and that the Mylar bag is tight against the food. Smaller bags can be stacked like bricks.

4) Mylar alone does not provide much physical protection. The best way to store food is combining Mylar with hard plastic containers such as five gallon buckets. Given the large size of the bag, seal them leaving plenty of room for resealing after use. Check you buckets regularly and don't be complacent. Rats will easily chew through plastic to get to the food inside.

WHEAT LENTILS RICE BEANS CORN
1.
OXIGEN ABSORBER
SODA BOTTLE
20 years
2.
OXIGEN ABSORBER
LENTILS DATE
LENTILS DATE
LENTILS DATE
3.
OXIGEN ABSORBER
RESEAL
4.

Recipes

Rice has to be one of the most versatile food staples. It stores well, has adequate nutritional value and is easy enough to cook. It is a fantastic "filler" for numerous recipes. Rice and lentils go together nicely too. Lentils have more protein and overall a more complete nutritional value. It combines especially well with brown rice.

In our household we do one variety of rice or another several times a week. It is out "go to" recipe when something needs to be cooked with whatever happens to be around. Rice and lentil stews are also popular.

1) The most typical recipe used in our house is Spanish organic rice, peas, tomatoes and carrots. Some lentils can go in there as well but rice alone with vegetables makes for a nice light meal. The rice and lentil combo seems to be more popular in winter and autumn. A bit of salt can be added if you want but it is not necessary. If there's some chicken in the fridge or some beef, it can be chopped and thrown in the mix.

2) For preparing yellow rice, a good amount of turmeric is added. It gives the rice a nice color and has several health benefits such as boosting antioxidants and being a natural anti-inflammatory. You want to stock up turmeric in your pantry so as to have the option of preparing white rice, yellow rice or rice and lentil stews.

3) During hot summer days a popular choice is going with rice (yellow or white), carrots and peas, wait until it cools down and then serve it with some tuna on top. This goes great with fresh tomatoes and green leafs.

4) For winter time you can go a bit more heavy on the lentils, make it maybe 70% lentils, 30% rice. Add some tomato sauce and a bit of white pepper. If you have some beef and potatoes to chop and throw in the pot it makes for a good hearty winter meal.

5) This isn't about going vegan. It's about not wasting food. If you are left with some 50/50 rice and lentil stew leftovers you can try doing some veggie burgers. No, they sure aren't meat burgers but if you are stuck eating rice and lentils after the end of the world for months at a time I bet you will want to give it a go. Simply put the leftovers in the fridge and when cool, scoop some, form a patty and put it in a pan, grill or skillet with a few drops of olive oil. Don't cook it! You just want to give it a light brown golden color. While still hot, put some cheese on top and let it melt. Add some tomato, lettuce and buns.

Not a real burger but still surprisingly good and worth a try!

RICE\LENTIL STEW

VEGGIE BURGER

6) Popular both for adult an kids, banana pancakes taste great and are simple enough to do.

You'll need a banana, a mature one a bit past its prime will do just fine. 1/3 cup of flour, 1 egg. Mix these together and you have some tasty banana pancakes. Home-made and free of any refined sugar. If you have some vanilla exact around, you can add a couple drops for a bit more flavour. A couple tablespoons of orange juice works fine too. If you have some fresh blueberries you can put some in the mix. The blueberries will give it that extra flavour to bite into.

This mix is good for four small pancakes. Mix it well and pour it on a pan. No oil or butter needed when using pans with a non-stick layer.

Cook it for a few minutes on each side at medium heat, checking often so as to not overcook it. Done!

7) Crepes (like a very thin pancake) are another way to go. The recipe is very easy.

1 Cup of flour, 2 cups of milk (you can use milk made with powdered milk), 3 eggs and 2 tablespoons of sugar. Mix well for a few minutes. You can do it by hand although an electric mixer is fasters and a bit better. For better results, put the mix on the fridge for 20 minutes before using.

Heat a pan and melt a bit of butter on it before pouring a spoonful of mix. Give it a few seconds and flip it to the other side. Flipping them with a flick of the wrist without messing them up is possible but it takes some practice. Before you do another crepe, melt another piece of butter. Crepes are supposed to be thinner than pancakes but taste great too. You can put whatever it is you like inside, roll them and eat them. Dulce de leche (type of caramel, but much better) is simply perfect for this. Talking about dulce de leche…

8) Dulce de leche can be made using a can of sweet condensed milk. Remove the paper label from the can and put it in a pot. Place a towel or dish cloth in the bottom before you fill it up with water so that is doesn't rattle when it starts boiling. Make sure the can is completely covered with water. Put a lid on and boil for two and a half to three hours or a bit more defending on how dark you want your dulce de leche.

Once the dulce de leche is done put it on a glass jar before it cools and keep it in the fridge for up to six months.

Wait until it cools and done! You have dulce de leche for crepes, pancakes, toast or anything else you want to try it on. There's nothing wrong with eating a spoonful or two straight out of the jar.

FLOUR
1. BANANA
1. EGG
1/3 CUP OF FLOUR
VANILLA\OJ
6.
COND MILK
1 CUP FLOUR
2 CUPS MILK
3 EGGS
2TBS. SUGAR
7.
COND MILK
8.

Make a Can Stove

The Fancy Feast stove, also known as the cat food can stove or tuna can stove is one of the most simple yet most effective stoves you can make. Pots sit on top of it so it requires no stand to be used. You can use a hole punch or you can just punch a few holes with the punch/reamer of your pocket knife or multi-tool. Either way, both work quite well.

1) A 3oz. tuna or cat food can works fine for most small pots. Keep in mind that since the can works also as the stand, if you want to use bigger pots a bigger can may be needed. You can use the punch in a Swiss army knife to punch the holes.

2) Punch two rows of 21 holes for a total of 42 (Hobo42). Go all the way with the punch and try to make the holes as big and as round as possible but don't worry if it's not perfectly rounded. The sharp edges on the inside will help heat the can faster and work as it's supposed to.

3) Denatured alcohol, grain alcohol or even rubbing alcohol can be used. 20 ml (4 tablespoons) should be enough to boil a large cup of water (about 300 ml).

4) Carefully lit the stove. Make sure to keep the alcohol bottle at a distance when you do this.

5) Give it two or three minutes until the can heats up. You want the evaporated alcohol to go out the side through the holes when you put a pot on top. If putting a pot on top of the stove simply extinguishes the flame, then it needs to heat up more. Lit it again and give it a bit more time before putting the pot on top.

6) With the pot on top, the stove should look like a regular gas burner with blue flames coming out the sides.

7) So as to get the water to boil faster, it's a good idea to use a lid. If one isn't available it can be improvised with aluminium foil.

Aluminium foil can also be used to make a wind shield around the stove.

8) Using a hole punch, punch two rows of sixteen holes each for a total of thirty two. Doing just one row of holes (16 holes) allows you to fill it up with more alcohol and will use less of it, burning longer. It will also require more time to heat up and more time to get water boiling.

Since making these stoves is so easy, make different models and see which one works best for you. Try making ones with more or less holes of different sizes, using one, two or three rows of holes depending on the size of the can.

1.
3oz. CAN
HOBO42
ALCOHOL
2.
3.
4.
5.
6.
7.
FOIL
LID
8.

Thermos Cooking and Shopping Cart Grill

Thermos cooking is a fantastic way of cooking food when you have little fuel and little water available. This makes it ideal for survivalists or preppers looking to cook using limited resources. It also requires a simple common thermos. Make sure the thermos is stainless steel and not one of the models made of glass on the inside.

1) Use a cup or two of food. You can somewhat eyeball this and it also depends on the food you're cooking but try leaving about two thirds of the thermos empty so as to fill it up with water.

On colder climates or when cooking tougher food like lentils, you also want to preheat your thermos by putting boiling water in it for a minute, take it out, and only then add the food.

Once you have the food inside quickly fill it up with boiling water. Close the thermos and give it a couple good shakes to mix it up. If the thermos isn't very good you can wrap it up with a towel so as to improve the heat retention.

Pasta cooks in about 15 to 20 minutes. Rice will take about 5 to 8 hours depending on the type of rice, ratio of rice to boiling water and even the barometric pressure. Lentils take 10 hours or a bit less if you pre-soaked them. Don't rush it and let the thermos do its thing. One of the nice things about thermos cooking is that you won't overcook the food. It will be warm and ready for you. You can even cook meat in a thermos. The smaller the bits of meat the faster it will cook, so cut them small!

2) Another improvised cooking method I've seen several times is using a shopping cart as a grill.

The cart can be turn sideways on the floor or rolled on top of the fire.

One cart I came across once had the side that goes up when they are stacked removed. It was later attached horizontally to the inside of the cart, jury rigged with wire or welded so as to be used as a grill. The bottom of the cart had some corrugated metal to hold the fire, effectively making a portable barbeque grill.

Tip: Post-collapse business idea: One person I saw once was using this BBQ-grill cart contraption to make a living, selling burgers on the street. He would park outside a couple factories in the industrial district and cater for the workers during lunchtime.

Selling affordable, tasty burgers to blue-collar workers, he couldn't grill those things fast enough.

RiCE
STEEL
BOIL
1.
DONE!

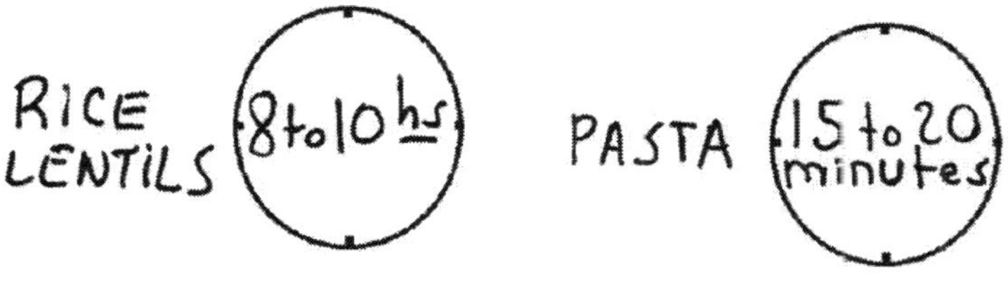
RICE
LENTILS
8 to 10 hrs
PASTA
15 to 20 minutes

2.

NOTES:

Chapter 11
First Aid and Sanitation

"If you are not your own doctor, you are a fool."
-Hippocrates

First Aid and Home Remedies

1) Gargling with warm salt water to treat a sore throat is one of the better known home remedies. A faster and in some ways better method is to open wide, pull the head back, stick your tongue out and say "ah" as you shake the salt shaker a couple times. The salt quickly dehydrates the area, killing the bacteria like it would kill a slug.

2) Super glue (Cyanoacrylate) is often used to close small wounds instead of stitches with good results. The wound needs to be properly cleaned first. Knife and other clean cuts are good candidates.

3) Butterfly (closure) strips can be improvised using ordinary medical tape. Simply cut a piece, twist it into a ribbon and use it to close the wound. The ribbon will minimize the contact area on the wound while keeping it closed. A strip can be placed on both sides for additional support. A neat trick if only one hand is available it to cut the strip, stick one side to keep it in place, twist the strip 360 degrees to create the ribbon and stick it on the other side of the wound.

4) When it comes to haemorrhages (bleeding) the first way to try to stop it is applying direct pressure[13]. When possible, elevate the wound above the heart. Pressure needs to be applied with a clean pad, gauze or cloth. Apply pressure until the bleeding stops. Don't remove it if it gets soaked. Instead, place another pad on top and keep applying direct pressure. Once the bleeding stops, tie the padding to keep it in place.

5) If the bleeding can't be stopped through direct pressure, a tourniquet may be needed[14 15]. Tourniquets can be effective when applied to limbs but it also means that the blood flow to the limb is interrupted. They can also cause skin, muscle and nerve damage. If left unattended the limb dies and may require amputation. This is why it's so important to write down the time in which the tourniquet is applied. Combat Application Tourniquet (CAT) have a slot for writing the time. Write "T" on the victim's forehead so that emergency response personnel know it was applied. Use the victim's own blood to do this if you don't have a pen.

Wide cordage (at least 2 inches wide) such as belts, straps and ties can be used. The tourniquet is applied two to four inches from the wound, between the wound and heart. Wrap it around the limb several times, keeping the material as flat as you can. Tie a knot, place the stick on top and tie another knot. Use a pen or stick to twist the tourniquet tight until the bleeding stops completely but don't keep turning once the bleeding stops. Secure the stick with the loose ends of the tourniquet.

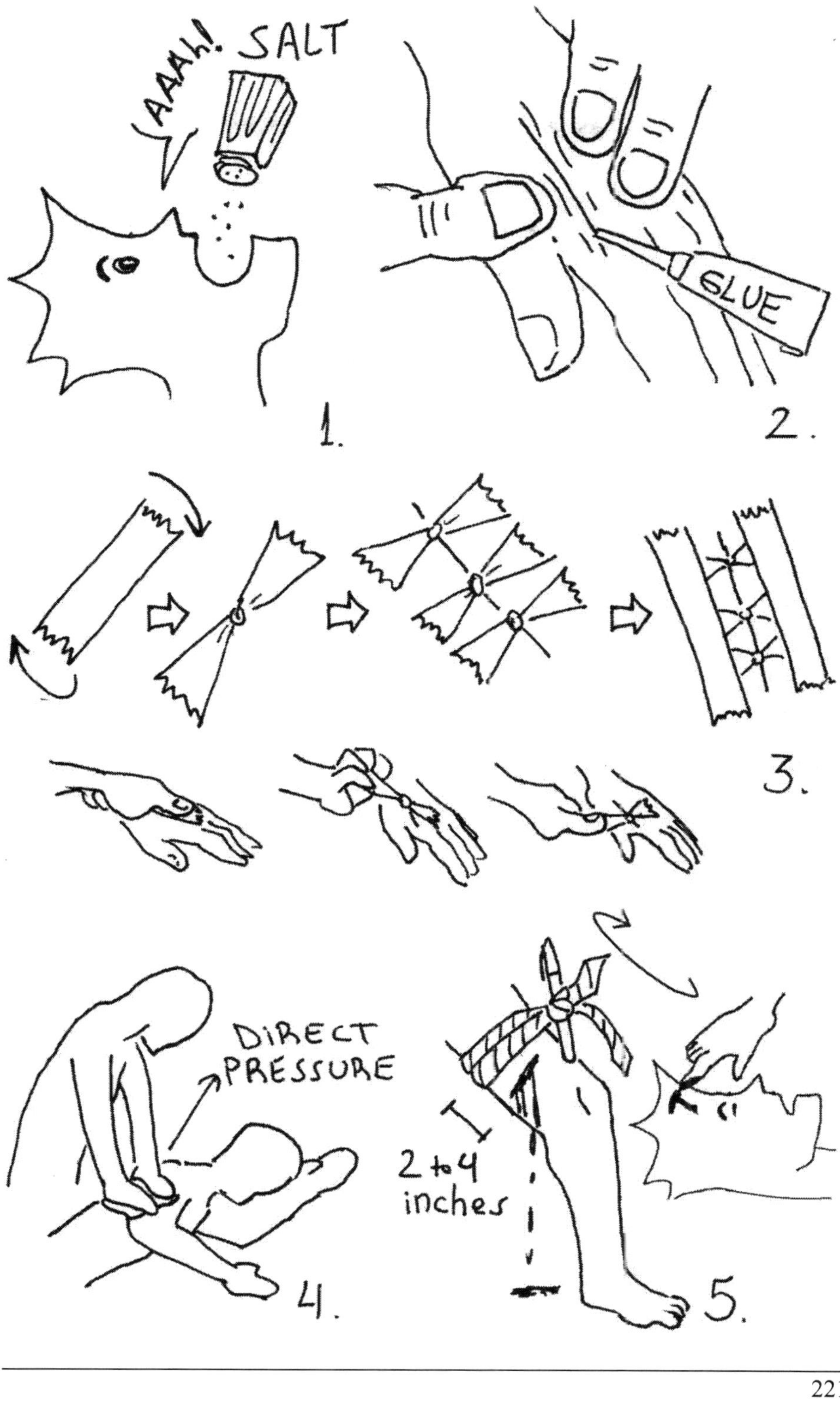
AAAH!
SALT
1.
GLUE
2.
3.
DIRECT PRESSURE
4.
2 to 4 inches
5.

6) A useful trick for dealing with minor injuries, if a finger gets smashed or otherwise crushed (hammer, pliers accident) apply pressure to it and keep it elevated above the head for several minutes.

7) Doing this greatly reduces the swelling and formation of blood blisters typical in this kind of injury. The swelling and in particular the blood blisters are a nuisance. Applying pressure in the injured area may prevent their appearance to a great degree.

8) Fevers are uncomfortable but high fevers can be downright dangerous. If the fever is too high, 40.0 or 41.5 °C (104.0 or 106.7 °F) or more, immediate medical attention is needed. This is known as Hyperpyrexia. The elevated temperature may damage organs, in particular the brain or even lead to death. The first course of action for fever[16] is rest, drinking plenty of fluids and medication such as paracetamol or ibuprofen.

A simple and effective way of reducing body temperature is through baths[17]. Start with a bath with warm water and slowly add cold water, bringing the temperature down gradually. Make sure you have a good thermometer to frequently check the progress.

9) For fevers that are less severe, a damp cloth placed on the forehead helps reduce the body temperature. Soak the cloth frequently to cool it down. You can also place a wet rag on the elbow pit (cubital fossa), that spot where nurses stick a needle to draw blood.

This method works particularly well in children due to their smaller bodies.

10) Bumps to the head and other forms of blunt force trauma are also fairly common. Applying an ice pack immediately after the injury occurs is one of the oldest, tried-and-true methods for reducing both pain, swelling and recovery time.

The cold temperature promotes vasoconstriction, the tightening of the blood vessels. As the blood vessels contract, less fluid flows towards the injured area reducing the swelling. Pain is also relieved as the nerves also tighten. The faster the cold pack is applied to the injured area, the less swelling the person will experience. Direct contact with the ice pack is to be avoided. The pack is often wrapped in a towel or dishcloth.

11) For some injuries where you expect almost immediate swelling such as in the face, wrapping the ice pack with a wet towel or cloth will transfer the cold to the injured area much faster. After a few minutes remove the pack so as to not freeze the skin on the injured area. Keep applying the ice pack frequently to minimize the swelling and bruising.

!@#
6.
7.
40°C
8.
9.
COLD
10.
11.

Honey has been used all over the world to treat wounds for thousands of years. Battlefield wounds in ancient Egypt have been treated with sugar. It has also been used in Africa and China.

Manuka honey[18] is commercialised and used for treating wounds given its additional antibacterial properties but common honey is adequate too.

Even common, refined sugar is used regularly to treat deep wounds[19 20]. It enhances macrophage migration, granulation, tissue formation and epithelialization. It works so well that sugar is sold by pharmaceutical companies under commercial names in the form of a sugar paste.

12) Rinse the wound with water. Remove any debris.

13) Elevate it above the head if possible so as to stop the bleeding.

14) Apply honey or sugar. Honey is gentler for skin injuries but the sugar's granulation and tissue formation may be better for deeper wounds. Cover with dressing and replace when needed, adding more sugar or honey.

15) This is a handy tip for parents with small children. Some of the medicine sold already comes with a syringe and indications on how to use it but many still come with the typical cup, which no baby in the world will ever drink from. Fortunately, a common syringe (without the needle!) can be used to administer medication to babies. Simply fill with as much medicine as you need, insert the plastic tip of the syringe in the corner of the mouth and gently pull back towards the ear. Press the syringe and the baby will swallow the liquid. This method works well because the medicine is administered behind the tongue, triggering the swallow reflex.

16) Olive oil works well for removing ear wax. It is commercially sold in pharmacies around the world under different brand names, specifically for loosening and removal of ear wax. This is a gentler, less aggressive approach compared to other ear drops that have more powerful solvents but that are more likely to irritate the ear as well.

Simply administer two or three drops of olive oil and massage the ear before going to bed. Within a couple days the wax dissolves and comes out the ear along with the olive oil.

Tip: On a personal note, a relative of mine underwent surgery in a private health facility in Buenos Aires. She was surprised to learn that the wound was to be treated with common refined sugar every time the dressing was replaced. According to her experience, it healed noticeably faster leaving less of a visible scar.

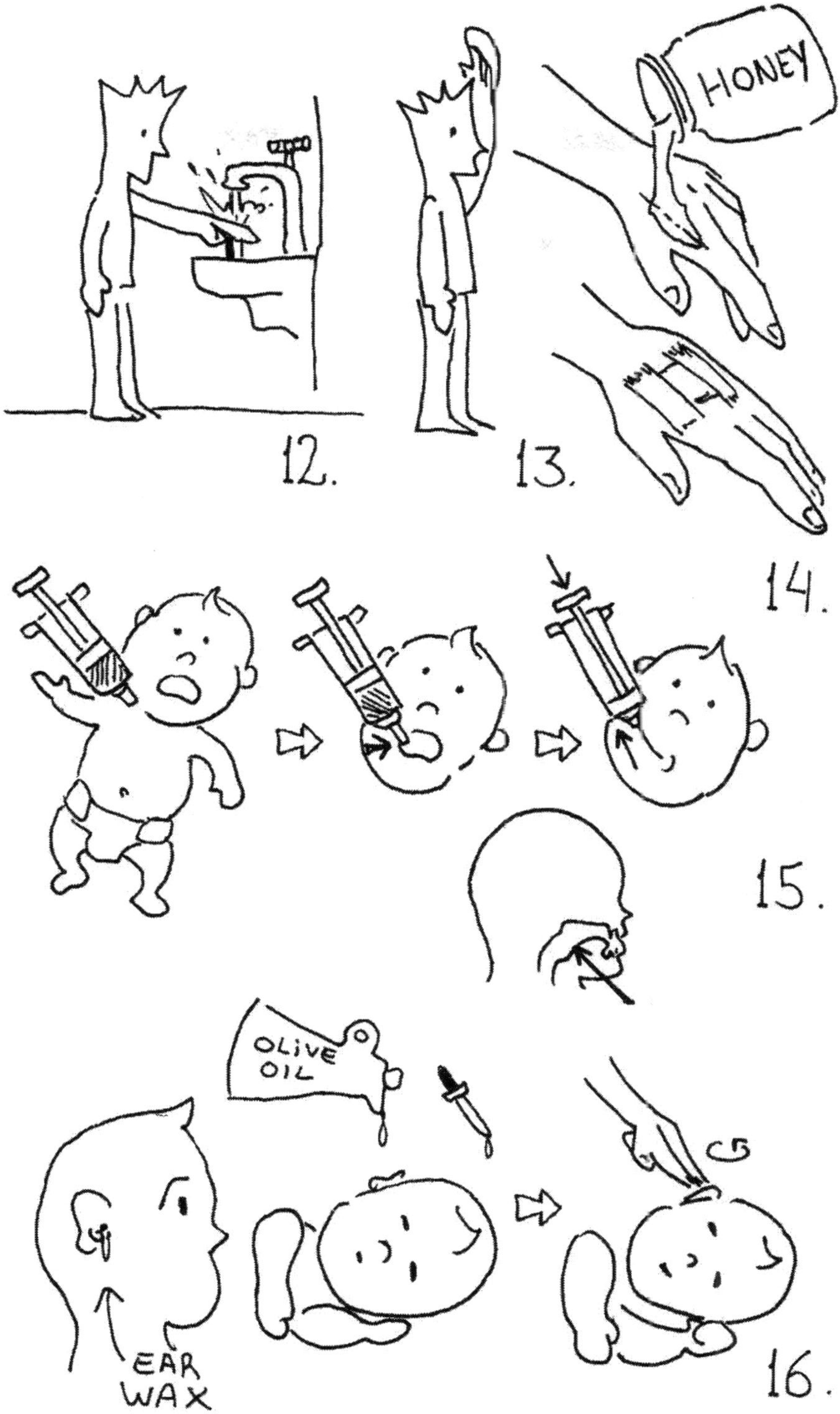
12.
13.
HONEY
14.
15.
OLIVE OIL
EAR WAX
16.

Fireman's Carry and Walk Assist

There may be times when you may have to either assist or carry a person.

Assisting a person is always preferable whenever possible since it's easier, faster and less likely to injure yourself or the casualty. Keep in mind that moving an unconscious person can injure the casualty further, cause spine damage or bleeding. Whenever possible, don't move the casualty and wait for first responders to arrive. Only attempt to move an unconscious person as a last resort.

1) Fireman's Carry[21] requires good shoulder and leg strength and it's easier to perform on a smaller person. Start by carefully rolling the casualty on their stomach, kneel in front of them and hook your arms under their armpit so as to lift them.

2) As you start lifting the casualty, bring your hands together around his back for a better grip. Keep your back straight and use your legs to rise the casualty to his feet.

3) Put your leg between the casualty's knees to help you support and stabilize him. Grab his right arm with your left hand, holding him by the wrist. Bring the hand over your head, putting your head under the casualty's armpit. Now bring the arm down to your left shoulder using his arm for leverage

4) Squat down putting your right arm around the casualty's right knee, bringing his torso over your shoulders so that the casualty's weight goes on them, distributing it as evenly as possible.

5) Get up using your legs and keeping your back as straight as possible to avoid injury. At this point you can grab the casualty's right arm with your right hand, freeing your left hand for using a weapon, opening doors, carrying gear, etc.

6) If the casualty can stand with assistance, help by putting one of his arms across your shoulder and holding the wrist with your opposite hand. Place your other arm around the casualty, holding under the armpit for additional support.

7) In certain situations dragging by the collar (or combat vest), is a fast way of moving a casualty, especially short distances. It is a simple technique that doesn't require a lot of skill or strength.

8) Dragging by the feet is uncomfortable and it risks hurting the head. It does help keep the spine in line though so in certain indoor surfaces with low friction (tiles, marble) it may be a viable alternative.

1.
2.
3.
4.
5.
6.
7.
8.

Ranger Roll

The Ranger Roll allows you to quickly pick up a person. As the name implies, it is intended for combat or similar situations where speed is the main priority. It could be enemy fire, an immediate safety hazard or some other life-threatening event. As fast as the Ranger Roll is, the technique presents two problems. First, it requires a lot of practice, dexterity and strength to perform. Second, it puts significant stress on the casualty, potentially making the injuries much worse. For spine and head injuries, even dragging the casually is a better alternative if at all possible.

It is still a valid technique but for specific high-risk situations where other methods just won't be fast enough.

1) Lift the right leg with your left arm putting one foot between the casualty's legs, keeping your knees slightly flexed.

2) Bring your right hand under the casualty's right leg. If the casualty is using cargo pants you can grab its contents for a better grip. Initiate a roll, aiming with your right shoulder to the left side of the casualty.

3) Commit to it so as to have enough momentum to make the casualty roll over you across your shoulders. Your head can roll over the casualty's torso but you want to avoid crushing him as much as possible. How much of you ends up rolling on top will also depend on the size and body type of both people. For a small, thin person it is easier to roll diagonally across them, rolling them across your back.

4) As you finish the roll you want to end up with your hips under you and your feet under your hips. You don't want to roll in such a way that you end up face down with the casualty on top of you.

5) Keep your legs under you as you finish the roll. Support yourself with one hand so as to get your body into a good position to get up, positioning the casualty comfortably across your shoulders.

6) Help yourself so as to get one leg up first. Hold the casualty's right arm with your left hand to keep him in place as you get up. Keeping your back straight, use your legs to get yourself up. Once you get up you can grab the casualty's right arm with your right hand, so as to have one hand free to use.

The Ranger Roll is easier to perform on smaller, lighter people.

Variations can be performed by first positioning yourself on the ground, holding the leg and then committing to the roll.

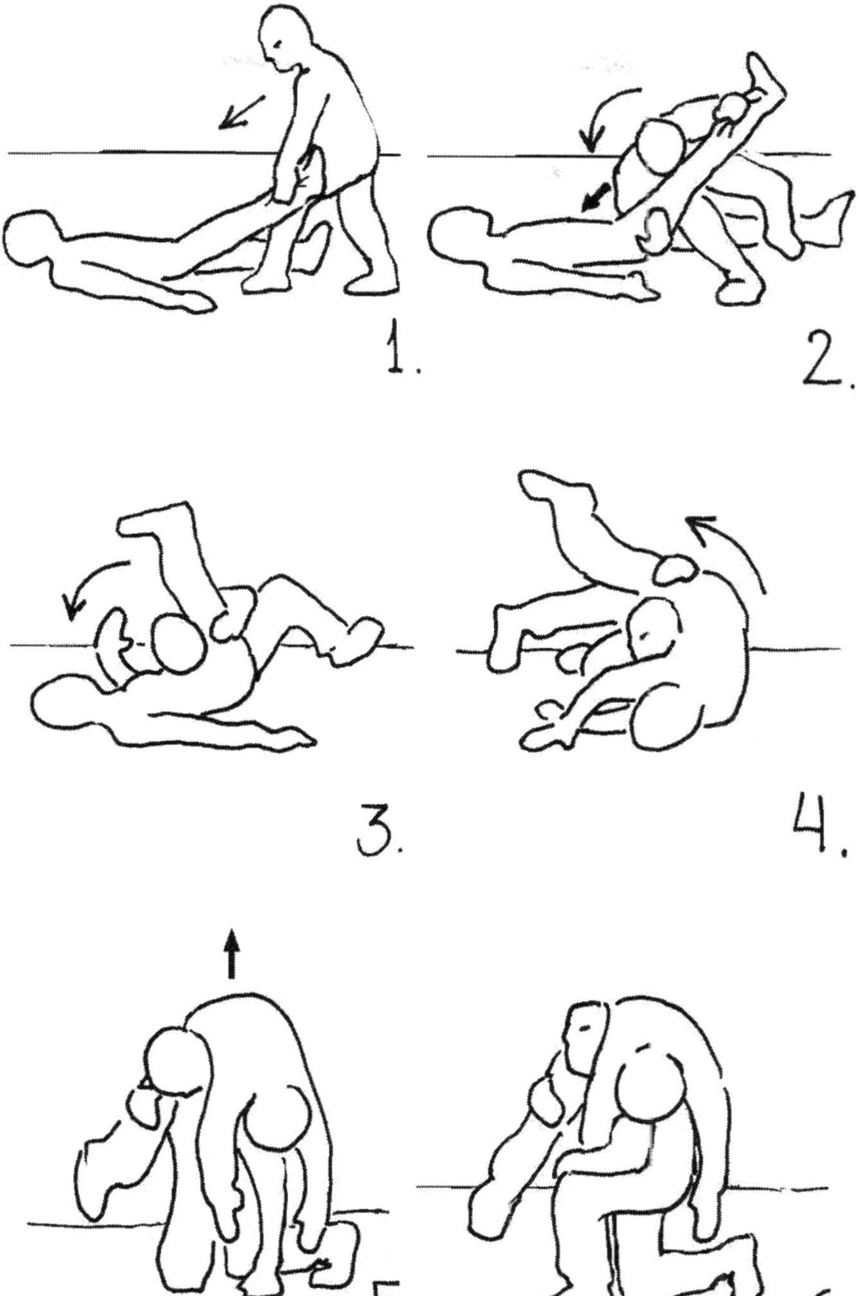
1.
2.
3.
4.
5.
6.

Homemade Hand Sanitizer

A great number of diseases can be avoided entirely by simply washing your hands. Access to safe water and correct hand sanitation alone can help save thousands of lives[22]. During disasters and long term financial downturns the spread of diseases will increase, sometimes significantly so. Hand sanitation is also important during flu pandemics. The CDC (Centers for Disease Control and Prevention[23]) advices that if soap and water are unavailable, use an alcohol-based hand sanitizer that contains at least 60% alcohol to clean hands. Always use commercial hand sanitizer when available (stock up!) but it may be sold out or hard to come by. Fortunately it is not that difficult to make your own hand sanitizer.

1) A 2oz spray bottle makes it easier to use the hand sanitizer, getting the right dosage on the palm of the hand. Fill with 2/3 of ethyl alcohol. This can be found in most places sold as "denatured alcohol", which means it has a very small percentage of a bittering or toxic additive to discourage consumption. Ideally, use the purest ethyl alcohol (ethanol, grain alcohol, drinking alcohol) you can find. Add 1/3 of Aloe Vera Gel. You may want to add 5 drops of lavender or tea tree oil.

2) Vodka and Whiskey have been used in the past as disinfectants[24], with whiskey working slightly better in some studies, although both of them have lower concentrations of alcohol than the recommended 60%. Some hair gels can be used as thickeners for the hand sanitizer, especially if they contain Aloe Vera.

3) Stir with a stick and shake to mix. The hand sanitizer is ready to use.

4) One shot on the palm is usually enough product to spread, rub your hands with it and disinfect them.

5) Wash hands properly with the product by rubbing them together, rub the palm and back of your hands, the wrists and in between the fingers.

6) It is not pepper spray by any means but the hand sanitizer spray can be used to at least surprise and momentarily distract an attacker. Alcohol in such concentrations can cause eye damage so even if inefficient for self defense, use only as a last resort. The good news is that hand sanitizer hasn't been banned anywhere (yet) and it is normal for people to carry a bottle in their pocket or purse.

7) When it comes to pandemics, also protect your face with a respirator and eyewear. Asians aren't shy about using surgical masks and respirators when necessary and neither should you. A collapsible respirator folds flat and is easy to carry in a purse or backpack.

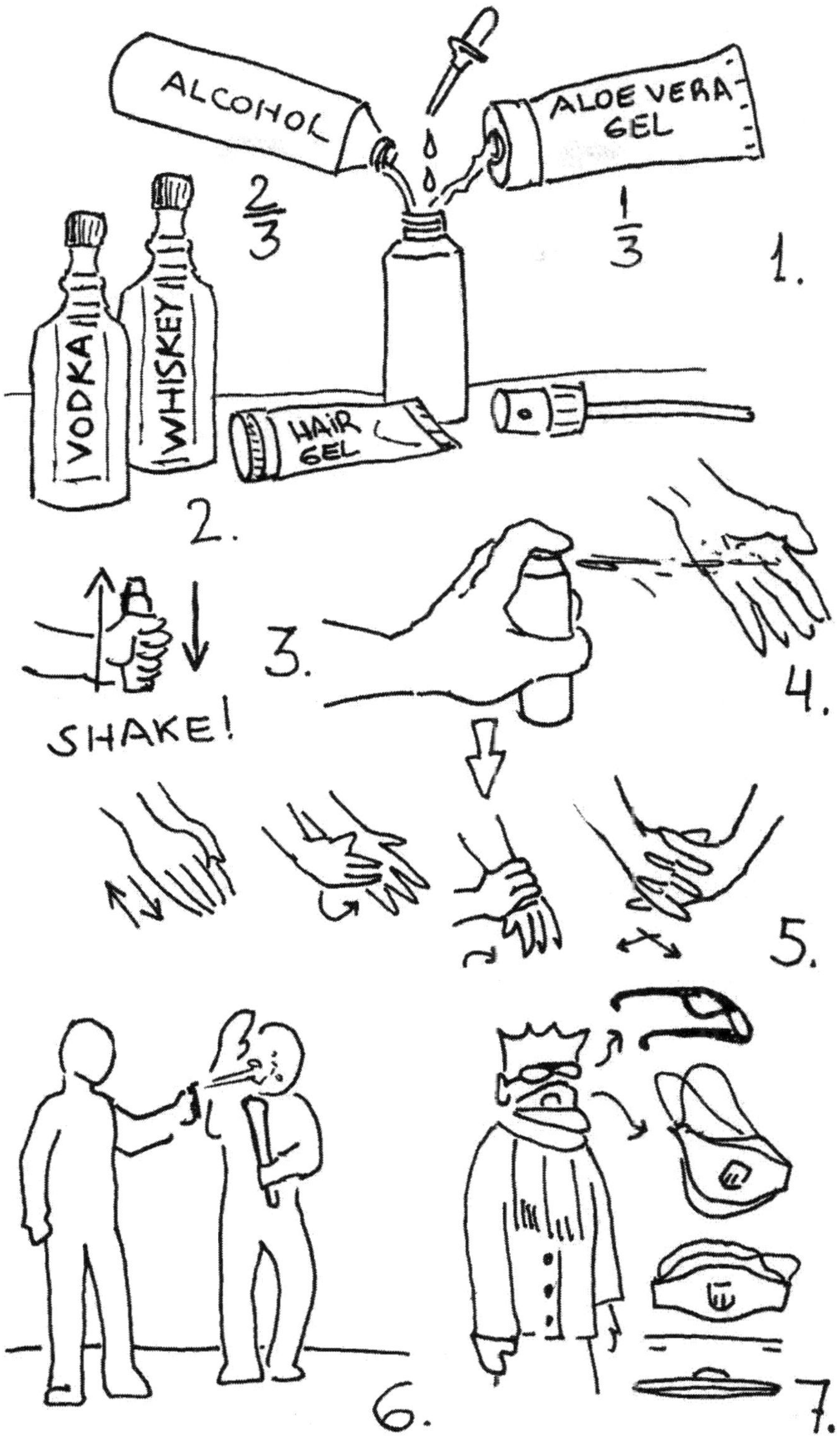
ALCOHOL
ALOE VERA GEL
2/3
1/3
1.
VODKA
WHISKEY
HAIR GEL
2.
SHAKE!
3.
4.
5.
6.
7.

Washing Clothes

During extended periods of time without power you need to find a way to wash your clothes so as to avoid diseases and boost morale.

For backpacking, emergencies or bugging out, it's good to know how to wash clothes on the go.

1) If the clothes are very dirty or muddy you want to give it a quick rinse to remove some of the larger chunks of dirt and mud. Once that's taken care of, apply soap or laundry detergent to the dirty spots you have left. Give it a few minutes to penetrate the fibres and loosen the stains a bit.

2) A simple improvised washing machine consists of a plunger and a bucket partially filled with water.

3) Put the dirty clothes in the bucket. If you have laundry detergent then use a couple tablespoons per bucket. Work the plunger up and down for a few minutes. Check the clothes and repeat as necessary until they are clean. Once they are clean empty the bucket, fill it with clean water and use the plunger again until the clothes no longer feel soapy.

4) Wring the clothes dry. Squeeze and twist the clothes to remove as much water as possible. Some natives in South America would hit rocks and trees with the clothes to dry them up. This method works well but it can damage your clothes. You can now hang the clothes up to dry.

5) Although a normal plunger can be used right away, you can make a few modifications so that it works even better. Cutting four or five holes allows water to jet throw them as the clothes are compressed. This forces the water through the fibers and therefore cleans the clothes better.

Many plungers currently available have a cone shaped tip that gets a nicer fit in the toilet to clear blockages. You want to cut this off and end up with the traditional cup shaped plunger. Then you can cut the holes to make it a more effective washing tool.

6) Manual portable clothes washers are available in the market. These are intended for boats, camping and recreational vehicles but would work great during an extended blackout as well. In principle it's the same thing, a bucket with water and clothes being flushed up and down. Of course that a dedicated basket with holes to keep the clothes in works far better as water is forced through the clothes in a more efficient manner. Other commercial manual washers look very much like a big plunger and have the holes on top which perform the task described earlier.

SOAP
1.
2.
3.
4.
5.
6.

Drying Clothes

This method works well not so much for drying large amounts of clothes but for quickly drying whatever it is you need to put on right away.

This method is ideal for hotels or anywhere else where you have dry towels available to use. But even if you are using your own towel, it's still better to have a wet towel that you can hang from your backpack and let it dry throughout the day than walk around wearing wet (or dirty) clothes.

1) Wring the clothes dry as well as you can. The more water you can get out before you use the towel the more water the towel will absorb.

The fabric of the clothes you are trying to dry makes a big difference too. Cotton will be the hardest to dry and thin synthetic fabric will dry almost perfectly once you're done. 50/50 blends and wool clothes have good enough results, especially merino wool underwear and t-shirts.

2) Place the clothes you wish to dry on top of the towel. You can use other cloths but cotton towels work best and absorb the most water. Make sure there are no wrinkles so as to have maximum contact area.

3) Roll the towel with the clothes inside. Make sure it's rolled as tight as possible but without moving the clothes out of place.

4) Step on the roll, making sure you step all over it. This will press the towel fabric against the clothes and absorb the water.

5) Grab one end of the roll and bang it against the floor. Then grab the other end and repeat the process. The inertia makes the water move away from the clothes and into the towel.

6) Unroll the towel and check your clothes. Most underwear and t-shirts should be pretty dry by now, especially those made of synthetic fabrics.

You can repeat the process to take even more water out. A different towel works best but you can also do it with the same towel you just used. It's still likely to absorb some more water.

7) At this point you can just put the clothes on. Whatever bit of humidity is left will dry on its own soon enough thanks to your body heat.

Try wearing the clothes for a few minutes before putting any pants or jacket on top.

Tip: If traveling by car, hang the clothes in a line across the back seat. Crack open the front and back windows. The flowing air will dry them in a matter of minutes in most climates. Secure your clothes well so as to not lose them!

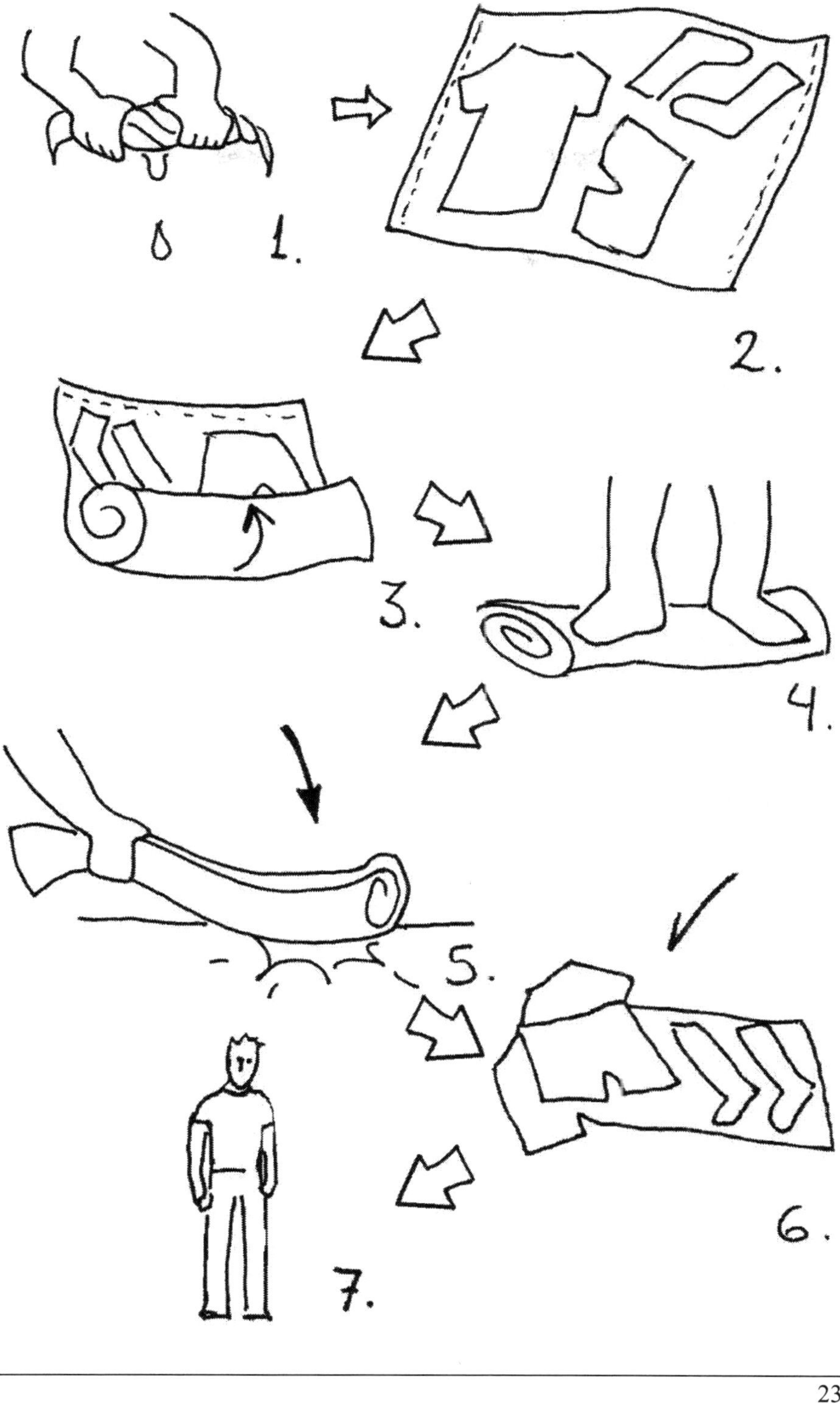
1.
2.
3.
4.
5.
6.
7.

NOTES:

Chapter 12
Improvisation and Practical skills

"To succeed, planning alone is insufficient.
One must improvise as well."
- Isaac Asimov, Foundation

Power Outages

Power outages tend to be short-term events but if the cause is a serious problem the power outage may last for days. During natural disasters, even if the damage is technically easy to repair, the number of incidents may delay the return of electricity as well.

A good supply of batteries, flashlights and some simple tricks will make life easier until the problem is resolved.

1) Get flashlights that can stand on their tail. This makes it easier to keep it pointed to the ceiling. If painted white (like most ceilings tend to be) the light bouncing back will illuminate the entire room. 100 Lumens is enough once your eyes adjust. 500-1000 lumens will light a room nicely.

2) Place several plastic bottles full of water in the freezer. Leave some space for the water to expand as it freezes without breaking the bottle. Once the light goes out, move the ice bottles to the vegetable drawers in the fridge. Put the products you wish to keep fresh in there and cover them with a plastic tarp. Food can easily be kept cold for at least two days using this method. The more ice bottles you have, the more time you can run your "ice box" like in the old days before people had fridges.

3) Different methods can be used to redirect the light of a flashlight so as to turn it into an improvised lantern. A small flashlight can simply be dropped into an empty milk jug. Make sure to clean it well first. Smaller bottles can be taped to the head of the flashlight. The bean hitting the bottom of the bottle will dissipate light nicely.

A simple method is to put some paper or medical tape on the light. This reduces the "throw" of a light making it more of a "flood" light.

A good way to improvise a small lantern is to wrap the tape like a cone.

4) For cooking, making repairs, walking a perimeter or anything that involves the use of both hands, a headlamp is just invaluable during a power outage. Have several around the house.

Tip: Buy a good solar charger. It will allow you to charge your cell phone, batteries, flashlights and other small devices.

1.
ICE BOTTLES
2.
PLASTIC TARP
IMPROVISED LANTERN
paper or medical tape
3.

Homemade Insecticide

Keep ants, cockroaches and other insects away from your food supply.

1) Homemade insecticide is effective and cheap to make. Borax or Boric Acid (not the same but both work) are often used along with sugar and water. At times it can be even more effective than commercial bait which may be required to contain bitter additives to discourage consumption by pets and children.

2) A fairly successful recipe is half a cup of sugar (brown sugar sometimes works best) 1 ½ tablespoons of borax. Mix the sugar and borax. Add about a cup of warm water and stir until both sugar and borax are completely dissolved. A teaspoon of honey makes the bait even more attractive. Dip cotton balls and use them as bait. The ants will drink from the cotton and take it back to the nest killing the rest. This will take two or three days, sometimes a week or more depending on the size of the nest and how resistant the ants are to the poison.

If after a week you don't get the desired results, increase the borax dose by another ½ tablespoon. If the ants don't eat the bait, then reduce the dose of borax and use only 1 tablespoon. The exact dosage needed will vary depending on the ants.

3) Using this recipe, you can also spray it directly on the ants. Add more water if needed but make sure both the borax and sugar are completely dissolved before using a spray bottle. This seems to work well on large ant trails. Besides eating the bait, the solution sticks to the ants and they consume it when cleaning themselves.

4) Other types of bait can be made using other food products. Borax can be used not only on ants, but also cockroaches. Peanut butter and pâté paste are good choices to try. Mix one part of borax to three or four parts of pâté or peanut butter. Make bait balls and place them where needed.

5) It is important to know what type of food the pest you are trying to eradicate likes. Ants may be attracted to sugar or protein depending on the type of ant or even depending on what the colony needs at that time. Once you know what the ants like, then you can start experimenting with borax. The most common mistake with homemade insecticide is putting too much borax and the ants not eating the bait. Be patient and start with a lower dosage. Even with doses as low as three or five percent it will kill ants eventually so be patient.

BORAX
SUGAR
8 PARTS SUGAR
1 PART BORAX
WATER
HONEY
1.
COTTON BALL
SUGAR + BORAX
2.
PEANUT BUTTER
3 PARTS
PÂTÉ
+
1 PART BORAX
4.
3.
?
5% BORAX
25% BORAX
5.

Homemade Body Armor

Body armor is affordable (cheaper than a good handgun) and easy enough to buy. Trusting your life to homemade body armor when dependable armor made to the correct specifications is available is not recommended. Having said that, in some scenarios there's simply no other choice. You either do without protection at all or you try making it yourself. If that's the case, then at the very least test your homemade armor until you believe it is safe, and indeed better than nothing.

Firearm projectiles have great penetration and are not easily stopped. Rifle rounds in particular are very hard to stop and even retail plates can only take a small number of hits before failing.

1) Owning a firearm means you envision the possibility of having to use it at some point for self-defense. If that's the case, then it's perfectly logical to have gear that also protects you in the event of getting shot. Body armor also makes a lot of sense for certain high risk situations such as rioting and civil unrest, security from looters after a disaster, cash transactions with strangers you only met online, visiting the ATM or bank and making large cash withdrawals during troubled times.

2) If concerned about the possibility of terrorist attacks, mass shootings and robberies, you can keep either a soft armor panel or hard ballistic plate in your briefcase or bag to be used as a shield.

3) If Kevlar isn't available, fiberglass and synthetic resin can be used to create plates capable of providing ballistic protection. Stack the fiberglass with coats of resin in between, clamp it down using two particle boards and let it cure. Using aluminium foil will keep the plate from getting stuck to the boards. Don't forget to use a respirator, gloves and eye protection when working with fiberglass.

Stacked one inch thick, the homemade fiberglass plate should stop most common handgun rounds but **will not be enough to stop rifle rounds**.

4) Incorporating one or two layers of ceramic tiles will improve the ballistic protection and have a better chance of stopping rifle rounds.

How effective all of this is depends on numerous factors, from the type of fabric used, how thick the plate is, the resin, if its epoxy resin or polyester resin (epoxy is usually stronger, but more expensive) the kind of tiles used and the specific round it gets shot with. Consider this a last resort, worst case scenario alternative. Experiment with different builds before you even consider trusting your life to a homemade armor plate.

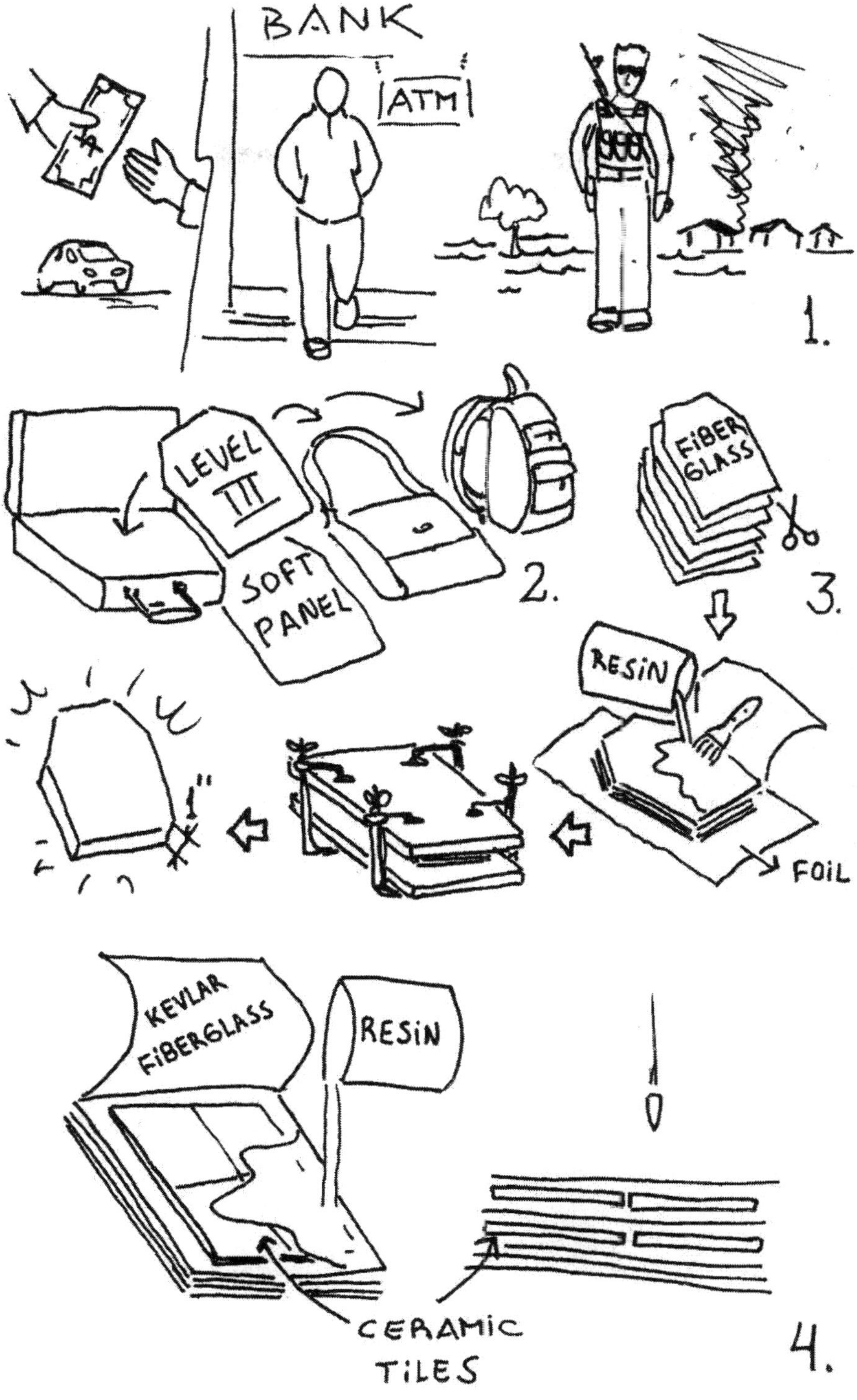
BANK
ATM
1.
LEVEL III
SOFT PANEL
2.
FIBER GLASS
3.
RESIN
FOIL
1"
KEVLAR FIBERGLASS
RESIN
CERAMIC TILES
4.

Knife Sharpening

Knives are essential survival tools but they aren't of much use if they don't have a good edge on them. Knives are typically sharpened at about 15 to 20 degree angle. Keeping that angle constant as you move the blade along the abrasive material is easier said than done. Sharpening a knife isn't rocket science but it is a skill that takes some time to develop. Be patient at first. Don't force it. Focus on getting the angle right.

1) Coffee mugs are typically made of fine grain ceramic, ideal for sharpening knives. Turn one upside down and the exposed ceramic on the bottom can be used to sharpen a knife. Work along the edge in circular movements.

2) Mineral oil is one of the most commonly used lubricants when using a sharpening stone but a bit of spit works in a pinch. Regularly rinse the stone to keep it unclogged.

3) Fine grit sandpaper (400 or finer) works well for sharpening knives. It is not as durable as a stone and will deteriorate fast, but it is easy to come by and found in most households. Hold it with tape against a hard even surface. For convex edge knives, you can use a mousepad or piece of leather so that the paper rolls along the edge. Work the blade away from the edge, moving in the direction of the spine of the knife so as to not cut into the sandpaper.

4) Nail buffers can be used to touch up a knife's edge. Use the buffer with the soft surface, the one intended to make nails shine. Move away from the edge, towards the tip to cover the entire length of the edge.

5) Check with your nail to see if your blade has a "wire edge". You'll feel the nail catch on something even if you can't see it with the naked eye. Do check both sides. Remove the wire edge by sharpening the blade towards the direction of the edge.

6) Know what type of blade you have so as to sharpen it properly. A) Convex Grind B) Hollow Grind C) Flat Grind.

7) Use a leather belt as a strop to polish the edge of the blade. Move the blade in the direction of the spine so as to not cut into the strop.

8) Toothpaste can be used on the belt as a polishing paste. Actual metal polishing paste found in most household's cleaning supplies works even better.

Tip: Rubbing metal polishing paste or toothpaste with a cloth also work great for restoring cloudy (oxidized) headlights in cars.

1.

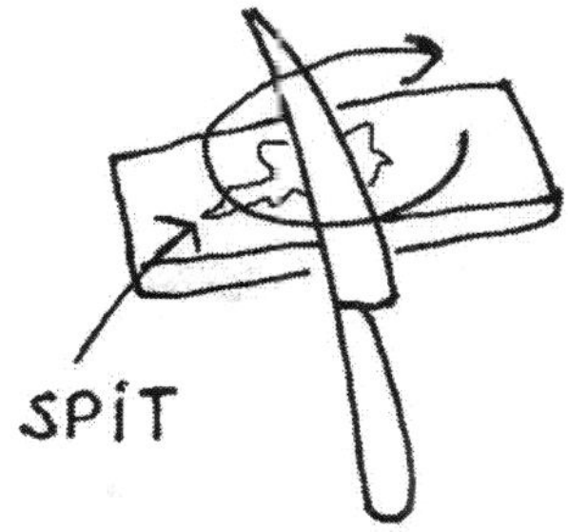

2.

3.

4.

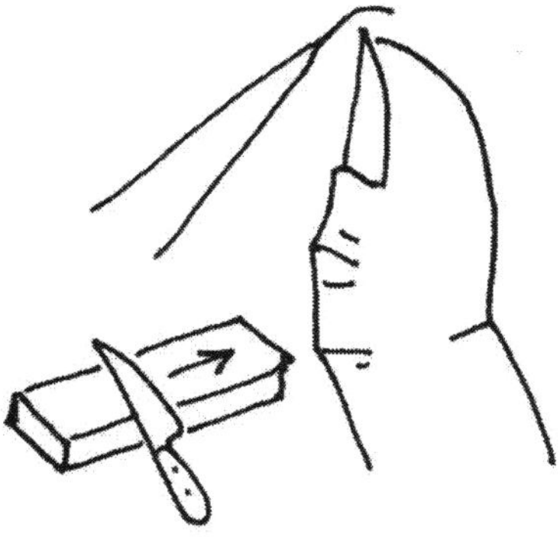

5.

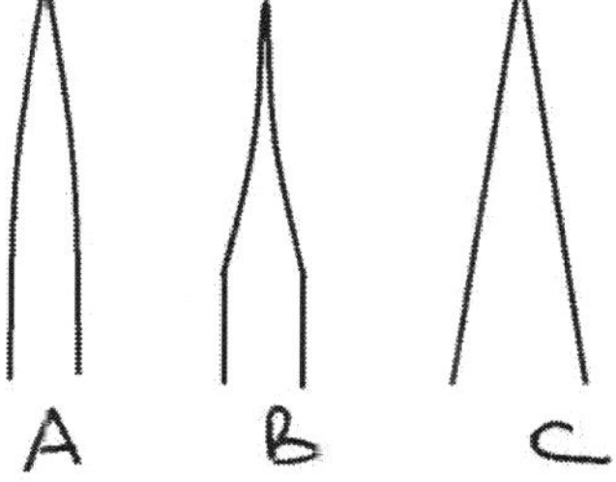

6.

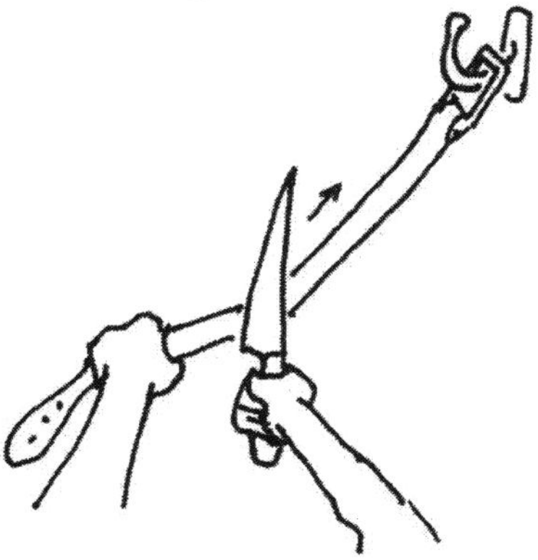

7.

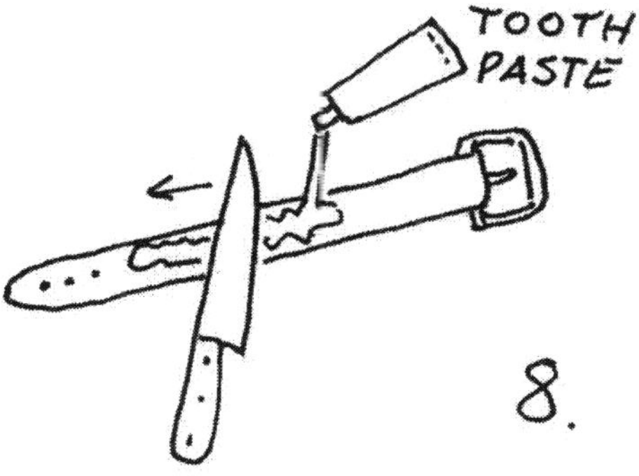

8.

Gun Cleaning

Modern firearms are reliable and can take a fair share of neglect. They still do require a minimum amount of maintenance. Some firearms can go for several hundred rounds or even thousands of rounds before suffering failures due to fouling but such practice is not recommended and can be downright dangerous. At the very least, guns should be cleaned and oiled after 300-500 rounds. Ideally, guns should be field stripped, inspected and cleaned after each use.

1) Guns require lubrication to work properly. Some are more dependent on it than others but metal on metal moving parts, rails and pivot points should be lubricated. Clean oil should be used but oil from the car's engine works in an emergency. A few drops from your car's oil dip stick should do the trick for field expedient cleaning and lubrication.

2) WD-40 or 3-in-One oil can be used to clean guns. Unload and field strip the firearm. Spray the inside of the barrel. Let it soak for a few minutes so as to penetrate and loosen the metal and gunpowder particles.

3) You can make a DIY bore snake. Traditionally, shoe laces are used but any other cord such as paracord will do the trick. Tie several knots, make them large enough to get a snug fit when going through the barrel. If you have a brass scrubber from the kitchen sink, you can cut small pieces and tie them down. This will help remove the metal and carbon buildup.

4) If you don't have a cleaning kit, rod, bore brush and patches, you can make small TP balls and push them down the barrel with a pencil. This works well in polygonal barrels which tend to be easier to clean.

5) Ed's Red is a well-known homemade bore cleaner that has enjoyed a fair amount of popularity over the years.

Automatic transmission fluid (ATF) can be used as a gun oil. It usually contains anti-wear additives as well as rust and corrosion inhibitors which make it suitable for this kind of use. ATF and acetone at a 50/50 rate makes for a good high penetration oil, well regarded among some machinists. Use it only on metal parts of the firearm since the red or green color can stain the wood stock and grip panels.

Ed's Red should be stored in metal, PET or PVC containers. A clean jam or mayonnaise glass jar can also be used.

Tip: Grease is a useful and cheap lubricant to have around. It doesn't dry up nearly as fast as regular oil does in a carry gun and it protects well against rust. Calcium-sulfonate grease is an excellent choice.

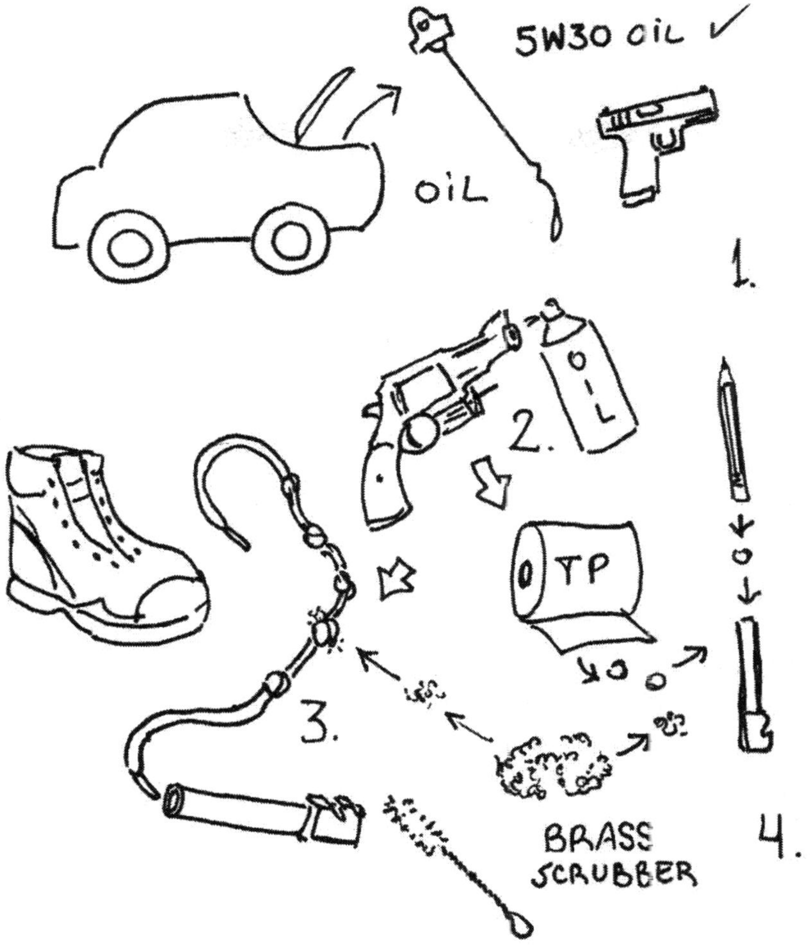

HOMEMADE BORE CLEANER 5.

HIGH PENETRATION OIL { 1 PART ATF
1 PART ACETONE

1 PART KEROSENE

1 PART MINERAL SPIRIT OR TURPENTINE

} ED'S RED

STORE IN METAL, PVC OR PET.
NOT IN HDPE CONTAINERS

Gun and Ammo Modifications

Before modifying a firearm make sure to **follow your local laws**. In the United States, you will need an approved ATF Form 1 before making a short barrel shotgun. Modifying firearms and ammunition can be very dangerous and should be done only by knowledgeable gunsmiths.

Shotguns are one of the most prolific firearms around the world. In many countries, shotguns can be found in nearly every farm.

Cutting the barrel and stock turns the shotgun into a more compact firearm. If you have more than one shotgun, a sawed-off shotgun can be a viable backup gun as an alternative to a proper handgun. Contrary to common belief, it does not make the gun more powerful (you lose velocity and energy with a shorter barrel) or make the pattern spread more. The gun is also far less controllable and accurate without the stock.

1) Cut the barrel with hacksaw or grinder. Blue and oil the exposed steel to keep it from rusting. Cut the stock with a saw leaving the pistol grip. Round up the grip with sandpaper. Use linseed oil to protect the wood.

2) Birdshot (top) is the most common type of shotshell and the one most likely to come across when scrounging for ammunition. It is intended for birds and has very little penetration. An "Improvised Slug" or DIY slug (bottom), although not as good as a real slug, can be a viable option for hunting large game or self-defense when all you have is birdshot shells.

3) A "Cut Shell" is a fast and easy way to make a field expedient "improvised slug", keeping the projectile together at greater distances. Simply cut around the plastic hull but not going all the way. Leave about 2mm to keep the shell together. Cut the exterior hull only, not the plastic wad inside. Cut Shells work best in single or double barrel guns, or fed one by one directly into the chamber of pump shotguns or auto loaders. Use cut shells on cylinder bore barrels and avoid full or modified chokes.

4)"Wax slugs" are made by melting wax (crayons work nicely), cutting the top of the shell to remove the shot, mixing the two together and refilling the shell. Once it cools it is ready to shoot.

5)"Glue Slugs" can be made in a similar manner without the need of fire. Wood glue can be used although resin being stronger will make for a better, stronger projectile. Glue slugs are the better choice for DIY slugs and can be loaded into shotgun magazines. Leave an even layer of glue on top so as to make sure there are no pellets protruding which could impact the primer of the shell it is up against in the tubular magazine.

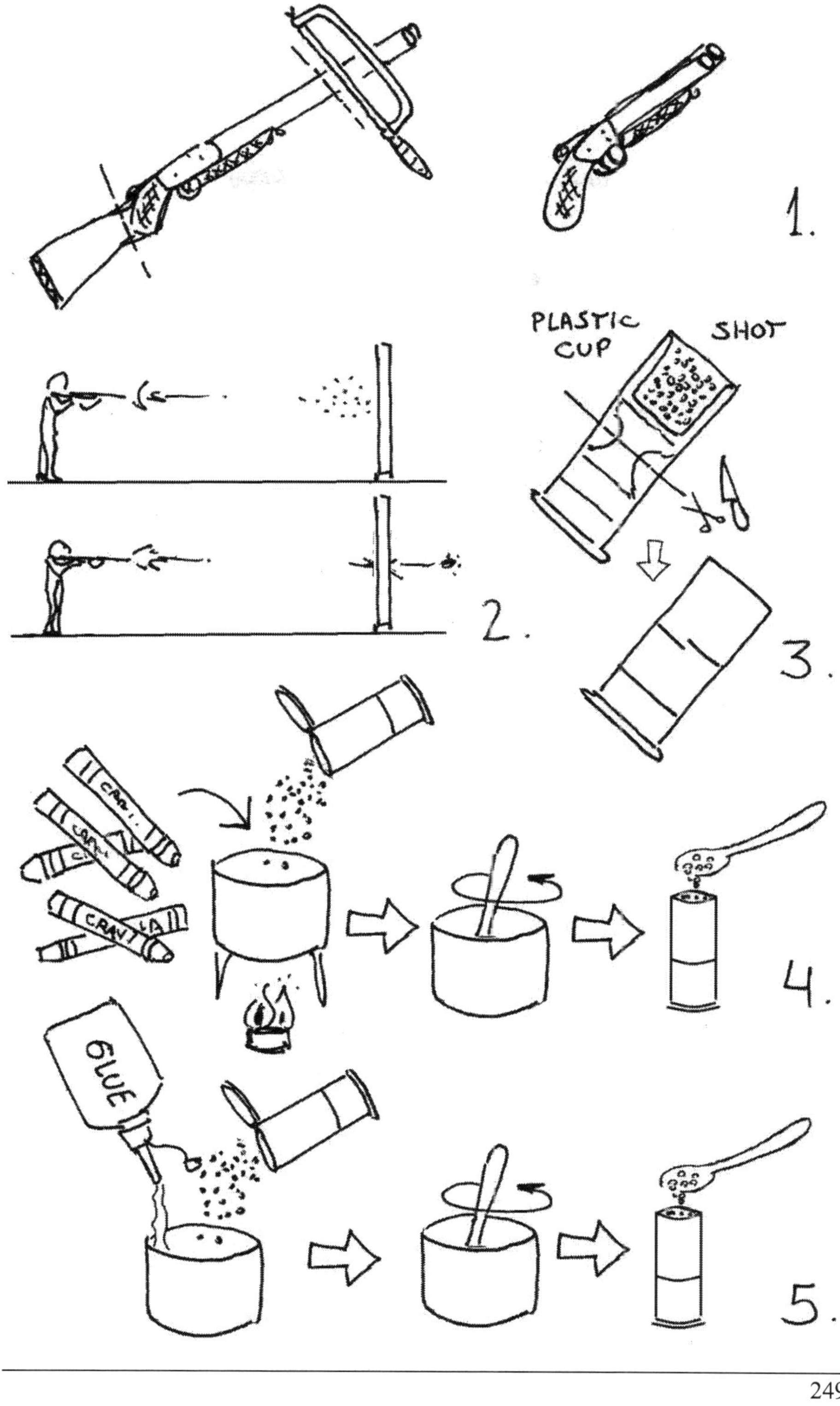
1.
PLASTIC CUP
SHOT
2.
3.
4.
GLUE
5.

Detecting Counterfeit Money

According to the United States Department of Treasury there's an estimated $70 million in counterfeit bills in circulation.

That's approximately 1 note in counterfeits for every 10,000 in genuine currency. With counterfeiters adopting sophisticated advances in technology, the Secret Service has called counterfeiting a growing threat to the financial system. Expect this problem to only get worse in periods of social or economic instability.

The Secret Service[25] advices people to check the following security features when handling cash:

1) Texture and feel. The quickest way to tell if a bill is fake is if it lacks the texture real money has due to the ink and printing process. The paper itself has a specific feel and weight. Even if you don't consciously pay attention to it you handle money all the time. Be suspicious if your gut feeling tells you the weight feels off or if it feels too thin or too thick.

2) 10, 20, 50 and 100 bills have color-shifting ink, so the lower-right denomination should change from copper to green when tilted.

3) When you hold a bill up to the light, for any 5, 10, 20, 50 and 100 bill, there's a watermark on the right side of the same portrait as the one on the bill. Some counterfeit bills have a hand-made watermark, but the portrait may look crude and lack detail compared to a real dollar.

4) When you hold a bill up to the light, look for the Inscribed Security Thread, a vertical band found on different places on each denomination. Here too, counterfeits may have the band, but it is likely to be on the wrong place or lack the finer details. New 100 bills have a visible 3D Security Ribbon.

5) The 2004 style $100 FRN has a color-shifting "Bell in the Inkwell". When you tilt the note, the copper inkwell changes from copper to green. This makes the bell seem to appear and disappear within the inkwell.

6) The Inscribed Security Thread band will have a different position and will glow in different colors for each denomination under UV light.

Tip: A small UV light in your keychain may be a valuable tool to use when quickly checking currency for counterfeits. For years I kept one in my chain when living in Argentina. I would constantly use it to check Pesos and US dollars. Money Counterfeit markers such as the ones used often in stores are cheap, simple and a quick way to check bills.

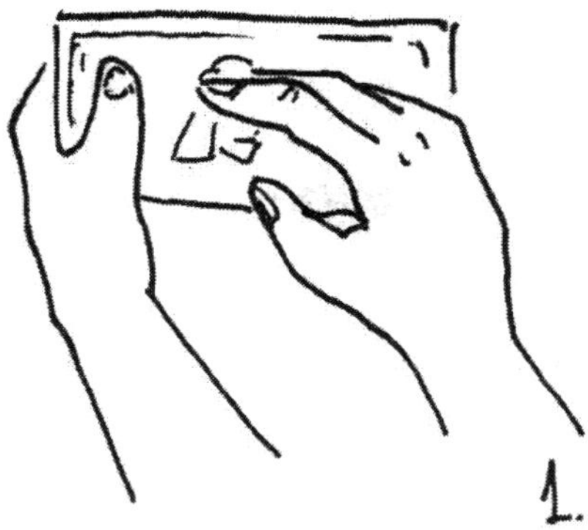

1.

2.

3.

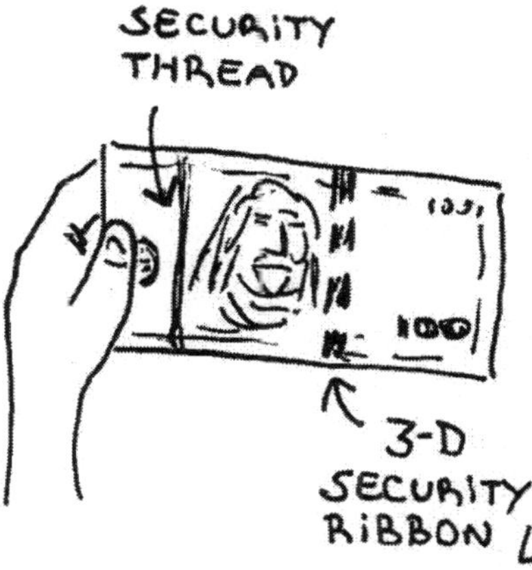

4.

5.

6.

Detecting Counterfeit Silver Coins

Gold and Silver have been a form of currency for over ten thousand years. Even today it is a well-established form of wealth that retains its value when fiat currencies crumble to pieces. This has happened before in nearly every country at one time or another and will happen again. Because of this, it's important to learn to spot fake gold and silver. These tests are mostly for silver, but some work for gold as well.

1) Silver and gold are non-magnetic. If a coin or a bar sticks to a magnet you know you have a fake. There's plenty of fake pre-65 American junk silver coming from China (yes, those too are counterfeited). Some of these are magnetic. A magnetic slide can be used to detect real silver. Silver has a property known as "diamagnetism", meaning it repels magnetics fields. This causes it to slide down noticeably slower than fake coins made out of non-magnetic metals.

2) Place a coin on the tip of your finger and lightly tap it with another coin. This is called a "Ping Test" and it's rather effective once you know the sound of real silver. Silver will have a sweet, long lasting high-pitched ring to it unlike other metals.

3) Knowing the correct specifications of the coin, verify its weight, dimensions and density. A deviation of weight of about 1% or 2% is to be expected. On larger coins, the deviation can be of up to 4% depending on wear but anything more than that is suspicious. Modern bullion such as American silver and gold eagles have small deviations. Greater deviation is more likely in older, worn coins.

4) Coin experts will check coins by looking for details with a jeweler's loupe. Pay particular attention to the rim and the font used. Details should match those of similar verified real coins.

5) A small drop of bleach will tarnish silver very fast, leaving a black spot. This may decrease the numismatic value (collector's value) of some coins. If the coin is silver plated then it will also pass the test unless you file a spot on an edge for testing. Acid tests work in a similar manner, with the drop of acid turning certain colors when reacting to real silver.

XRF Analyzers, ultrasonic thickness gauge and Precious Metals Verifiers are very reliable and often used by expert precious metal dealers.

6) Place an ice cube on top of the silver coin. Silver is the best conductor of heat for all the metals. This means the ice will visibly melt very fast, especially compared to a similar ice cube placed right next to it.

MAGNETIC
1.
PING!
2.
11.01 oz
3.
2001
4.
BLEACH
5.
6.

Reality-Based Preparedness

So you've reached the end of this book, maybe learned a thing or two, revised some tricks you already knew but at the end of the day you are not left feeling like 007 or some swimsuit model-looking kickass assassin that terrorises the Russian mob. There was no tip on how to build a satellite phone using coconuts or a hand grenade using a butane lighter.

That's fine. Reality is far more boring than fiction, even when things do go south. But the skills explained here are very much real and proven, which is probably why you may have known some already. Many of these, especially regarding awareness and security, you'd be wise to integrate to your normal everyday habits. Others like improvisation during storms and blackouts, you are also likely to use on occasions.

As for fighting and self-defense, unfortunately these too are realities you may one day be forced to face. It will be fast, violent and your brain will go from "this can't be happening" to "why is this happening?" in a microsecond. How well you handle these situations will certainly be a matter of training and how committed you've been to preparing for that moment. Luck also plays a role, but above all it will be about the sheer will to fight and prevail by any means necessary, using anything and everything you've got. Most people in the developed world will be lucky enough to navigate through life never knowing true violence, but that doesn't mean it can't happen. If it does, chances are it won't be some grand event worthy of the next blockbuster movie but it will be over a parking spot, over a hat you're wearing with a phrase deemed politically incorrect by some or just because someone lost his marbles and decided to open fire on your church, office or while grabbing a burger with your family any given Sunday. These are far more likely to happen than you suddenly living like a frontier trapper in the Taiga river valley.

That's just the way life is during the good times. We're not talking about the truly bad ones, the terrible reality many preppers believe they are getting ready for when in fact they are not. Ask people in eastern Ukraine how life changed for them. Ask Venezuelans, Syrians, South Africans or the people in New Orleans during Hurricane Katrina in 2005.

Enjoy the good times while happily preparing for the bad ones.

Don't forget about the "happily" part. It is much more important than most people give it credit for.

-Fernando

About the author

Fernando "FerFAL" Aguirre is a survival and emergency preparedness author that has lived through the 2001 socio-economic collapse of Argentina. He is the editor of The Modern Survivalist website and The Modern Survivalist YouTube channel.

Fernando is recognized in the survival and preparedness community for his first-hand experience and practical approach to preparedness.

He published his first book "The Modern Survival Manual: Surviving the Economic Collapse" in 2009. Due to the continuing instability and growing social unrest, Fernando bugged out of Argentina with his family in 2011. This experience is the topic of his second book, "Bugging Out and Relocating: When Staying Put is not an Option".

Fernando has lived in Argentina, United States, Spain and Northern Ireland. He resides in a small town by the sea with his wife, their three children and Spike, their English Bull Terrier.

Bibliography

-“The “Walking Stick” Method of Self-Defence” by Anonymous (Author)

-“Principles of Personal Defense” by Jeff Cooper

-“Esgrima Criolla – Ilustrado” by Lopez Osornio, Mario

-“L’arte di ben maneggiare la spada” by Francesco Fernando Alfieri

-“ Martial Arts For Agents Of The Law” by Mike Young

-“Massad Ayoob's Greatest Handguns of the World” by Massad Ayoob

-“Wartime Farm” by Ginn, Peter; Goodman, Ruth; Langlands, Alexander

-“Manual del Aventurero” by Rudger Nehberg

-“Home Herbal” by Penelope Ody

-“Gray's Anatomy” by Henry Gray

-“Manual de Armas y Tecnicas para la Defensa” by Alejandro A. Reynoso

-“Home Invasion” by Rudolph Zinn

-“The Parkour & Freerunning Handbook” by Dan Edwardes

References

1)"3 de cada 10 hogares sufrieron hechos de inseguridad"

https://www.perfil.com/noticias/sociedad/una-cifra-preocupante-3-de-cada-10-hogares-sufrieron-hechos-de-inseguridad.phtml

2) Physical Activity and Adults WHO

https://www.who.int/dietphysicalactivity/factsheet_adults/en/

3) Range estimation - Marine Corps Base Camp Lejeune

https://www.lejeune.marines.mil

4) Police Facilitation of Mass Protests

https://sfbos.org/police-facilitation-mass-protests

5) Crowd Safety and Risk Analysis

https://www.gkstill.com/Support/crowd-density/CrowdDensity-1.html

6) What do you need in a Survival Kit?

https://www.redcross.org/get-help/how-to-prepare-for-emergencies/survival-kit-supplies.html

7) Survival Rates Similar for Gunshot, Stabbing Victims Whether Brought to the Hospital by Police or EMS, Penn Medicine Study Finds

https://www.pennmedicine.org/news/news-releases/2014/january/survival-rates-similar-for-gun

8) Tips for Improving Effectiveness in Forcible Entry

https://www.fireengineering.com/content/dam/fe/online-articles/documents/FEU/Gustin-April-June08.pdf

9) How to Use a Belt to Barricade a Door During a Shooting

https://www.insideedition.com/headlines/13353-how-to-use-a-belt-to-barricade-a-door-during-a-shooting

10) CDC-Make Water Safe

https://www.cdc.gov/healthywater/emergency/pdf/make-water-safe-H.pdf

11) EPA - Emergency Disinfection of Drinking Water

https://www.epa.gov/ground-water-and-drinking-water/emergency-disinfection-drinking-water

12) CDC- Solar Disinfection

https://www.cdc.gov/safewater/solardisinfection.html

13) Emergencies and First Aid - Direct Pressure to Stop Bleeding

https://www.health.harvard.edu/staying-healthy/emergencies-and-first-aid-direct-pressure-to-stop-bleeding

14) Army Study Guide- Apply A Tourniquet

https://www.armystudyguide.com/content/Prep_For_Basic_Training/Prep_for_basic_first_aid/apply-a-tourniquet.shtml

15) High velocity gunshot injuries to the extremities: management on and off the battlefield

https://www.ncbi.nlm.nih.gov/pmc/articles/PMC4596205/

16) NHS Treating a fever (high temperature) in children

https://www.nhs.uk/conditions/pregnancy-and-baby/treating-high-temperature-children/

17) Treating Fever in Children

https://www.webmd.com/first-aid/fever-in-children-treatment#1

18) WebMD Manuka Honey

https://www.webmd.com/a-to-z-guides/manuka-honey-medicinal-uses#1

19) BBC The Hidden Healing Power of Sugar

http://www.bbc.com/future/story/20180328-how-sugar-could-help-heal-wounds

20) Honey and Sugar in Open Wound Management

https://www.mspca.org/angell_services/honey-and-sugar/

21) How to Do a Fireman's Carry

https://www.wikihow.com/Do-a-Fireman's-Carry

22) Handwashing: Clean Hands Save Lives

https://www.cdc.gov/handwashing/

23) When & How to Wash Your Hands

https://www.cdc.gov/handwashing/when-how-handwashing.html

24) Can liquor be used as an emergency antiseptic?

https://www.straightdope.com/columns/read/2978/can-liquor-be-used-as-an-emergency-antiseptic/

25) Secret Service-Know Your Money

https://www.secretservice.gov/data/KnowYourMoney.pdf

Printed in Great Britain
by Amazon

54168343R00154